By Evelyn Waugh

Novels

DECLINE AND FALL

VILE BODIES

BLACK MISCHIEF

A HANDFUL OF DUST

SCOOP

PUT OUT MORE FLAGS

WORK SUSPENDED

BRIDESHEAD REVISITED

SCOTT-KING'S MODERN EUROPE

THE LOVED ONE

HELENA

MEN AT ARMS

LOVE AMONG THE RUINS

OFFICERS AND GENTLEMEN

THE END OF THE BATTLE
(Unconditional Surrender)

THE ORDEAL OF GILBERT
PINFOLD

Biography

ROSSETTI

EDMUND CAMPION

MSGR. RONALD KNOX

Autobiography

A LITTLE LEARNING

Travel

LABELS

REMOTE PEOPLE

NINETY-TWO DAYS

WAUGH IN ABYSSINIA

ROBBERY UNDER LAW

WHEN THE GOING WAS GOOD

A TOURIST IN AFRICA

Short Stories

CHARLES RYDER'S SCHOOLDAYS AND OTHER STORIES

BASIL SEAL RIDES AGAIN

Journalism

A LITTLE ORDER
(Edited by Donat Gallagher)

THE ESSAYS, ARTICLES AND REVIEWS OF EVELYN WAUGH
(Edited by Donat Gallagher)

WHEN THE GOING
WAS GOOD

WHEN THE GOING
WAS GOOD

by
EVELYN WAUGH

LITTLE, BROWN AND COMPANY

BOSTON · NEW YORK · TORONTO · LONDON

LIBRARY OF CONGRESS CATALOG CARD NO. 84-080133

REPUBLISHED APRIL 1984

10   9   8   7   6   5   4   3

MV NY

PRINTED IN THE UNITED STATES OF AMERICA

Contents

Preface   **7**

Chapter One

   A PLEASURE CRUISE IN 1929   **11**

Chapter Two

   A CORONATION IN 1930   **73**

Chapter Three

   GLOBE-TROTTING IN 1930–1   **137**

Chapter Four

   A JOURNEY TO BRAZIL IN 1932   **187**

Chapter Five

   A WAR IN 1935   **247**

Preface

THE following pages comprise all that I wish to preserve of the four travel books I wrote between the years 1929 and 1935: *Labels, Remote People, Ninety-two Days* and (a title not of my own choosing) *Waugh in Abyssinia*. These books have now been out of print for some time and will not be reissued. The first three were published by Messrs Duckworth & Co., the fourth by Longmans, Green & Co. There was a fifth book, *Robbery under Law*, about Mexico, which I am content to leave in oblivion, for it dealt little with travel and much with political questions. 'To have travelled a lot,' I wrote in the Introduction to that book, 'to have spent, as I have done, the first twelve years of adult life on the move, is to this extent a disadvantage. At the age of thirty-five one needs to go to the moon, or some such place, to recapture the excitement with which one first landed at Calais. For many people Mexico has, in the past, had this lunar character. Lunar it still remains, but in no poetic sense. It is a waste land, part of a dead or, at any rate, a dying planet. Politics, everywhere destructive, have here dried up the place, frozen it, cracked it, and powdered it to dust. In the sixteenth century human life was disordered and talent stultified by the obsession of theology; today we are plague-stricken by politics. This is a political book.' So let it lie in its own dust. Here I seek the moon landscape.

From 1928 until 1937 I had no fixed home and no possessions which would not conveniently go on a porter's barrow. I travelled continuously, in England and abroad. These four books, here in fragments reprinted, were the record of certain journeys, chosen for no better reason than that I needed money at the time of their completion; they were pedestrian, day-to-day accounts of things seen and people met, interspersed with commonplace information and some rather callow comments. In cutting them to their present shape, I have sought to leave a purely personal narrative in the hope that there still lingers round it some trace of vernal scent.

Each book, I found on re-reading, had a distinct and slightly

7

grimmer air, as, year by year, the shades of the prison-house closed. In *Labels* I looked only for pleasure. Not uncritically I examined the credentials of its varied sources and watched the loss and gain of other seekers. Baroque, the luxurious and surprising; cookery, wine, eccentric individuals, grottoes by day, the haunts of the underworld at night; these things I, like a thousand others, sought in the Mediterranean.

How much we left unvisited and untasted in those splendid places! 'Europe could wait. There would be a time for Europe,' I thought; 'all too soon the days would come when I needed a man at my side to put up my easel and carry my paints; when I could not venture more than an hour's journey from a good hotel; when I needed soft breezes and mellow sunshine all day long; then I would take my old eyes to Germany and Italy. Now, while I had the strength, I would go to the wild lands where man had deserted his post and the jungle was creeping back to its old strongholds.' Thus 'Charles Ryder'; thus myself. These were the years when Mr Peter Fleming went to the Gobi Desert, Mr Graham Greene to the Liberian hinterland; Robert Byron – vital today, as of old, in our memories; all his exuberant zest in the opportunities of our time now, alas! tragically and untimely quenched – to the ruins of Persia. We turned our backs on civilization. Had we known, we might have lingered with 'Palinurus'; had we known that all that seeming-solid, patiently built, gorgeously ornamented structure of Western life was to melt overnight like an ice-castle, leaving only a puddle of mud; had we known man was even then leaving his post. Instead, we set off on our various stern roads; I to the Tropics and the Arctic, with the belief that barbarism was a dodo to be stalked with a pinch of salt. The route of *Remote People* was easy going; the *Ninety-two Days* were more arduous. We have most of us marched and made camp since then, gone hungry and thirsty, lived where pistols are flourished and fired. At that time it seemed an ordeal, an initiation to manhood.

Then in 1935 came the Italian invasion of Abyssinia and I returned there, but no longer as a free traveller. As a war correspondent, lightly as I took my duties and the pretensions of my colleagues, I was in the livery of the new age. The ensuing book betrayed the change. I have omitted many pages of historical summary and political argument. Re-reading them, after the experience of recent years, I found little to retract. Hopes proved dupes; it is possible that present fears may be liars. This is not the place in which to attempt to disentangle the *post hoc* from the *propter hoc* of disaster.

My own travelling days are over, and I do not expect to see many travel books in the near future. When I was a reviewer, they used, I remember, to appear in batches of four or five a week, cram-full of charm and wit and enlarged Leica snapshots. There is no room for tourists in a world of 'displaced persons'. Never again, I suppose, shall we land on foreign soil with letter of credit and passport (itself the first faint shadow of the great cloud that envelops us) and feel the world wide open before us. That is as remote today as 'Yorick's' visit to Paris, when he had to be reminded by the landlord that their countries were at war. It will be more remote tomorrow. Some sort of reciprocal 'Strength-through-Joy', *dopo-lavoro* system may arise in selected areas; others, not I, gifted with the art of pleasing public authorities may get themselves despatched abroad to promote 'Cultural Relations'; the very young, perhaps, may set out like the *Wandervogels* of the Weimar period; lean, lawless, aimless couples with rucksacks, joining the great army of men and women without papers, without official existence, the refugees and deserters, who drift everywhere today between the barbed wire. I shall not, by my own wish, be among them.

Perhaps it is a good thing for English literature. In two generations the air will be fresher and we may again breed great travellers like Burton and Doughty. I never aspired to being a great traveller. I was simply a young man, typical of my age; we travelled as a matter of course. I rejoice that I went when the going was good.

E.W.

Stinchcombe
1945

WHEN THE GOING WAS GOOD

CHAPTER ONE

A Pleasure Cruise in 1929

(From *Labels*)

IN February 1929 London was lifeless and numb, seeming to take its temper from Westminster, where the Government was dragging out the weeks of its last session. Talking films were just being introduced, and had set back by twenty years the one vital art of the century. There was not even a good murder case. And besides this it was intolerably cold. The best seller of the preceding months had been Mrs Woolf's *Orlando*, and it seemed as though Nature were setting out to win some celestial Hawthornden Prize by imitation of that celebrated description of the Great Frost. People shrank, in those days, from the icy contact of a cocktail glass, like the Duchess of Malfi from the dead hand, and crept stiff as automata from their draughty taxis into the nearest tube-railway station, where they stood, pressed together for warmth, coughing and sneezing among the evening papers.

So I packed up all my clothes and two or three solemn books, such as Spengler's *Decline of the West*, and a great many drawing materials, for two of the many quite unfulfilled resolutions which I made about this trip were that I was going to do some serious reading and drawing. Then I got into an aeroplane and went to Paris where I spent the night with some kind, generous, and wholly delightful Americans. They wanted to show me a place called 'Brick-Top's', which was then very popular. It was no good going to Brickey's, they said, until after twelve, so we went to Florence's first. We drank champagne because it is one of the peculiar modifications of French liberty that one can drink nothing else.

Then we went to an underground public house called the New York Bar. When we came in all the people beat on the tables with little wooden hammers, and a young Jew who was singing made a joke about the ermine coat which one of our party was wearing. We drank some more, much nastier, champagne and went to

11

Brick-Top's, but when we got there, we found a notice on the door saying, 'Opening at four. Bricky', so we started again on our rounds.

We went to a café called *Le Fétiche*, where the waitresses wore dinner-jackets and asked the ladies in the party to dance. I was interested to see the fine, manly girl in charge of the cloakroom very deftly stealing a silk scarf from an elderly German.

We went to the Plantation, and to the Music Box, where it was so dark we could hardly see our glasses (which contained still nastier champagne), and to Shéherazade, where they brought us five different organs of lamb spitted together between onions and bay leaves, all on fire at the end and very nice to eat.

We went to Kasbek which was just like Shéherazade.

Finally, at four, we went to Brick-Top's. Brick-Top came and sat at our table. She seemed the least bogus person in Paris. It was broad daylight when we left; then we drove to the Halles and ate fine, pungent onion soup at *Le Père Tranquille*, while one of the young ladies in our party bought a bundle of leeks and ate them raw. I asked my host if all his evenings were like this. He said, no, he made a point of staying at home at least one night a week to play poker.

It was during about the third halt in the pilgrimage I have just described that I began to recognize the same faces crossing and re-crossing our path. There seemed to be about a hundred or so people in Montmartre that night, all doing the same round as ourselves.

Only two incidents of this visit to Paris live vividly in my memory.

One of these was the spectacle of a man in the Place Beauveau, who had met with an accident which must, I think, be unique. He was a man of middle age and, to judge by his bowler hat and frock coat, of the official class, and his umbrella had caught alight. I do not know how this can have happened. I passed him in a taxi-cab, and saw him in the centre of a small crowd, grasping it still by the handle and holding it at arm's length so that the flames should not scorch him. It was a dry day and the umbrella burnt flamboyantly. I followed the scene as long as I could from the little window in the back of the car, and saw him finally drop the handle and push it, with his foot, into the gutter. It lay there smoking, and the crowd peered at it curiously before moving off. A London crowd would have thought that the best possible joke, but none of the witnesses laughed, and no one to whom I have told this story in England has believed a word of it.

The other incident happened at a night club called *Le Grand Écart*. To those who relish the flavour of 'Period', there is a rich opportunity for reflection on the change that came over this phrase when the Paris of Toulouse-Lautrec gave place to the Paris of M. Cocteau. Originally it means the 'splits' – that very exacting figure in which the dancer slides her feet farther and farther apart until her body rests on the floor with her legs straight out on either side of her. It was thus that La Goulue and La Mélonite – 'the Maenad of the Decadence' – were accustomed to complete their *pas seul*, with a roguish revelation of thigh between black silk stocking and frilled petticoat. It is not so today. It is the name of a night club with little coloured electric bulbs, decorated with coils of rope and plate glass mirrors; on the tables are little illuminated tanks of water, with floating sheets of limp gelatine in imitation of ice. Shady young men in Charvet shirts sit round the bar repairing with powderpuff and lipstick the ravages of grenadine and *crème de cacao*. I was there one evening in a small party. A beautiful and splendidly dressed Englishwomen – who, as they say, shall be nameless – came to the next table. She was with a very nice-looking, enviable man who turned out later to be a Belgian baron. She knew someone in our party and there was an indistinct series of introductions. She said, 'What did you say that boy's name was?'

They said, 'Evelyn Waugh.'

She said, 'Who is he?'

None of my friends knew. One of them suggested that she thought I was an English writer.

She said, 'I knew it. He is the one person in the world I have been longing to meet.' (You must please bear with this part of the story: it all leads to my humiliation in the end.) 'Please move up so that I can come and sit next to him.'

Then she came and talked to me.

She said, 'I should never have known from your photographs that you were a blond.'

I should not have known how to answer that, but fortunately there was no need as she went straight on. 'Only last week I was reading an article by you in the *Evening Standard*. It was so beautiful that I cut it out and sent it to my mother.'

I said, 'I got ten guineas for it.'

At this moment the Belgian baron asked her to dance. She said, 'No, no. I am drinking in the genius of this wonderful young man.' Then she said to me, 'You know, I am psychic. The moment I came into this room tonight I *knew* that there was a *great personality* here, and I knew that I should find him before the evening was over.'

I suppose that real novelists get used to this kind of thing. It was new to me and very nice. I had only written two very dim books and still regarded myself less as a writer than an out-of-work private schoolmaster.

She said, 'You know, there is only one other great genius in this age. Can you guess his name?'

I suggested Einstein? No ... Charlie Chaplin? No ... James Joyce? No ... Who?

She said, 'Maurice Dekobra. I must give a little party at the Ritz for you to meet him. I should feel I had at least done something to justify my life if I had introduced you two great geniuses of the age. One must do something to justify one's life, don't you think, or don't you?'

Everything went very harmoniously for a time. Then she said something that made me a little suspicious, 'You know, I so love your books that I never travel without taking them all with me. I keep them in a row by my bed.'

'I suppose you aren't by any chance confusing me with my brother Alec? He has written many more books than I.'

'What did you say his name was?'

'Alec.'

'Yes, of course. What's your name, then?'

'Evelyn.'

'But ... but they said you wrote.'

'Yes, I do a little. You see, I couldn't get any other sort of job.'

14

Her disappointment was as frank as her friendliness had been. 'Well,' she said, 'how very unfortunate.'

Then she went to dance with her Belgian, and when she sat down she went to her former table. When we parted she said vaguely, 'We're sure to run into one another again.'

I wonder. And I wonder whether she will add this book, and with it this anecdote, to her collection of my brother's works by the side of her bed.

My next move was to Monte Carlo, where I had arranged to join a ship called the *Stella Polaris*.

I had decided to get out at Monaco because, I was told, the hotels were cheaper, and it would be more convenient for boarding the ship.

The station at Monaco is very small and unpretending. The only porter I could find belonged to an hotel with a fairly reputable-sounding name. He took my suitcase and led me through the falling snow, down the hill to his hotel. It was a *pension* in a side street. There was a small lounge full of basket chairs in which elderly Englishwomen sat sewing. I asked the porter whether there was not a better hotel at Monaco. Why, yes, he said, all the hotels in Monaco were better than this one. So he picked up my suitcase again and we went out into the snow, pursued by a manageress, and soon reached a larger hotel facing the harbour.

After luncheon the snow stopped, and the afternoon turned out intensely cold but bright and clear. I took a tram up the hill to Monte Carlo. The sound of firing came from the bastion below the promenade where '*Tir aux Pigeons*' was advertised. Some kind of match was in progress; the competitors were for the most part South Americans with papal titles. They made very interesting gestures with their elbows as they waited for the little cages to collapse and release the game; they also had interesting gestures of vexation and apology when they missed. But this was rare. The standard of marksmanship was high, and while I was there only three birds, fluttering erratically with plucked tail and wings, escaped the guns, to fall to the little boys below, who wait for them on the beach or in rowing-boats and pull them to pieces with their fingers. Often when the cages fell open the birds would sit dazed among the débris, until they were disturbed with a bowl; then they would rise clumsily and be brought down, usually by the first barrel, when they were about ten feet from the ground. On the balcony above the terrace sat one of the Casino pigeons, privileged and robust, watching the destruction without apparent emotion. The only convincing recommendation which I heard of this sport came from one of the visitors at the Bristol who remarked that it was not cricket.

There was a heavy fall of snow every night I was at Monaco, sometimes continuing nearly until midday, but always, within an hour of it stopping, every trace had disappeared. The moment that the last flake had fallen there appeared an army of busy little men in blue overalls armed with brooms and hoses and barrows; they sluiced and scraped the pavements and brushed up the lawns; they climbed up the trees with ladders and shook down the snow from the branches; the flower beds had been overlaid with wire frames, straw, and green baize counterpanes; these were whipped off, revealing brightly flowering plants which were replaced, the moment they withered in the frost, by fresh supplies warm from the hot-houses. Moreover, there was no nonsense about merely tidying the unseemly deposit out of the way; one did not come upon those dirty drifts and banks of snow which survive in odd corners of other places weeks after the thaw. The snow was put into barrows and packed into hampers and taken right away, across the frontier perhaps, or into the sea, but certainly well beyond the imperium of the Casino.

The arrival of the *Stella Polaris* caused excitement. She came in late in the evening, having encountered some very heavy weather on her way from Barcelona. I saw her lights across the harbour and heard her band faintly playing dance music, but it was not until next morning that I went to look more closely at her. She was certainly a very pretty ship, standing rather high in the water, with the tall, pointed prow of a sailing yacht, white all over except for her single yellow funnel.

Every Englishman abroad, until it is proved to the contrary, likes to consider himself a traveller and not a tourist. As I watched my luggage being lifted on to the *Stella* I knew that it was no use keeping up the pretence any longer. My fellow passengers and I were tourists, without any compromise or extenuation.

The *Stella Polaris* is a Norwegian-owned six-thousand-ton motor yacht, carrying, when full, about two hundred passengers. As one would expect from her origin, she exhibited a Nordic and almost glacial cleanliness. I have never seen anything outside a hospital so much scrubbed and polished. She carried an English doctor and nurse; otherwise the officers and crew, hairdresser, photographer, and other miscellaneous officials were all Norwegian. The stewards came of that cosmopolitan and polyglot race, Norwegian, Swiss, British, Italian, which supply the servants of the world. They maintained a Jeeves-like standard of courtesy and efficiency which was a particular delight to the English passengers, many of whom had been driven abroad by the problem of servants in their own homes. The passengers, too, were of all nationalities, but British strongly predominated, and English was the official language of the ship. The officers seemed to speak all languages with equal ease; several of them had first gone to sea in windjammers; sitting out between dances after dinner, while the ship ran on smoothly at fifteen knots into the warm darkness, they used to tell hair-raising stories of their early days, of typhoons and calms and privations; I think that when they were getting a little bored by their sheltered lives they found these reminiscences consoling.

I soon found my fellow passengers and their behaviour in the different places we visited a far more absorbing study than the places themselves.

One type which abounds on cruising ships is the middle-aged widow of comfortable means; their children are safely stored away at trustworthy boarding-schools; their servants are troublesome; they find themselves in control of more money than they have been used to; their eyes stray to the advertisements of shipping companies and find there just that assembly of phrases – half poetic, just perceptibly aphrodisiac – which can produce at will in the unsophisticated a state of mild unreality and glamour. 'Mystery, History, Leisure, Pleasure.' There is no directly defined sexual appeal. That rosy sequence of association, desert moon, pyramids, palms, sphinx, camels, oasis, priest in high minaret chanting the evening prayer, Allah, Hichens, Mrs Sheridan, all delicately point the way to sheik, rape, and harem – but the happily dilatory mind does not follow them to this forbidding conclusion; it sees the direction and admires the view from afar.

I do not think these happier travellers are ever disappointed in anything they see. They come back to the ship from each expedition with their eyes glowing; they have been initiated into strange mysteries, and their speech is rich with the words of the travel bureau's advertising manager; their arms are full of purchases. It is quite extraordinary to see what they will buy. I suppose it is the housekeeping habit run riot after twenty years of buying electric-light bulbs and tinned apricots and children's winter underwear. They become adept in bargaining and may be seen in the lounge over their evening coffee, lying prodigiously to each other, like the fishermen of comic magazines, comparing prices and passing their acquisitions from hand to hand amid a buzz of admiration and competitive anecdote. I wonder what happens to all this trash. When it reaches England and is finally unpacked in the grey light of some provincial morning, has it lost some of its glamour? Does it look at all like the other bric-à-brac displayed in the fancy goods emporium down the street? Is it distributed among relatives and friends to show that they are not forgotten during the voyage? – or is it treasured, every bit of it, hung upon walls and displayed on occasional tables, a bane to the house-parlourmaid but a continual reminder of those magical evenings under a wider sky, of dance music and the handsome figures of the officers, of temple bells heard across the water, of the inscrutable half light in the bazaars, of Allah, Hichens, and Mrs Sheridan?

But there were many kinds of passenger on board. I made friends with a young couple named Geoffrey and Juliet.

There was a series of land excursions organized on board the *Stella* by a patient and very charming Norwegian ex-sea-captain in a little office on the promenade deck, and one of the questions most exhaustively discussed among the passengers was whether these were worth while. At Naples, where I set out entirely alone with a very little knowledge of Italian, I wished very much that I had joined one of the parties.

We ran into the bay early on Sunday morning, and moored alongside the quay. There was a German-owned tourist ship in the harbour, which we were to see several times during the next few weeks, as she was following practically the same course as ourselves. She was built on much the same lines as the *Stella*, but the officers spoke contemptuously of her seaworthiness. She had capsized, they said, on the day she was launched, and was now ballasted with concrete. She carried a small black aeroplane on her deck, and the passengers paid about five guineas a time to fly over the harbour. At night her name appeared on the boat deck in illuminated letters. She had two bands which played almost incessantly. Her passengers were all middle-aged Germans, unbelievably ugly but dressed with courage and enterprise. One man wore a morning coat, white trousers, and a beret. Everyone in the *Stella* felt great contempt for this vulgar ship.

By the time that we had finished breakfast, all the formalities of passport and quarantine offices were over, and we were free to go on shore when we liked. A number of English ladies went off in a body, carrying prayer-books, in search of the Protestant church. They were outrageously cheated by their cab driver, they complained later, who drove them circuitously and charged them 85 lire. He had also suggested that instead of going to matins they should visit some Pompeian dances. I, too, was persecuted in a precisely similar way. As soon as I landed a small man in a straw hat ran to greet me, with evident cordiality. He had a brown, very cheerful face, and an engaging smile.

'Hullo, yes, you sir. Good morning,' he cried. 'You wanta one nice woman.'

I said, no, not quite as early in the day as that.

'Well, then, you wanta see Pompeian dances. Glass house. All-a-girls naked. Vair artistic, vair smutty, vair French.'

I still said no, and he went on to suggest other diversions rarely associated with Sunday morning. In this way we walked the length of the quay as far as the cab rank at the harbour entrance. Here I took a small carriage. The pimp attempted to climb on to the box, but was roughly repulsed by the driver. I told him to drive me to the cathedral, but he took me instead to a house of evil character.

'In there,' said the driver, 'Pompeian dances.'

'No,' I said, 'the cathedral.'

The driver shrugged his shoulders. When we reached the cathedral the fare was 8 lire, but the supplement showed 35. I was out of practice in travelling, and after an altercation in which I tried to make all the wrong points, I paid him and went into the cathedral. It was full of worshippers. One of them detached himself from his prayers and came over to where I was standing.

'After the Mass. You wanta come see Pompeian dances?'

I shook my head in Protestant aloofness.

'Fine girls?'

I looked away. He shrugged his shoulders, crossed himself, and relapsed into devotion ...

At dinner that evening at the Captain's table the lady next to me said, 'Oh, Mr Waugh, the custodian at the museum was telling me about some very interesting old Pompeian dances which are still performed, apparently. I couldn't quite follow all he said, but they sounded well worth seeing. I was wondering whether you would care to –'

It was one of the exasperating traits of the Neapolitan cab drivers to nod happily at their directions, drive on an elaborate and I have no doubt circuitous route until they arrived before the façade of the building whose frescoes I wished to see, and then, turning round on the box, smile genially, make the motion of locking a door, and say, '*Chiusa, signore*'. The Church of San Severo was the only one I succeeded in entering that afternoon, and it amply repaid the trouble we took to find it. The name was new to my driver, but after many inquiries we found a small door in a back street. He left the carriage and went off to fetch the custodian, returning after a great delay with a lovely little bare-footed girl who carried a bunch of large keys. We left the slum and stepped into a blaze of extravagant baroque. The little girl pattered round, enumerating the chapels and tombs in a voice of peculiar resonance. The sculpture there is astonishing, particularly Antonio Corradini's 'La Pudicizia' – a gross female figure draped from head to foot in a veil of transparent muslin. I do not see how imitative ingenuity can go further; every line of face and body is clearly visible under the clinging marble drapery; the hands and feet alone are bare, and the change of texture between the marble which represents flesh and the marble which represents flesh closely covered with muslin is observed with a subtlety which defies analysis.

While I was going round, my driver took the opportunity of saying a few prayers. The action seemed slightly out of place in this church, so cold and ill-kept and crowded with all but living marble.

When I had made a fairly thorough tour, the little girl lit a candle and beckoned me to a side door, her face, for the first time, alight with genuine enthusiasm. We went down a few steps and turned a corner. It was completely dark except for her candle, and there was a strong smell of putrefaction. Then she stepped aside and held up the light for me to see the object of our descent. Two figures of death stood upright against the wall in rococo coffins, their arms folded across their chests. They were quite naked and dark brown in colour. They had some teeth and some hair. At first I thought they were statues of more than usual virtuosity. Then I realized that they were exhumed corpses, partially mummified by the aridity of the air, like the corpses at St Michan's in Dublin. There were man and woman. The man's body was slit open, revealing a tangle of dry lungs and digestive organs. The little girl thrust her face into the aperture and inhaled deeply and greedily. She called on me to do the same.

'Smell good,' she said. 'Nice.'

We went up into the church.

I asked her about the corpses. 'They are the work of the priest,' she said.

Catania looked dirty and uninviting from the sea. A motor boat came out to meet us full of harbour officials, quarantine officers, passport inspectors, and so on, most of them in very fine uniforms with cloaks and swords and cocked hats. The companion ladder was let down for them, but there was some swell on in the harbour and they found difficulty in boarding. As the boat rose towards the ladder the officials stretched out their hands to the rail and towards the massive Norwegian seaman who was there to assist them. Some succeeded in catching hold, but each time their courage failed them just when the boat was at its highest; instead of stepping firmly from the motor boat, they gave a little hop and then let go. It was not a very exacting feat; all the passengers returning from Taormina accomplished it without mishap, including some very elderly ladies. The Sicilians, however, soon abandoned the attempt, and contented themselves with driving twice round the ship as though to show that they had never really intended coming on board, and then returned to their offices.

Geoffrey and I went ashore for an hour or two. The people seemed urban and miserable, particularly the children, who hung about in little joyless groups at the street corners as only grown men do in happier places.

That evening we headed east with two clear days at sea before reaching Haifa. During these days Juliet developed pneumonia, so I saw little of Geoffrey. Deck games broke out all over the ship.

A committee was formed, of which I found myself a very helpless member, to organize these sports into a tournament. It was interesting to notice that while the English, on the whole, threw themselves zealously into all the business of organizing, scoring, and refereeing, they were disposed to treat the games themselves with discernible casualness and frivolity. The other nationalities, however, and particularly the Scand-inavians, devoted every energy wholeheartedly to the cause of victory.

We reached Haifa during the night after the second day of sports. Lately its name has appeared in the newspapers as the scene of anti-Jewish rioting. It seemed very peaceful on the morn-ing of our arrival; there was no other big shipping in the harbour and a light fall of rain kept most of the inhabitants indoors.

Warned by my experience in Naples, I had arranged to go with the organized expedition to Nazareth, Tiberias, and Mount Carmel. Accordingly, I landed immediately after breakfast with the rest of the *Stella* party. The cars were waiting for us on the quay-side. I was put into the front seat of a Buick next to the driver, who had a sallow, intellectual face and European clothes. Most of the other drivers wore the *tarboosh*; the dragoman in charge of the expedition had huge moustaches that stood out from his face, so that the ends were clearly visible from behind him like the horns of a bison. Later we passed several families in Arab costume and a convoy of camels. They seemed out of place in this landscape, for, except for an occasional clump of cactus by the side of the road, these misty purple hills, this gentle downpour of rain, this plethora of Jews, these drab conifers, might surely have been from some grouse-laden corner of the Scottish highlands.

The driver of our motor car was a restless and unhappy man. He smoked 'Lucky Strike' cigarettes continuously, one after the other. When he lit a new one he took both hands off the wheel; often he did this at corners; he drove very fast and soon outdistanced all the other cars. When we most nearly had accidents he gave a savage laugh. He spoke almost perfect English with an American accent. He said he could never eat or drink when he was out with the car; he smoked instead; last month he had driven a German gentleman to Baghdad and back; he had felt ill after that. He never smiled except at the corners, or when, as we swept through a village, some little child, its mother wailing her alarm, darted in front of us. Then he would stamp on the accelerator and lean forward eagerly in his seat. As the child skipped clear of our wheels, he would give a little whistle of disappointment through his teeth and resume his despondent but polite flow of anecdote. This man had no religious beliefs, he told me, no home, and no nationality. He was an orphan brought up in New York by the Near East Relief Fund; he did not know for certain, but he supposed his parents had been massacred by the Turks. He liked America; there were a lot of rich people there, he said. After the war he had tried to get American citizenship, but they had turned him out. He had some very bitter trouble about some 'papers'; I could not quite understand what. They had sent him to colonize Palestine. He did not like Palestine because there were so few rich people there. He hated the Jews because they were the poorest of all, so he had become a Mohammedan. He was allowed a dozen wives but remained unmarried. Women took up time and money. He wanted to get rich and then spend all his time going from one place to another until he died. Perhaps if he became very rich they would let him become an American citizen. He would not settle in America, but he would like, when he travelled about, to say he was American; then everyone would respect him. He had been to London once; that was a good town, full of rich people. And Paris; that was nice, too, plenty of rich people there. Did he like his present job? What else was there to do in a stinking place like the Holy Land? His immediate ambition was to get a job as steward in a ship; not a stinking little ship, but one full of rich people like the *Stella Polaris*.

We went to Cana of Galilee, where a little girl was offering wine jars for sale. They were the authentic ones used in the miracle. If they were too big she had a smaller size indoors; yes, the small ones were authentic, too. Then we drove on to Tiberias, a small fishing village of cubic houses on the Sea of Galilee. There were the ruins of some kind of fort and a white domed public bath of steaming mineral water. We were led into this bath. In the court-yard a kind of picnic was going on; an Arab family sitting on the ground and eating bread and raisins. It was almost dark in the bath; the naked bathers lay about in the steam undisturbed by our intrusion. We lunched at Nazareth in an hotel managed by Germans, and ate omelettes, rissoles, and pork, and drank an uncommendable wine called Jaffa Gold. During luncheon the rain stopped. We went to visit the holy places. We were shown the site of the Annunciation and Joseph's Workshop; both these were caves. A cheerful Irish monk with a red beard opened the gates for us. He was as sceptical as ourselves about the troglodytic inclinations of the Holy Family. The attitude of my fellow travellers was interesting. This sensible ecclesiastic vexed them. They had expected someone very superstitious and credulous and medieval, whom they would be able to regard with discreet ridicule. As it was, the laugh was all on the side of the Church. It was we who had driven twenty-four miles, and had popped our tribute into the offertory box, and were being gently humoured for our superstition.

Outside the church a brisk trade was done in olive-wood paper-weights. Small boys flung themselves at our feet and began cleaning our shoes. A nun sold lace doyleys. An old woman wanted to tell our fortunes. We struggled through these Nazarenes and got back to the cars. Our driver was smoking by himself. The other drivers were ignorant fools, he said. He wasn't going to waste his time talking to them. He looked with derision at the souvenirs we had bought.

'They are of no interest,' he said, 'none whatever. But if you really wished to buy them you should have told me. I could have got them for you at a tenth of the price.' He lunged out with a spanner and rapped an old man over the knuckles who was trying to sell us a fly-whisk. Then we drove on. The hills were covered with asphodel and anemones and cyclamen. We stopped him, and I got out to pick a bunch for Juliet.

'They will all die before you get back to the ship,' said the driver.

Poor Geoffrey had spent the day with the ship's doctor securing the services of a nurse. They secured a squat young woman of indeterminable nationality, who spoke English of a sort and had had hospital training. She spent the first half-hour scrubbing Juliet and tumbling her from one side of the bed to the other till her temperature rose to formidable heights. Then she scraped her tongue with a nail file. Then she was very sick and retired to her cabin, and poor Geoffrey, who had been up all the night before, shared another night's vigil with the stewardess (whom the nurse addressed as 'sister'). They sent this nurse back by train from Port Said. It was the first time she had been at sea. Despite the fact that she had spent the whole of her voyage prostrate in her cabin, she expressed the utmost delight in her experience and applied to the doctor for a permanent position on board. After she had gone Geoffrey found an odd document in the cabin. It was a sheet of the ship's notepaper. At the very top, above the crest, was a line of very unsteady pencil handwriting. 'Pneuminia (*La Grippe*) is a very prevalent epidemic Disease in the spring it is.'

Many of the passengers left the *Stella* at Haifa and went on to Egypt by way of Damascus and Jerusalem, rejoining her eight days later at Port Said. The others stayed on board for the night and left next morning by train for Cairo and Luxor. Geoffrey, Juliet, and I, and the two other invalids, were alone on board after the first day at Port Said. Everyone on board values this week of inaction in the middle of the cruise. The officers change into plain clothes and go shopping at Simon Arzt; the sailors and stewards go ashore in jolly batches of six and seven. It is about the only opportunity they have for prolonged land excursions; several of them went up to Cairo for the day. Those who are on duty are employed in renewed prodigies of cleaning, polishing, and painting. We were filled up with fuel and water. The band played on shore in one of the cafés. The Captain gave luncheon-parties to officials and friends. The sun was brilliant and warm without being too hot, and for the first time we were able to sit comfortably on deck without scarves or greatcoats, and watch the continual coming and going of the big ships in the canal basin.

The only disturbing element in this happy week was Juliet, who was by this time very seriously ill. The doctor pronounced her unfit for travel, and she was accordingly lowered in a stretcher and taken ashore to the British hospital. I accompanied the procession, which consisted of the ship's doctor, carrying warm brandy and a teaspoon, an officer, Geoffrey, half distracted with anxiety, a dense mob of interested Egyptians, Copts, Arabs, Lascars, and Sudanese, and a squad of ambulance men, two of whom fought the onlookers while the others bundled Juliet – looking distressingly like a corpse – into a motor van. These last men were Greeks, and refused all payment for their services. It was sufficient reward that they were allowed to wear uniform. They must be the only people in the whole of Egypt who have ever done anything for nothing. I met one of them some weeks later marching with a troop of Boy Scouts, and he fell out of the ranks and darted across the road to shake my hand and ask me news of Juliet.

It was a melancholy journey to the hospital, and a still more melancholy walk back with Geoffrey. The British hospital lies at the far end of the sea front. We passed a game of football, played enthusiastically upon an uneven waste of sand, by Egyptian youths very completely dressed in green and white jerseys, white shorts, striped stockings, and shiny black football boots. They cried ''ip-'ip-'ooray' each time they kicked the ball, and some of them blew whistles; a goat or two wandered amongst them, nosing up morsels of lightly buried refuse.

We stopped on the terrace of the Casino Hotel for a drink, and a conjuror came and did tricks for us with live chickens. These are called 'gully-gully men' because of their chatter. They are the worst possible conjurors but excellent comedians. They squat on the ground, making odd clucking noises in their throats and smiling happily, and proceed with the minimum of deception to pop things in and out of their voluminous sleeves; their final trick is to take a five-piastre piece and drop that up their sleeve, but it is a good entertainment the first two or three times. There was a little Arab girl in the town who had taught herself to imitate them perfectly, only, with a rare instinct for the elimination of inessentials, she used not to bother about the conjuring at all, but would scramble from table to table in the cafés, saying, 'Gully-gully', and taking a chicken in and out of a little cloth bag. She was every bit as amusing as the grown-ups and made just as much money. On this particular afternoon, however, Geoffrey was not to be consoled so easily, and the performance seemed rather to increase his gloom. We went back to the ship, and I helped him pack up his luggage and move it to his hotel.

Two days later I decided to join him.

The hotel where Geoffrey and I stayed was on the front – a brand new concrete building kept by a retired English officer and his wife. It was recommended by all the British colony in Port Said on the grounds that it was the only place where you could be certain of not meeting any 'gyppies'. The people we did meet were certainly very British but far from gay. Few people stay in Port Said except for some rather dismal reason. There were two genial canal pilots who lived at Bodell's permanently, and there was an admirable young lawyer just down from Cambridge who added immeasurably to our enjoyment; he was spending his holiday from the Temple in investigating the night life of Alexandria, Port Said, and Cairo. As some people can instinctively find the lavatories in a strange house, this young man, arriving at the railway station of any town in any continent, could instantly orientate himself towards its disreputable quarter. But apart from him and the pilots, the other guests at Bodell's were all people on their way through who had been obliged to leave their ships by the illness of wives or children. There was a planter from Kenya with a small daughter and governess; he was returning home for the first time after fourteen years; his wife was lying desperately ill in the hospital. There was a captain in the Tank Corps, on his way

27

out to India for the first time, whose wife had developed appendicitis and had been rushed to the operating theatre. There was a soldier's wife taking her children home for the hot season; her youngest son had developed meningitis. I grew to dread the evenings at home, when we all sat round in wicker arm-chairs dolefully discussing the patients' progress, while the gentle Berber servants, with white gowns and crimson sashes, stole in and out with whiskies and sodas, and Mr Bodell attempting to cheer us up with an ancient gramophone and an unintelligible gambling game played with perforated strips of cardboard.

Geoffrey, the Cambridge solicitor, and I spent two or three evenings investigating the night-town, called by the residents 'red lamp district'. It lies at the farthest extremity of the town on the shore of Lake Menzaleh, round the little wharf and goods yard of the Menzaleh canal, separated from the shops and offices and hotels by a mile or so of densely populated Arab streets. It is very difficult to find by day, but at night, even without our solicitor's peculiar gifts, we should have been led there by the taxis full of tipsy sailors and stewards, or grave, purposeful Egyptians, that swept by us in the narrow thoroughfare.

We set out after dinner one evening, rather apprehensively, with a carefully calculated minimum of money, and life-preservers of lead, leather, and whalebone, with which our solicitor, surprisingly, was able to furnish us; we left watches, rings, and tie-pins on our dressing-tables, and carefully refrained from alarming Juliet with the knowledge of our destination. It was an interesting walk. An absurd tram runs up the Quai du Nord, drawn by a mare and a donkey. We followed this for some way and then struck off to the left through Arab Town. These streets presented a scene of astonishing vivacity and animation. Little traffic goes down them and there is no differentiation of pavement and road in the narrow earthen track; instead, it is overrun with hand-barrows selling, mostly, fruit and confectionery, men and women bargaining and gossiping, innumerable bare-footed children, goats, sheep, ducks, hens, and geese. The houses on either side are wooden, with overhanging balconies and flat roofs. On the roofs are ramshackle temporary erections for store-rooms and hen-houses. No one molested us in any way, or, indeed, paid us the smallest attention. It was Ramadan, the prolonged Mohammedan fast during which believers spend the entire day from sunrise to sunset without food or drink of any kind. As a result the night is spent in feverish feasting; nearly everyone carried a little enamelled bowl of a food resembling some kind of milk pudding, into which he dipped between bites of delicious-looking ring-shaped bread. There were men with highly decorated brass urns selling some kind of lemonade; there were women carrying piles of cakes on their heads. As we progressed the houses became more and more tumble-down and the street more narrow. We were on the outskirts of the small Sudanese quarter where a really primitive life is led. Then suddenly we came into a rough, highly-lighted square with two or three solid stucco-fronted houses and some waiting taxis. One side was open to the black, shallow waters of the lake, and was fringed with the masts of the little fishing-boats. Two or three girls in bedraggled European evening dress seized hold of us and dragged us to the most highly-lighted of the buildings; this had 'Maison Dorée' painted across its front, and the girls cried, 'Gol'-'ouse, gol'-'ouse,' 'Vair good, vair clean.' It did not seem either very good or very clean to me. We sat in a little room full of Oriental decorations and drank some beer with the young ladies. Madame joined us, a handsome Marseillaise in a green silk embroidered frock; she cannot have been more than forty, and was most friendly and amusing. Four or five other young ladies came in, all more or less white; they sat very close together on the divan and drank beer, making laudably little effort to engage our attention. None of them could talk any English, except, 'Cheerioh, Mr American'. I do not know what their nationality was. Jewesses, Armenians, or Greeks, I suppose. They cost 50 piastres each, Madame said. These were all European ladies. The other, neighbouring houses, were full of Arabs – horrible, dirty places, she said. Some of the ladies took off their frocks and did a little dance, singing a song which sounded like ta-ra-ra-boom-de-ay. There was a jolly-sounding party going on upstairs, with a concertina and glass-breaking, but Madame would not let us go up. Then we paid for our drinks and went out.

Then we went next door to a vastly more plebeian house called Les Folies Bergères, kept by a gross old Arab woman who talked very little French and no English. She had a licence for eight girls, but I do not think hers was a regular establishment. On our arrival a boy was sent out into the streets, and he brought back half a dozen or so Arab girls, all very stout and ugly and carelessly daubed with powder and paint. All round were the little alleys where the freelance prostitutes lived. These were one-roomed huts like bathing cabins. The women who were not engaged sat at their open doors sewing industriously, and between stitches looking up and calling for custom; many had their prices chalked on the door-posts – 25 piastres in some cases, but usually less. Inside iron bedsteads were visible, and hanging banners worked with the crests of British regiments.

On our way back we came upon another gaily illuminated building called Maison Chabanais. We went in, and were surprised to encounter Madame and all her young ladies from the Maison Dorée. It was, in fact, her back door. Sometimes, she explained, gentlemen went away unsatisfied, determined to find another house, then as often as not they found the way round to the other side, and the less observant ones never discovered their mistake.

While we were at Port Said, Ramadan came to an end with the feast of Bajiram. All the children were given new clothes – those that could not afford a frock wearing a strip of tinsel or bright ribbon, and paraded the streets on foot or in horse-cabs. The streets of Arab Town were illuminated and hung with flags, and everyone devoted himself to making as much noise as he could. The soldiers fired cannonade after cannonade of artillery; civilians beat drums, blew whistles and trumpets, or merely rattled tin pans together and shouted. This went on for three days.

There was a fair and two circuses. Geoffrey and I and the head of the hospital went to the circus one evening, much to the bewilderment of one club. The hospital nurses were very shocked at our going. 'Think of the poor animals,' they said. '*We* know the way the gyppies treat their animals.' But, unlike European circuses, there were no performing animals.

We were the only Europeans in the tent. The chairs were ranged on rather unstable wooden steps ascending from the ring to a considerable height at the back. Behind the back row were a few heavily curtained boxes for the women; there were very few there; most of the large audience consisted of young men. A number of small boys were huddled between the front row and the ringside, and a policeman was employing his time in whisking these off the parapet with a cane. The seats seemed all to be the same price; we paid 5 piastres each and chose places near the back. Attendants were going about between the rows selling nuts, mineral waters, coffee, and hubble-bubbles. These were of the simplest pattern, consisting simply of a coconut half full of water, a little tin brazier of tobacco, and a long bamboo mouthpiece. The doctor warned me that if I smoked one of these I was bound to catch some frightful disease; I did so, however, without ill effect. The vendor keeps several alight at a time by sucking at each in turn. We all drank coffee, which was very thick and sweet and gritty.

The show had begun before we arrived, and we found ourselves in the middle of a hugely popular comic turn; two Egyptians in European costume were doing cross-talk. It was, of course, wholly unintelligible to us; now and then they smacked each other, so I have no doubt it was much the same as an English music-hall turn. After what seemed an unconscionable time the comedians went away amid thunderous applause, and their place was taken by a very pretty little white girl in a ballet dress; she cannot have been more than ten or twelve years old; she danced a Charleston. Later she came round and sold picture postcards of herself. She turned out to be French. To those that enjoy moralizing about such things there is food for reflection in the idea of this African dance, travelling across two continents from slave to gigolo, and gradually moving south again towards the land of its origin.

Then there were some Japanese jugglers, and then an interminable comic turn performed by the whole company. They sang a kind of doleful folk song and then, one at a time, with enormous elaboration of 'business', came in and lay down on the ground; after all the grown-ups were settled the little girl came in and lay down too; finally a tiny child of two or three tottered in and lay down. All this took at least a quarter of an hour. Then they all got

31

up again, still singing, one at a time in the same order, and went out. After that there was an interval, during which everyone left his place and strolled about in the ring as people do at Lord's between the innings. After this a Negro of magnificent physique appeared. First he thrust a dozen or so knitting-needles through his cheeks, so that they protruded on either side of his head; he walked about among the audience bristling in this way and thrusting his face into ours with a fixed and rather frightful grin. Then he took some nails and hammered them into his thighs. Then he stripped off everything except a pair of diamanté drawers, and rolled about without apparent discomfort on a board stuck with sharp carving-knives.

It was while he was doing this that a fight began. It raged chiefly round the exit, which was immediately below our seats. The heads of the combatants were on a level with our feet, so that we were in a wholly advantageous position to see everything without serious danger. It was difficult to realize quite what was happening; more and more of the audience joined in. The Negro got up from his board of knives, feeling thoroughly neglected and slighted, and began addressing the crowd, slapping his bare chest and calling their attention to the tortures he was suffering for them. The man on my right, a grave Egyptian with a knowledge of English, with whom I had some conversation, suddenly stood up, and leaning across all three of us struck down with his umbrella a resounding blow on the top of one of the fighting heads; then he sat down again with unruffled gravity and devoted himself to his hubble-bubble.

'What is the fight about –' I asked him.

'Fight?' he said. 'Who has been fighting? I saw no fight.'

'There.' I pointed to the seething riot in the doorway which seemed to threaten the collapse of the entire tent.

'Oh, that!' he said. 'Forgive me, I thought you said "fight". That is only the police.'

And sure enough, when the crowd eventually parted some minutes later, there emerged from its depths two uncontrollably angry police constables whom the onlookers had been attempting to separate. They were ejected at last to settle their quarrel outside; the crowd began sorting out and dusting their fallen fezes;

everything became quiet again, and the big Negro resumed his self-lacerations in an appreciative calm.

Various forms of acrobatics followed in which the little French girl displayed great intrepidity and style. It was in full swing when we left, and apparently continued for hours nightly until the last comer felt he had had his money's worth. One day after this we saw the French child in the town, seated at a table in the confectioner's with her manager, eating a great many chocolate éclairs with a wan and emotionless face.

During Bajiram, the railway sold return tickets to Cairo at half price, so the solicitor and I went up for a night in a very comfortable Pullman carriage.

We arrived in the late afternoon and went to look for an hotel. All the hotels in Egypt are bad, but they excuse themselves upon two contrary principles. Some maintain, legitimately, that it does not really matter how bad they are if they are cheap enough; the others, that it does not really matter how bad they are if they are expensive enough. Both classes do pretty well. We sought out one of the former, a large, old-fashioned establishment under Greek management in the Midan el-Khaznedar, called the Hotel Bristol et du Nil, where rooms even in the high season are only 80 piastres a night. My room had three double beds in it under high canopies of dusty mosquito netting, and two derelict rocking chairs. The windows opened on a tram terminus. None of the servants spoke a word of any European language, but this was a negligible defect since they never answered the bell.

Dennis – as it would be more convenient to name my companion – had been to Cairo before and was anxious to show me the sights, particularly, of course, those of the 'red light district'.

The whole quarter was brilliantly illuminated in honour of the holiday. Awnings of brightly coloured cotton, printed to imitate carpets, were hung from window to window across the streets. Rows of men and women sat on chairs outside the houses watching the dense crowds who sauntered up and down. Many small cafés were occupied by men drinking coffee, smoking, and playing chess. This district, in addition to its disreputable trade, is the centre of a vivid social life; men were dancing deliberate and rather ungainly folk dances in some of the cafés. There was plenty of music on all sides. Except for a picket of military police, we saw no Europeans; nobody stared at us or embarrassed us in any way, but we felt ourselves out of place in this intimate and jolly atmosphere, like gate-crashers intruding on a schoolroom birthday party. We were just about to go when Dennis met an acquaintance – an Egyptian electrical engineer who had been in the ship with him coming out. He shook us both warmly by the hand and introduced the friend who was with him; they linked their arms with ours and all four of us paraded the narrow street in this way, chatting amicably. The engineer, who had been trained in London for some important post connected with telephones, was very anxious that we should form a good impression of his town, and was alternately boastful and apologetic. Did we find it very dirty? We must not think of them as ignorant people; it was a pity it was a holiday; if we had come at any other time he could have shown us things people never dreamed about in London; did we love a lot of girls in London? He did. He showed us a pocketbook stuffed with photographs of them; weren't they peaches? But we must not think Egyptian girls were ugly. Many had skins as fair as our own; if it had not been a holiday, he could have shown us some beauties.

He seemed a popular young man. Friends greeted him on all sides and he introduced us to them. They all shook hands and offered us cigarettes. As none of them spoke any English these encounters were brief. Finally he asked us if we would like some coffee, and took us into one of the houses.

'This is not so dear as the others,' he explained, 'some of them are terrible what they charge. Just like your London.'

It was called the High Life House, the name being painted up in English and Arabic characters on the door. We climbed a great many stairs and came into a small room where three very old men were playing on oddly shaped stringed instruments. A number of handsomely dressed Arabs sat round the walls munching nuts. They were mostly small landed proprietors, our host explained, up from the country for the festival. He ordered us coffee, nuts, and cigarettes and gave half a piastre to the band. There were two women in the room, a vastly fat white creature of indistinguishable

race, and a gorgeous young Sudanese. Would we like to see one
of the ladies dance, he asked. We said we would, and suggested
the Negress. He was puzzled and shocked at our choice. 'She has
such a dark skin,' he said.

'We think she is the prettier,' we said.

Courtesy overcame his scruples. After all, we were guests. He
ordered the Negress to dance. She got up and looked for some
castanets without glancing in our direction, moving very slowly.
She cannot have been more than seventeen. She wore a very short,
backless, red dance dress with bare legs and feet, and numerous
gold bracelets round her ankles and wrists. These were quite
genuine, our host assured us. They always put all their savings
into gold ornaments. She found her castanets and began dancing
in an infinitely bored way but with superb grace. The more inflammatory her movements became, the more dreamy and detached her expression. There was no suggestion of jazz about her
art – merely a rhythmic, sinuous lapsing from pose to pose, a
leisurely twisting and vibrating of limbs and body. She danced for
a quarter of an hour or twenty minutes, while our host spat nut-
shells contemptuously round her feet; then she took up a
tambourine and collected money, giving a faintly discernible nod
at each donation.

'On no account give her more than half a piastre,' said our
host.

I had nothing smaller than a 5-piastre piece, so I put that into
her collection, but she received it with unmoved indifference. She
went out to conceal her winnings and then sat down again, and,
taking a handful of nuts, began munching and spitting, her eyes
half closed and her head supported on her fist.

Our host was clearly finding us something of an encumbrance
by now, so after prolonged exchanges of courtesy and good
fellowship we left him for the European quarter. Here we picked
up a taxi and told him to drive us to a night club. He took us to
one called Peroquet, which was full of young men in white ties
throwing paper streamers about. This was not quite what we were
looking for, so we drove on right out of the town and across the
river to Gizeh. The place of entertainment here was called
Fantasio, and there was a finely liveried commissionaire outside.

A number of slot machines in the vestibule, however, removed any apprehensions about its smartness. The tables were divided into pens by low wooden partitions; about three-quarters of them were empty. On a stage at the end of the hall a young Egyptian was singing what sounded like a liturgical chant in a doleful tenor. With brief pauses, this performance continued as long as we were there. There was a magnificent-looking old sheik in one of the boxes, incapably drunk.

After half an hour of the Fantasio even Dennis's enthusiasm for night life became milder, so we engaged an open horse-carriage and drove back under the stars to the Bristol and Nile.

Shortly before Easter the doctors pronounced Juliet fit to move, so we packed up and left Port Said for Cairo. Before going we made our adieux to the various people who had befriended us. This was no modern, informal leave-taking, but a very solemn progression from house to house with little packs of calling cards marked 'p.p.c.' in the corner. I had heard scathing comments from time to time at Port Said dinner-parties on people who neglected these polite observances.

The journey was unremarkable except to Juliet, who was not used to the ways of Egyptian porters. These throw themselves upon one's baggage like Westminster schoolboys on their Shrove Tuesday pancake, with this difference, that their aim is to carry away as small a piece as possible; the best fighter struggles out happily with a bundle of newspapers, a rug, an air-cushion, or a small attaché case; the less fortunate share the trunks and suitcases. In this way one's luggage is shared between six or seven men, all of whom clamorously demand tips when they have finally got it into the train or taxi. Juliet was shocked to see her husband and myself defending our possessions from attack with umbrella and walking-stick; when the first onslaught was thus checked and our assailants realized that we had not newly disembarked, we were able to apportion it between two of them and proceed on our way with dignity.

We had booked rooms at Mena House on the grounds that desert air and a certain degree of luxury were essential to Juliet's recovery. The road out to it is a great place for motor-speeding, and there is usually a racing car or so piled up at the side of the road any time one goes along, for Egyptians, particularly the wealthier ones, are reckless with machinery. We passed two on our way out with Juliet, one about two hundred yards from the road in a field of cucumbers, with two *fellahin* eyeing it distrustfully. Trams run all the way out to the pyramids, crowded and slow and very little used by Europeans or Americans. At the tram terminus there are a mob of dragomans, a great number of camels and mules for hire, a Greek-owned café, a picture-postcard shop, a photographic shop, a curiosity shop specializing in scarabs, and Mena House. This is a large building in pseudo-Oriental style, standing in a vast and lovely garden. The pyramids were a quarter of a mile away, impressive by sheer bulk and reputation; it felt odd to be living at such close quarters with anything quite so famous – it was like having the Prince of Wales at the next table in a restaurant; one kept pretending not to notice, while all the time glancing furtively to see if they were still there. The gardens were grossly luxuriant, a mass of harsh greens and violets. Round the house they were studded with beds, packed tight with brilliantly coloured flowers, like Victorian paper-weights, while behind and beyond were long walks bordered by gutters of running water, among orchards and flowering trees heavy with almost overpowering scent; there were high cactus hedges and a little octagonal aviary, and innumerable white-robed gardeners, who stood up from their work and bowed and presented buttonholes when a visitor passed them.

There was plenty of life at Mena, particularly at the week-ends. The residents were mostly elderly and tranquil, but for luncheon and tea all kinds of people appeared. Huge personally conducted luxury tours of Americans and northern Englishmen, Australians in jodphurs with topees and fly-whisks, very smart Egyptian officers with vividly painted motor cars and astonishing courtesans – one in a bright green picture frock led a pet monkey on a gold chain; it wore a jewelled bracelet round its neck and fleaed its rump on the terrace while she had her tea. On Easter Monday they had what they called a gymkhana, which meant that all the prices were raised for that afternoon. Apart from this it was not really a success. There was a gentlemen's camel race which was very easily won by an English sergeant who knew how to ride, and a ladies' camel race for which there were no competitors, and a ladies' donkey race won by a noisy English girl of seventeen, and a gentlemen's donkey race for which there were no competitors, and an Arabs' camel race the result of which had clearly been arranged beforehand, and an Arabs' donkey race which ended in a sharp altercation and the exchange of blows. There was an English tourist who tried to make a book; he stood on a chair and was very facetious, but gave such short odds that there were no takers. There was a lady of rank staying in the hotel who gave away the prizes – money to the camel- and donkey-boys and hideous works of Egyptian art to the Europeans. On another evening there was a ball, but that too was ill attended, as it happened to coincide with a reception at the Residency, and no one was anxious to advertise the fact that he had not been invited there.

Geoffrey's and my chief recreations were swimming and camel-riding. We used to ride most days for two hours, making a wide circle through the Arab village and up the ancient track past the Sphinx and the smaller pyramids. To please their customers, the boys called their beasts by American names – 'Yankydoodle', 'Hitchycoo', 'Red-Hot Momma'. They were most anxious to please in every way, even to seizing our hands and foretelling by the lines in our palms illimitable wealth, longevity, and fecundity for both of us.

Geoffrey, Juliet, and I went round the local antiquities with a kindly old Bedouin called Solomon.

One Friday, Solomon came to tell us about some religious dances that were to be performed in the neighbourhood; did we want to see them? Juliet did not feel up to it, so Geoffrey stayed at home with her and I went off alone with Solomon. We rode to the farther end of the plateau on which the pyramids stand, and then down into a sandy hollow where there were the entrances to several tombs. Here we left our camels in charge of a boy and climbed into one of the holes in the hillside. The tomb was already half full of Arabs; it was an oblong chamber cut in the rock and decorated in places with incised hieroglyphics. The audience were standing round the walls and packed in the recesses cut for the coffins. The only light came through the door – one beam of white daylight. The moment we arrived the dance began. It was performed by young men, under the direction of a sheik; the audience clapped their hands in time and joined in the chant. It *was* a dull dance, like kindergarten Eurhythmics. The youths stamped their feet on the sandy floor and clapped their hands and swayed slowly about. After a short time I signed to Solomon my readiness to leave, and attempted to make as unobtrusive a departure as possible so as not to disturb these ungainly devotions. No sooner, however, had I reached the door than the dance stopped and the whole company came trooping out crying for 'bakshish'. I asked Solomon whether it was not rather shocking that they should expect to be paid by an infidel for keeping their religious observances. He said, rather sheepishly, that some tip was usual to the sheik. I asked where the sheik was. 'Sheik. Me sheik,' they cried, all running forward and beating their chests. Then the old man appeared. I gave him the piastres and they promptly transferred their attention to him, seizing his robes and clamouring for a share. We mounted our camels and rode away. Even then two or three urchins pursued us on foot crying, 'Bakshish! Bakshish! Me sheik!'

As we went back I asked Solomon, 'Was that a genuine religious dance?'

He pretended not to understand.

'You did not like the dance?'

'Would they have done that dance if you had not brought me?'

Solomon was again evasive. 'English and American lords like to see dance. English lords all satisfied.'

'I wasn't satisfied,' I said.

Solomon sighed. 'All right,' he said, which is the Arab's reply to all difficulties with English and American lords. 'Better dance another day.'

'There won't be another day.'

'All right,' said Solomon.

One day I went alone to Sakkara, the enormous necropolis some way down the Nile from Mena. There are two pyramids there, and a number of tombs; one of them, named unpronounceably the Mastaba of Ptahhotep, is exquisitely decorated in low relief. Another still more beautifully sculptured chamber is called more simply the Mastaba of Ti. As I emerged from this vault I came upon a large party of twenty or thirty indomitable Americans dragging their feet, under the leadership of a dragoman, across the sand from a charabanc. I fell in behind this party and followed them underground again, this time into a vast subterranean tunnel called the Serapeum, which, the guide explained, was the burial-place of the sacred bulls. It was like a completely unilluminated tube-railway station. We were each given a candle, and our guide marched on in front with a magnesium flare. Even so, the remote corners were left in impenetrable darkness. On either side of our path were ranged the vast granite sarcophagi; we marched very solemnly the full length of the tunnel, our guide counting the coffins aloud for us; there were twenty-four of them, each so massive that the excavating engineers could devise no means of removing them. Most of the Americans counted aloud with him.

One is supposed, I know, to think of the past on these occasions; to conjure up the ruined streets of Memphis and to see in one's mind's eye the sacred procession as it wound up the avenue of sphinxes, mourning the dead bull; perhaps even to give licence to one's fancy and invent some personal romance about the lives of these garlanded hymn-singers, and to generalize sagely about the mutability of human achievement. But I think we can leave all that to Hollywood. For my own part I found the present spectacle infinitely stimulating. What a funny lot we looked, trooping along that obscure gallery! First the Arab with his blazing white ribbon of magnesium, and behind him, clutching their candles, like penitents in procession, this whole rag-tag and bobtail of self-improvement and uplift. Some had been bitten by mosquitoes and bore swollen, asymmetrical faces; many were footsore, and limped and stumbled as they went; one felt faint and was sniffing 'salts'; one coughed with dust; another had her eyes inflamed by the sun; another wore his arm in a sling, injured in heaven knows what endeavour; every one of the party in some way or another was bruised and upbraided by the thundering surf of education. And still they plunged on. One, two, three, four ... twenty-four dead bulls; not twenty-three or twenty-five. How could they remember twenty-four? Why, to be sure, it was the number of Aunt Mabel's bedroom at Luxor. 'How did the bulls die?' one of them asks.

'What did he ask?' chatter the others.

'What did the guide answer?' they want to know.

'How *did* the bulls die?'

'How much did it cost?' asks another. 'You can't build a place like this for nothing.'

'We don't spend money that way nowadays.'

'Fancy spending all that burying bulls ...'

Oh, ladies and gentlemen, I longed to declaim, dear ladies and gentlemen, fancy crossing the Atlantic Ocean, fancy coming all this way in the heat, fancy enduring all these extremities of discomfort and exertion; fancy spending all this money, to see a hole in the sand where, three thousand years ago, a foreign race whose motives must for ever remain inexplicable interred the carcasses of twenty-four bulls. Surely the laugh, dear ladies and gentlemen, is on us.

But I remembered I was a gate-crasher in this party and remained silent.

I drove down to Helwan for a couple of nights.

We went to Masr el Atika, Old Cairo or Babylon, the Coptic settlement built in the days of persecution within the walls of the old Roman garrison station. In this constricted slum there are five medieval Coptic churches, a synagogue, and a Greek Orthodox convent. The Christians seem to differ in decency very little from their pagan neighbours; the only marked sign of their emancipation from heathen superstition was that the swarm of male and juvenile beggars were here reinforced by their womenfolk, who in the Mohammedan quarters maintain a modest seclusion. The churches, however, were most interesting, particularly Abu Sergh, which has Corinthian columns taken from a Roman temple, Byzantine eikons, and an Arabic screen. It is built over the cave where the Holy Family – always troglodytic – are said to have spent their retirement during Herod's massacre of the innocents. The deacon, Bestavros, showed us over. When

41

he had finished his halting exposition and received his tip, he said, 'Wait one minute. Get priest.'

He hurried into the vestry and brought out a patriarchal old man with a long grey beard and large greasy bun of grey hair, obviously newly awakened from his afternoon nap. This priest blinked, blessed us, and held out his hand for a tip; then, lifting up his skirts, he tucked the two piastres away in a pocket and made off. At the vestry door he stopped. 'Go getting bishop,' he said.

Half a minute later he returned with a still more venerable figure, chewing sunflower seeds. The pontiff blessed us and held out his hand for a tip. I gave him two piastres. He shook his head.

'He is a bishop,' explained Bestavros, 'three piastres for a bishop.'

I added a piastre and he went away beaming. Bestavros then sold me a copy of a history of the church written by himself. It is such a very short work that I think it worth reproducing here with spelling and punctuation exactly as it was printed.

A BRIEF HISTORY

of

ABU SARGA CHURCH

By

MESSIHA BESTAVROS

ABU SARGA CHURCH

This Church was built in the year A.D. 1171 by a man whose name was Hanna El Abbah the secretary of Sultan Salah-El-Din El-Ayoubi.

The Church contains 11 marble pillars each containing a panting of one of the apostles and one granite pillar without capital, panting or cross alladvig Judes who betrayed our Lord.

The alter for the holy comminion contains 7 Maszaic steps (the 7 degrees of bishops). The screen of the alter is made of carved ivory.

On the North of wich were are tow nice penals of carved wood: one shows the last supper and the other Bethlehm. On there Southern sides St Demetrius, St Georges and St Theodore.

The cript was cut out of a solid rock 30 years B.C. Mearly which was used as a shelter for strangers. When the Holy Family moved from Jernsalim to Egypt to hide themselves from King Herod they found this cript where they remained until the death of King Herod.

When St Mark started preaching in Alexandria at 42 A.D. and we the Pharos who embraced the religion of Christ used this criot as a church for a period of 900 years till this church built on its top. On the other side of the cript you can see the fount where Christian children are baptised by emersion in water for 3 times. This church contains manu Byzantian painitings of the 9th & 10th centuries.

MESIHA BESTAVROS,
Deacon.

I left Port Said in the P. & O. ship *Ranchi* for Malta. On leaving Egypt, as a final nip of avarice, one is obliged to pay a few shillings 'quarantine tax'. No one seems to know anything about this imposition, what statute authorized it and how much of what is collected ever finds its way into the treasury, or what bearing it has upon 'quarantine'. Many residents maintain that it is purely a bit of fun on the part of the harbour officials, who have no legal right to it whatever.

Thanks to the kind offices of the local manager, I was able to obtain a second-class berth. The residents in Port Said said: 'You meet a first-rate lot of people travelling second class since the war. A jolly sight better than in the first class, particularly on the ships from India – the first class is all *nouveaux riches*. You'll find second class on the *Ranchi* as good as first class on a foreign line. My wife travels second class when she goes home.'

But my motive really was less the ambition to meet nice people than to save money. After my extravagances at Mena House I was beginning to get worried about money, so I thought of an ingenious device. Before leaving Cairo I wrote – on the notepaper of the Union Club, Port Said – to the managers of the two leading hotels in Valletta, the Great Britain and the Osborne, between whom, I was told, there existed a relationship of acute rivalry, and enclosed a publisher's slip of Press cuttings about my last book; I said to each that I proposed to publish a travel diary on my return to England; I had heard that his was the best hotel in the island. Would he be willing to give me free accommodation during my visit to Malta in return for a kind reference to his establishment in my book? They had not had time to answer by the time I embarked at Port Said, but I went on board hoping that at Valletta I should experience some remission of the continual draining of money that I had suffered for the last two months.

The *Ranchi* was advertised to sail some time on Sunday and was expected early in the afternoon. On Sunday morning she was announced for nine o'clock that evening. Finally she came in well after midnight and stayed only two hours. During those two hours the town, which, as usual, was feeling the ill-effects of its Saturday night at the Casino, suddenly woke again into life. Simon Arzt's store opened; the cafés turned on their lights and dusted the tables; out came the boot-cleaners and postcard sellers; the passengers who had stayed on board through the canal came ashore and drove round in two-horse carriages; those who had left the ship at Aden for a few hours at Cairo, and had spent all that afternoon on the quay in a fever of apprehension that they might miss her, scuttled on board to their cabins; half the residents of Port Said had business of some kind to transact on board. I went down to the harbour in a bustle that was like noon in the city of London. The sudden brightness of the streets and the animation on all sides seemed quite unreal. I went on board, found my steward and my cabin, disposed of my luggage, and went on deck for a little. The passengers who had done the Suez–Cairo–Port Said dash were drinking coffee, eating sandwiches, and describing the pyramids and Shepheard's Hotel. 'Two pounds ten, simply for a single bed and no bathroom. Think of that!' they said with obvious pride. 'And we rode on camels – you should just have seen me. How Katie would have laughed, I said. And the camel-boy told my fortune, and we had a coffee made actually in the temple of the Sphinx. You *ought* to have come. Well, yes, perhaps it was a little exhausting, but then we've plenty of time at sea to make up for it. And there was the sweetest little boy who cleaned our shoes. And we went into a mosque where the Mohammedans were all saying their prayers – so quaint. And would you believe it – at Shepheard's they charged 15 piastres – that's over three shillings – for a cup of early morning tea, and not very good tea at that. You *ought* to have come, Katie!'

Before we sailed, I went down to my cabin and went to bed. The man who was sharing it with me, a kindly, middle-aged civil

44

engineer, was already undressing; he wore combinations. I woke once when the engines started, dozed and woke again as we ran clear of the breakwater and began to roll, and then fell soundly asleep, to wake next morning on the high seas with a hundred Englishmen all round me, whistling as they shaved.

We had cold, sunless weather and fairly heavy seas during the next two days. I rather wished that I had gone first class. It was not that my fellow passengers were not every bit as nice as the Port Said residents had told me they would be, but that there were so many of them. There was simply nowhere to sit down. The lounge and smoking-room were comfortable and clean and well ventilated and prettily decorated and all that, but they were always completely full. On the decks there were no deck-chairs except those the passengers provided for themselves; the three or four public seats were invariably occupied by mothers doing frightful things to their babies with jars of vaseline. It was not even possible to walk round with any comfort, so confined and crowded was the single promenade deck. Children were everywhere. It was the beginning of the hot season in India, and the officers' wives were taking them back to England in shoals; the better sort lay and cried in perambulators; the worse ones fell all over the deck and were sick; these, too, appeared in the dining-room for breakfast and luncheon and were encouraged by their mothers to eat. There was an awful hour every evening at about six o'clock, when the band came down from the first-class deck to play Gilbert and Sullivan to us in the saloon; this visitation coincided exactly with the bathing of the elder children below; the combination of soap and salt water is one of the more repugnant features of sea travel, and the lusty offspring of sahib and memsahib shrieked their protest till the steel rafters and match-board partitions echoed and rang. There was no place above or below for a man who values silence.

The other passengers were mostly soldiers on leave or soldiers' wives, leavened with a few servants of first-class passengers, some clergymen, and three or four nuns. The valets wore neat blue suits throughout the voyage, but the soldiers had an interesting snobbism. During the day, though cleanly shaved and with carefully brushed hair, they cultivated an extreme freedom of dress, wearing khaki shorts and open tennis shirts and faded cricket blazers. At dinner, however, they all appeared in dinner jackets and stiff shirts. One of them told me that the reason he travelled second class was that he need not trouble about clothes, but that he had to draw the line somewhere. On the other side of the barrier we could see the first-class passengers dressed very smartly in white flannels and parti-coloured brown and white shoes. Among them there was a youth who knew me hurrying back to contest a seat in the Conservative interest at the General Election. He kept popping over the rail to have cocktails with me and tell me about the lovely first-class girls he danced and played quoits with. He cost me quite a lot in cocktails. He often urged me to come over and see all the lovely girls and have cocktails with him. 'My dear chap,' he used to say, 'no one will dare to say anything to you while you're with *me*. I'd soon fix it up with the Captain if they did.' But I kept to my own bar. Later this young man, in his zeal to acquit himself splendidly before the first-class girls, clambered up one of the davits on the boat deck. He was reported to the Captain and seriously reprimanded. P. & O. ships are full of public school spirit. He did very badly indeed in the election, I believe, reducing an already meagre Conservative poll almost to extinction.

Just before luncheon on the third morning, we came in sight of Malta. There was some delay about landing because one of the passengers had developed chicken-pox. There was only one other passenger disembarking. We had to go and see the medical officer in the first-class saloon. He had infinite difficulties about the pronunciation of my name. He wanted to know the address I was going to in Malta. I would only tell him that I had not yet decided between the two hotels. He said, 'Please decide now. I have to fill in this form.'

I said I could not until I had seen the managers.

He said, 'They are both good hotels, what does it matter?'

I said, 'I want to get in free.'

He thought I was clearly a very suspicious character, and told me that on pain of imprisonment, I must report daily at the Ministry of Health during my stay at Valletta. If I did not come the police would find me and bring me. I said I would come, and he gave me a quarantine form to keep. I lost the form that evening and never went near the Ministry of Health and heard no more about it.

We went ashore in a lighter and landed at the Custom House. Here I was met by two young men, both short, swarthy, and vivacious, and each wearing a peaked cap above a shiny English suit. One had 'The Osborne Hotel' in gold on his cap, the other 'The Great Britain Hotel'. Each held in his hand a duplicate letter from me, asking for accommodation. Each took possession of a bit of my luggage and handed me a printed card. One card said:

THE OSBORNE HOTEL
STRADA MEZZODI

Every modern improvement. Hot water. Electric light.
Excellent Cuisine.

PATRONISED BY H.S.H. PRINCE LOUIS OF BATTENBERG AND THE DUKE OF BRONTE

The other said:

THE GREAT BRITAIN HOTEL
STRADA MEZZODI

Every modern improvement. Hot and cold water. Electric light.
Unrivalled cuisine. Sanitation.

THE ONLY HOTEL UNDER ENGLISH MANAGEMENT

(a fact, one would have thought, more fit to be concealed than advertised).

I had been advised in Cairo that the Great Britain was really the better of the two, so I directed its representative to take charge of my luggage. The porter of the Osborne fluttered my letter petulantly before my eyes.

'A forgery,' I explained, shocked at my own duplicity. 'I am afraid that you have been deluded by a palpable forgery.'

The porter of the Great Britain chartered two little horse-carriages, conducted me to one, and sat with the luggage in the other. There were low, fringed canopies over our heads so that it was impossible to see out very much. I was aware of a long and precipitous ascent, with many corners to turn. At some of these I got a glimpse of a baroque shrine, at others a sudden bird's-eye view of the Grand Harbour, full of shipping, with fortifications beyond. We went up and round, along a broad street of shops and more important doorways. We passed groups of supremely ugly Maltese women wearing an astonishing black headdress, half veil and half umbrella, which is the last legacy to the island of the conventional inclinations of the Knights of St John. Then we turned off down a narrow side street and stopped at the little iron and glass porch of the Great Britain Hotel. A little dark passage led into a little dark lounge, furnished like an English saloon bar, with imitation leather arm-chairs, bowls of aspidistra on fumed oak stands, metal-topped tables, and tables with plush coverings, Benares brass work, framed photographs, and ashtrays stamped with the trade-marks of various brands of whisky and gin. Do not mistake me; it was not remotely like an old-fashioned hotel in an English market town; it was a realization of the picture I have always in my mind of the interiors of those hotels facing on to Paddington station, which advertise '5s. Bed and Breakfast' over such imposing names as Bristol, Clarendon, Empire, etc. My heart fell rather as I greeted my host in this dingy hall, and continued to fall as I ascended, storey by storey, to my bedroom. The worst of it, however, was in this first impression, and I think I am really doing my duty honourably to the proprietor in warning people of it and exhorting them not to be deterred. For I can quite conscientiously say that the Great Britain *is* the best hotel in the island. I went later to look at the Osborne and felt that I had done better than H.S.H. Prince Louis of Battenberg and the Duke of Bronte. The food at the Great Britain was good; the servants particularly willing and engaging. One evening, being tired and busy, I decided to dine in my room. At Mena House, where there were hosts of servants and a lift, the dinner was brought up in one load and left outside the door; at the Great Britain every course was carried separately up three flights of stairs by the panting but smiling *valet de chambre*.

Before I left, the proprietor of the hotel asked me, rather suspiciously, what I intended to say about him.

They had had another writer, he told me, who had come to stay as his guest; he wrote for a paper called *Town and Country Life*; he had written a very nice piece indeed about the Great Britain. They had had the article reprinted for distribution.

The proprietor gave me a copy.

That, he said, was the kind of article that did a house good. He hoped mine would be as much like that as I could make it.

It began: 'The beautiful and prolific foliage, exotic skies, and glorious blue waters, a wealth of sunshine that spells health and happiness, and the facilities for enjoying outdoor sports, all the year round, are a few of the reasons that has made Malta so popular. Picturesque scenery, and people, complete as fascinating an array of attractions as the heart of the most blasé, could wish for.' It continued in this way for a column, with the same excess of punctuation; then it gave a brief survey of Maltese history and a description of the principal sights, for another column. Then it started on the Great Britain Hotel. 'No expense,' it said, 'has been spared to make the Public Rooms as comfortable as possible ... the Management boasts that its meals equal in the excellence of its food, cooking and serving, those served at London's hostelries and restaurants ... special pains are taken to see that all beds are most comfortable and only best material used ...' and so on for a column and a half. It finished: 'The luxuries of modern civilization have all been embodied in the building and organization of the Great Britain Hotel, Valletta, Malta, where the visitor is able to revel in the joys of a healthy happy stay amidst the fascinations of a modern palace set in Nature's own setting of sea and foliage, and here are to be obtained sunshine and warmth the whole year round.'

I will not be outdone in gratitude. If my appreciation is more temperately expressed it is none the less genuine. Let me state again, the Great Britain may be less suitably placed for golfers than Gleneagles; the gambling may be better from the Normandie; one can shop more conveniently from the Crillon, the Russie is set in a prettier square, one meets more amusing company at the Cavendish, one can dance better at the Berkeley and sleep better at Mena and eat better at the Ritz, but *the Great Britain Hotel, Valletta, Malta, is the best on the island*; further comparisons seem rather to confuse the issue.

I spent too little time in Malta. Most of my days were spent in exploring Valletta, with the aid of a small book called *Walks in Malta*, by F. Weston, which I bought for two shillings at Critien's, the big stationer's shop. I found it a slightly confusing book at first until I got used to the author's method; after that I became attached to it, not only for the variety of information it supplied, but for the amusing Boy-Scout game it made of sightseeing. 'Turning sharply to your left you will notice ...' Mr Weston prefaces his comments, and there follows a minute record of detailed observation. On one occasion, when carrying his book, I landed at the Senglea quay, taking it for Vittoriosa, and walked on for some time in the wrong town, hotly following false clues and identifying 'windows with fine old mouldings', 'partially defaced escutcheons', 'interesting ironwork balustrades', etc., for nearly a mile, until a clearly non-existent cathedral brought me up sharp to the realization of my mistake.

Presently I began making enquiries at the shipping offices for a berth from Malta in any direction, and was told that these could rarely be guaranteed. Preference was always given to passengers booking a long passage. One just had to take one's chance. I was getting a little impatient with the proprietor of the Great Britain, who had, in the last two days, developed a habit of popping suddenly out of his office whenever I sat down to have a drink, and saying, ''Ullo, 'ullo. And 'ow's that book getting along? You don't seem to be seeing much of the island,' adding encouragingly: 'You couldn't see a 'alf of it, not if you was to spend a life-time 'ere, you couldn't.' I became aware of a slight claustrophobic itch, and in this mood one day, less than a week after my arrival, I leant over the Cavalier of St James, looking down into the Grand Harbour. Then I saw below, among the fishing-boats and cargo ships and nondescript official launches and lighters, a very radiant new arrival; a large white motor vessel, built like a yacht with broad, clean decks and a single yellow funnel. I took the funicular down to the Custom House and looked at her from the quay. She was the *Stella Polaris*, on her second cruise from the one I had abandoned at Port Said. As I stood there the motor launch left her side and ran up to the quay, the Norwegian cross fluttering at her stern. Three or four passengers landed, carrying cameras and sunshades. With them was the purser. I greeted him. Was there a spare berth? He said there was. The *Stella* was not due to sail until next afternoon, but within an hour I had made my adieux at the Great Britain, assured the proprietor that he should have my warmest commendations to the British public, and moved my luggage down to the harbour. That afternoon I unpacked, sent a vast pile of clothes to the laundry, folded and hung up my suits, set in order the mass of papers I had accumulated, notes, photographs, letters, guide-books, circulars, sketches, caught and killed two fleas I had picked up in the Manderaggio, and went above, very contentedly, to renew my acquaintance with the deck bar steward.

On our way east we stopped for the day at Crete. The little harbour of Candia was too small for the *Stella*, so we anchored outside in the bay, well sheltered by the headland of Cape Paragia and the island of Dia. Inside the fortified breakwater, with its finely carved Venetian lion, lay a jumble of ramshackle shipping – a small fishing fleet, two or three coastal sailing-boats, and some incredibly dissolute tramp steamers which ply between Piraeus and the islands. A cargo of wine was being loaded into one of these, bottled in goat-skins.

There is one main street in the town and a labyrinth of divergent alleys. There is the façade of a ruined Venetian palace, and a battered Venetian fountain carved with lions and dolphins. There is also a mosque, built up in places with capitals and fragments of carved stone work from other Venetian buildings. The top has been knocked off the minaret and the building has been turned into a cinematograph, where, by an odd coincidence, a film was being exhibited named *L'Ombre de Harem*. The shops sold, mostly, hunks of very yellow and grey meat, old Turkish watches, comic German picture-postcards, and brightly patterned lengths of printed cotton.

I accompanied a party of fellow passengers to the museum to admire the barbarities of Minoan culture.

One cannot well judge the merits of Minoan painting, since

51

only a few square inches of the vast area exposed to our consideration are earlier than the last twenty years, and their painters have tempered their zeal for reconstruction with a predilection for covers of *Vogue*.

We chartered a Ford car and drove with a guide to Cnossos, where Sir Arthur Evans (our guide referred to him always as 'Your English Lord Evans') is rebuilding the palace. At present only a few rooms and galleries are complete, the rest being an open hillside scarred with excavations, but we were able to form some idea of the magnitude and intricacy of the operation from the plans which were posted up for our benefit on the chief platform. I think that if our English Lord Evans ever finishes even a part of his vast undertaking, it will be a place of oppressive wickedness. I do not think that it can be only imagination and the recollection of a bloodthirsty mythology which makes something fearful and malignant of the cramped galleries and stunted alleys, these colonnades of inverted, conical pillars, these rooms that are mere blind passages at the end of sunless staircases; this squat little throne, set on a landing where the paths of the palace intersect; it is not the seat of a lawgiver nor a divan for the recreation of a soldier; here an ageing despot might crouch and have borne to him, along the walls of a whispering gallery, barely audible intimations of his own murder.

There was one pretty incident of my visit which I only discovered later. I took a camera with me to Cnossos and left it in the car when we went over the excavations. I remember being mildly surprised later in the day, when I came to photograph the harbour, to see by the number that I had exposed more of the film than I thought. When it came back from the ship's photographic shop after being developed I was surprised to find a picture I had never taken; it was just recognizable as the Ford car in which we had driven to Cnossos, with the driver sitting very upright at the wheel. He must have induced one of his friends to take it while we were at the palace, and I thought it argued a nice nature in the man. He could not have hoped either to receive a print or even to see our surprise when the result of his little joke became visible. I like to think that he wished to add a more durable bond to our relationship than the fleeting obligation of two hours' hire; he wanted to emphasize his individual existence as a separate thing from the innumerable, impersonal associations of the tourist. I am sure he was amused at the thought of the little surprise he had stored up for us, when we cursorily paid him his fare and went back to our ship. Perhaps he experienced something of the satisfaction which those eccentric (and regrettably rare) benefactors derive from sending bank-notes anonymously to total strangers. If only his technical ability had come up to his good nature, I would have reproduced his portrait in this book, but I am afraid that, in the only form I possess, it would do him no further credit.

We spent the night at anchor and sailed early next morning so as to pass the Cyclades in daylight.

We passed a new island, recently erupted from the sea – a heap of smoking volcanic matter, as yet quite devoid of life. Then past Naxos, Paros, and Mykonos into the Aegean, and so north to the Dardanelles, making fifteen knots through a calm sea. 'Can't you just see the quinqu*i*-remes?' said an American lady to me, as we leant on the rail, near each other. 'From distant Ophir,' she added, 'with a cargo of ivory, sandalwood, cedarwood, and sweet white wine.'

We were in the Hellespont when we awoke next morning, and passed Suvla Bay and Gallipoli before noon. The sea was pale green and opaque with the ice water that was coming down from the Black Sea. The Sea of Marmora was choppy; we ran under cold winds and a grey sky, broken by fitful bursts of sunlight.

It was getting dark by the time that we came to the mouth of the Golden Horn. A low sea mist was hanging about the town, drifting and mingling with the smoke from the chimneys. The domes and towers stood out indistinctly, but even in their obscurity formed a tremendous prospect; just as the sun was on the horizon it broke through the clouds, and, in the most dramatic way possible, threw out a great splash of golden light over the minarets of St Sophia. At least, I think it was St Sophia. It is one of the delights of one's first arrival by sea at Constantinople to attempt to identify this great church from the photographs among which we have all been nurtured. As one approaches, dome after dome comes into view, and receives, each in its turn, little gasps of homage. Finally, when the whole immense perspective has been laid before us, two buildings contend for recognition. The more imposing one is the Mosque of Ahmed I. One can identify it by its distinction, unique except for the Kaaba at Mekka, of having six minarets. A more convincing way, however, of carrying one's point, is to say, 'That' – pointing wherever you choose – 'is Agia Sophia.'

'Agia' will always win the day for one. A more recondite snobbism is to say 'Aya Sophia', but except in a very sophisticated circle, who will probably not need guidance in the matter at all, this is liable to suspicion as a mere mispronunciation.

Next day, with only about two hours to spare, we went to the Serai, the palace of the Sultans, now converted into a public museum; the attendants are mostly the survivors of the royal eunuchs. One was a dwarf; he had a funny little shrivelled-up, sexless face and a big black overcoat which brushed the ground and came very near to tripping him up once or twice. None of them were as big and fat as I had imagined. In the bad times before the secure establishment of the Kemalist régime, I am told that there was a big demonstration meeting held by the agitated eunuchs to protest against the abolition of polygamy.

The most striking thing about the Serai is its astonishing discomfort. It somewhat resembles Earls Court Exhibition, consisting, not of a single building, but of a large enclosed area, laid out roughly with lawns and trees, and strewn fortuitously with kiosks and pavilions of varying date and design. It is simply a glorified nomad encampment. Constantinople is by no means warm. The site was chosen for its political and geographical importance rather than for the serenity of its climate. It is exposed to cold winds from the Steppes, and snow is not uncommon. Yet, in the five centuries of Turkish occupation, it seems never to have occurred to the sultans, with vast wealth and unlimited labour at their disposal, to provide any kind of covered corridor between the various rooms of their chief residence. Their highest aspirations towards physical luxury were confined to sprawling among gaudy silk cushions and munching sweetmeats while the icy wind whistled through the lattice-work over their heads. No wonder they took to drink. The treasures of the royal household, however, are staggering. Some idea of the economy of the Serai can be gained from the fact that the officials of the Kemalist party, when making a tour of the buildings in the first months of their occupation, came upon a room stacked from floor to ceiling with priceless sixteenth-century porcelain, still in the original wrappings in which it had arrived by caravan from China. It had been no one's business to unpack it, and there it had lain through the centuries. Theft and embezzlement must have been continuous and unchecked in the household. The astonishing thing is the amount of treasure that has survived the years of imperial bankruptcy. There are huge uncut emeralds and diamonds, great shapeless drops full of flaws, like half-sucked sweets; there is a gold throne set with cabuchons of precious stone; a throne of inlaid mother-o'-pearl and tortoiseshell; there are cases of jewelled pipe mouthpieces, and of dagger-hilts, watches, cigar-holders, snuff boxes, hand-mirrors, brushes, combs – twenty or thirty of each, all supremely magnificent; there is a dressing-table presented by Catherine the Great, encrusted all over, every inch of it, with rose-coloured paste jewels; there is a dressing-table presented by Frederick the Great, covered with alabaster and amber; there is an exquisite Japanese garden and temple made of filigree gold and enamel; there is a model paddle steamer, made of red and white gold with diamond port-holes and ruby and emerald pennons; there is the right hand and the skull of St John the Baptist; there are jewels to be worn in turbans and jewels to be worn round the neck on chains and jewels to be worn by women and jewels to be played with and tumbled listlessly between the fingers from hand to hand. The guide made a round estimate of each object in turn as being worth 'more than a million dollars'. One cannot help doubting, however, whether, in the prolonged period of Turkish insolvency, some depredations were not made upon this hoard. It would have been so easy to prize out a cabuchon emerald or so with the finger-nail and replace it with a jujube, that I feel it must have been done from time to time – who knows how often?

Immediately in front of me in our tour of inspection there

travelled a very stout, rich lady from America, some of whose conversation I was privileged to overhear. Whatever the guide showed her, china, gold, ivory, diamond or amber, silk or carpet, this fortunate lady was able casually to remark that she had one like that at home. '*Why*,' she would say, 'whoever would have thought that *that* was of any value. I've got three like that, that Cousin Sophy left me, bigger, of course, but just the same pattern, put away in one of the store-rooms. I must have them out when I get back. I never looked on *them* as being anything much.'

But she had to admit herself beaten by the right hand and skull of St John the Baptist.

We sailed next afternoon just before sunset.

The chief subject of conversation on board that evening was an accident which had occurred in the harbour. The ferry steamer which travels between Galata and Scutari, on the other side of the Bosphorus, had run on to the rocks in the morning mist; the passengers had been removed without loss of life, but only just in time. There was a newcomer in the *Stella* – a very elegant Greek who wore an Old Etonian tie and exhibited an extensive acquaintance with the more accessible members of the English peerage. He had been on board the ferry boat at the time of the disaster, and he gave a very interesting account of his experience. The ship had been crowded with labourers going across to their work. At the first impact the Captain and his chief officer leaped into the only boat and made off. Later in the day the Captain resigned his command, on the grounds that this was the third time it had happened in eighteen months and his nerves were not what they had been. Left to themselves the passengers, who were a motley race of Turks, Jews, and Armenians, fell into a state of mad panic. The only helpful course would have been to sit absolutely firm and hope for rescue. Instead they trotted moaning from side to side, swaying the ship to and fro and shaking it off the rocks on which it was impaled. My informant sat, frozen with terror, on one of the seats, in expectation of almost immediate capsize. He was here met by a stout little man, strutting calmly along the deck with a pipe in his mouth and his hands plunged into the pockets of his ulster. They observed each other with mutual esteem as the frenzied workmen jostled and shouted round them.

'I perceive, sir,' said the man with the pipe, 'that you, too, are an Englishman.'

'No,' answered the Greek, 'only a damned foreigner.'

'I beg your pardon, sir,' said the Englishman, and walked to the side of the ship, to drown alone.

Fortunately, however, there was no drowning. Boats came out from the shore and removed all the passengers before the ship foundered.

The Greek was travelling only as far as Athens. I spent most of next day in his company. He asked me searching questions about 'aestheticism' at Oxford. He had been at the House, but re-marked with a shade of regret that he had not found any 'aestheticism' in his day. Was it because of 'aestheticism' that Oxford did so badly at athletics? I said, no, the evil was deeper than that. I didn't mind telling another Oxford man, but the truth was, that there was a terrible outbreak of drug-taking at the University.

'Cocaine?'

'Cocaine,' I said, 'and worse.'

'But do the dons do nothing to stop it?'

'My dear man, the dons are the origin of the whole trouble.'

He said that there had been practically no drug-taking at the House in his time.

He renewed the attack later in the day. Would I come down to his cabin to have a drink?

I said I would have a drink with him by all means, but in the deck bar.

He said, 'I can see you are Scottish because of your blue eyes. I had a very dear friend who was a Scotchman. You remind me a little of him.'

Later, he said, would I come to his cabin to look at a silver Turkish inkpot. I said no, but I would love to see it on deck. It was very ugly.

When he disembarked he invited me to luncheon at the Grande Bretagne. I said, yes, but next day he did not turn up.

We arrived just before dinner and moored in Phaleron Bay.

I had been to Athens once before, at a time when I had never been farther from England than Paris. I shall not easily forget the romance of my first arrival. I came from Marseilles in the *Patris II*, a Hellenic national ship of fairly recent construction. It was in winter and we had rough weather most of the way. I shared a cabin with a Greek currant merchant who did not move from his bed during the five days' voyage. The only other English-speaking first-class passenger was a blustering American engineer. I sat on deck most of the time, feeling rather ill and reading James's *Varieties of Religious Experience*. At intervals the American and I drank *mastika*. He said if one ever drank *mastika* one returned to Greece; sometimes I went and looked over at the 'deck passengers', huddled under improvised tents, scratching their feet, and always eating. Piraeus was our first stop. Sun had set and the harbour was all alight when we came in. There was a long delay before we could land. The rowing boats came out all round us packed so tight that one could have walked ashore, all the boatmen shouting for custom. The friends I was visiting had come out to meet me, and sat bobbing below and shouting up, 'Evelyn'. They had brought their valet with them to deal with the luggage – a man of singular ferocity who had been a hired assassin at Constantinople under the old régime. He and the boatmen took up the cry 'EE-lin! EE-lin!'

Then my luggage got into the hands of the wrong boatman, and he and that valet had a fight which the valet won very easily by means of an outrageous but wholly conclusive foul blow. Then we went ashore and drove very quickly from Piraeus to Athens, along a road cleft and scarred as if by bombardment, in a very ramshackle Morris car which had no lamps or brakes or hooter, but was freed from police molestation by a diplomatic number and a little Union Jack between the places where the headlights ought to have been.

It was the Orthodox Christmas Day, and the streets were full of people shaking hands and kissing and letting off fireworks in each other's eyes. We went straight to a night club kept by a one-legged Maltese, who gave us cocktails made out of odd drugs and a spirit of his own distilling.

Later the *première danseuse* of the cabaret came out and sat at our table and warned us on no account to touch the cocktails. It was too late.

Later still I drove round the city in a taxi-cab on I forgot what errand, and then back to the night club. The taxi-driver followed me to our table. I had given him as a tip over ten pounds in drachmas, my watch, my gloves, and my spectacle-case. It was too much, he protested.

The rest of my visit was rather overshadowed by this introduction to Athenian life. That was in my undergraduate days, and it makes me feel unnaturally old to recall them.

But even now, in comparative maturity, my second visit to Athens coincided with my introduction to a new sort of drink. As soon as I landed I took a taxi into the town, to visit a friend called Alastair who lived at this time in a little house in the eastern quarter, under the slopes of Lycabettus, in a side street off the Kolonaki Square. This house was full of mechanical singing birds and eikons, one of which, oddly enough the most modern, had miraculous powers. One of Alastair's servants gave notice, on the grounds that it used to stretch an arm out of the picture and bang him over the head when he neglected his work. Alastair was not yet dressed. I told him that I had had a late night, drinking after the ball with some charming Norwegians, and felt a little shaken. He then made me this drink, which I commend to anyone in need of a wholesome and easily accessible pick-me-up. He took a large tablet of beet sugar (an equivalent quantity of ordinary lump sugar does equally well) and soaked it in Angostura Bitters and then rolled it in Cayenne pepper. This he put into a large glass which he filled up with champagne. The excellences of this drink defy description. The sugar and Angostura enrich the wine and take away that slight acidity which renders even the best champagne slightly repugnant in the early morning. Each bubble as it rises to the surface carries with it a red grain of pepper, so that as one drinks one's appetite is at once stimulated and gratified, heat and cold, fire and liquid, contending on one's palate and alternating in the mastery of one's sensations. I sipped this almost unendurably desirable drink and played with the artificial birds and musical boxes until Alastair was ready to come out. I had another friend in Athens called Mark, and with these two I spent two delightful days.

We drove along the Eleusis road, pursued at times by savage sheep-dogs, and then turned off by the cart road below Mount Aegaleos to an isolated café overlooking the bay of Salamis. It was Sunday afternoon, and there were several other parties sitting under the Hawaiian thatched arbour. There was a photographer making little tin-type photographs which, when developed, usually revealed his own thumb print and little else. There were two students, male and female, in football shorts and open shirts, with rugged staffs and haversacks. There was a very happy family of Athenian bourgeoises. They had a baby with them. This they first sat on the table, then on the top of their car; then they put it upside down on a chair; then it was lifted on to the roof of the café, then it was put astride a clothes line and rocked gently backwards and forwards, then it was put into the bucket of the well and let down out of sight, then it was given a bottle of gaseous lemonade, a more perilous drink in Athens than in any town in the world. To all these efforts towards its entertainment it responded with chirrups of happy laughter and big, frothy bubbles dribbling down its chin. There was also a limousine containing two very *mondaine* young ladies, who would not come into the open, but sat back hardly visible among cut velvet upholsteries and were waited upon by two adolescent military officers; now and then the window would be let down and jewelled fingers would appear, haughtily discarding a sheet of silver paper or a banana skin.

Mark and Alastair and I sat in the shade and drank a carafe of resinated white wine and ate Turkish delight, while the photographer capered before us with his camera and caused us to purchase enough copies of his thumb print to convict him of any crime in the Greek statute book.

We went back to the *Stella* for dinner and then returned to see the night life. First we went to an underground café decorated with pseudo-Russian frescoes. Here we saw most of the English colony, engaged in those fervent intrigues, part social, part political, part personal, which embellish and enrich Athenian life more than that of any capital in Europe. But the entertainment was confined to one pianist in Georgian peasant dress. We asked if there was to be no cabaret. 'Alas,' said the manageress. 'Not tonight. Last night there was a German gentleman here, and he bit the girls so terribly in the legs that tonight they say they will not dance!'

From there we went to the Folies Bergères, which was very chic and Parisian; the waiter tried to induce us to order champagne, and a Hungarian Jewess performed Oriental dances in a Chu-Chin-Chow slave market costume, modestly supplemented with pink cotton tights. Mark's boredom soon became uncontrollable, so we called for our bill, paid them half what they demanded (which they accepted with every manifestation of gratitude), and left.

We walked across the gardens to the poorer part of the town. Of the many smells of Athens two seem to me the most character-istic – that of garlic, bold and deadly like acetylene gas, and that of dust, soft and warm and caressing like tweed. It was in this dusty smell that we walked in the garden, but garlic met us at the bottom of the steps which led from the street to the door of the *ΜΠΑΡ ΘΕΛΛΑΤΟΕ*; it was garlic sweetened, however, by the savour of roast lamb. There were two lambs impaled horizontally on spits, sizzling over an open charcoal fire. The atmosphere was one of Dickensian conviviality. Only men were present, most of them peasants come up from the country for the night. They all smiled greetings to us, and one of them sent three mugs of beer across to our table. This began a tremendous round of cere-monious health-drinking which was still going on by the time we left. It is the commendable practice of the Greeks never to serve drink without food, usually a little bit of garlic sausage, or bad ham on the end of a match; these appear in little saucers, and our table was soon strewn with them.

Two men in the corner were playing guitars of a kind, and others were dancing, with very severe expressions on their faces but a complete lack of self-consciousness. They were Pyrrhic dances of indefinable antiquity. Four of them danced together, going through the various figures with great solemnity. If one of them made a false move it was as though he had dropped a catch in an English cricket match; they accepted his apologies in as sporting a spirit as they could assume, but it clearly was a grave wrong, not lightly to be dismissed or expiated except by prodigies of accuracy in the future. Moreover, as in cricket, the amateur status was jealously preserved. So far from taking a hat round after the performance, the dancers themselves paid a few half-pence to the band. There was keen competition to dance, the fours being already made up and eagerly waiting for their turn to take the floor. The only fight which occurred that evening was occasioned by one rather tipsy young man attempting to perform out of his turn. They all set on him and pummelled him for his bad manners, but later it was made up and they drank his health.

As the evening went on the conversation became more animated. I was unable to follow it, but Alastair said it was mostly about politics; an uninstructed discussion but full of high feeling. There was an elderly man with a curly grey beard who was much moved. He roared and pounded on the table with his fist; he pounded on his glass, broke it, and cut himself. He stopped arguing and began to cry. Immediately everyone else stopped arguing too and came over to comfort him. They wrapped a grubby handkerchief round his hand, which was not, I think, at all seriously injured. They gave him beer and bits of bad ham on matches; they patted him on the back and put their arms round his neck and kissed him. Soon he was smiling again and the discussion was resumed, but as soon as he showed signs of excitement, they warned him with smiles, by moving his mug farther across the table.

At last, after a great many adieux, we climbed up the steps again into the fresh air, and so home under the orange-trees through the warm darkness that smelled like tweed.

Next morning Alastair had to go to the Chancery to decode telegrams, so Mark and I went shopping in Shoe Lane – the street in the old Turkish quarter where all the second-hand dealers have their stalls. Mark continued some negotiations which, he told me, had already been protracted for three weeks, concerning the purchase of a grotto constructed by Anatolian refugees out of cork and looking-glass and pieces of sponge;

only the price prevented me from buying a marble statuette of an association footballer.

The *Stella* was sailing at noon for Venice, and I narrowly escaped missing the last launch from the shore, Mark delaying me by the gift of three religious postcards, a balloon, and a basket of black olives.

Immediately after luncheon we passed through the Corinth canal, which, for some reason I could not understand, attracted many of the passengers more than anything they had yet seen on their travels. It took some time to go through, but they remained on deck, photographing it and talking about it and making water-colour sketches of its featureless stone sides, while I went to my cabin and dozed; I had a good deal of sleep to make up and this seemed an opportunity.

We reached Corfu early next morning.

When, after my first visit to Greece, I stopped there for a few hours (in a vile ship called the *Yperoke*, where I was travelling second class in barely conceivable discomfort), it seemed to me then one of the most beautiful places I had ever seen. So much was I impressed, that when, later, I found myself writing a novel about someone very rich, I gave her a villa in Corfu, as I thought that, when I was rich, that was one of the first things I would buy.

The chief merchandise of the island seemed to be live tortoises and olive-wood animals, made by the convicts in the prison. Several passengers in the *Stella* bought tortoises, few of which survived the voyage; tortoise races became an added attraction to the deck games. The chief disability suffered by tortoises as racing animals is not their slowness so much as their defective sense of direction. I had exactly the same difficulty when I used to take part in sports at my school, and was repeatedly disqualified for fouling the other competitors.

I drove in a horse-carriage along the Vide Imperatore Guglielmo, which is bordered by groves of olive, rose, and orange-trees, to the little balustraded platform called, in the old style, Canone Point, or, in its Hellenized version, *ΣΤΟΠ ΚΑΝΟΝΙ*. This is the extreme point of the peninsula that runs out from the town, enclosing the fiord called Lake Kaliki-copulo. There used to be a battery here of one gun. Now there is a café-restaurant. The bank falls steeply down to the water, where there are two tiny islands, the one wooded, containing a villa that was once, I think, a monastery; the other is very small and is completely occupied by a minute chapel, two cypress-trees, and a parsonage. It is accessible from the beach by stepping-stones. I went down to it. There were two little bells in the tower, and, inside, some quite black eikons and a hen laying an egg. The priest appeared magically, rowing a boat full of vegetables from the opposite bank. His son sat in the stern with bare legs crossed under him, nursing a tin of Californian peaches. I gave some money to the church expenses and climbed up the hill path to the café. One or two other passengers had arrived from the *Stella*. I joined them, and ate sponge fingers and drank some delicious Corfiote wine, that looks like the juice of blood oranges and tastes like cider and costs, or should cost when one is not obviously a tourist, about twopence. A band appeared, of two guitars and a fiddle. The fiddler was quite young but blind. They played, 'Yes, Sir, That's my Baby', in the oddest way conceivable, and laughed aloud with pleasure at the money they collected.

During the days on our way back to Monte Carlo we were rarely out of sight of land for long.

I do not think I shall ever forget the sight of Etna at sunset; the mountain almost invisible in a blur of pastel grey, glowing on the top and then repeating its shape, as though reflected, in a wisp of grey smoke, with the whole horizon behind radiant with pink light, fading gently into a grey pastel sky. Nothing I have ever seen in Art or Nature was quite so revolting.

Monte Carlo was practically deserted; the Sporting Club was closed; the Russian ballet had packed up and left for their last season in London; the dress shops had either already closed or were advertising their end of the season sales; there were shutters up in most of the villas and hotels; a few invalids encumbered the promenades in their bath-chairs; Mr Rex Evans had ceased to sing. And I wondered, as I pottered about those serene and sunny streets or sat drowsily in the shade of the Casino Gardens, at that provision of destiny which has made rich people so rigidly liturgical in their movements that they will come to Monte Carlo

in the snow because that is the time ordained for their arriva
rubric and calendar, and will leave as soon as it becomes habita
for their grubby great shambling cities in the north; and how u
like rich people are to the lilies of the field, who do not divid
time by any metrical system, but will joyfully put out buds at the
first intimation of spring, and lose them, almost immediately, in
the intervening frost.

On Norwegian Independence Day, the *Stella* was dressed with
hundreds of little flags. That evening there were speeches at
dinner, and after the dancing a party, given by the officers and
the Scandinavian passengers. The first officer made a patriotic
speech in Norwegian and then in English, and then he made a
speech in English in praise of England and then translated his
speech into Norwegian. Then I made a speech in English in
praise of Norway, and one of the passengers translated my
speech into Norwegian; then she made a speech in English and
Norwegian in praise of England and Norway and quoted
Kipling. It was all delightful. Then we went down to the lower
deck, where the crew were having a tremendous supper of
Norwegian *delicatessen* and sugar cakes and champagne; one of
them was in a rostrum made of flags; he was delivering a patriotic
speech. Then we all drank each other's health and danced; it was
by no means a calm sea. Then we went up to the Captain's cabin
and ate a dish called *eggdosis*, but I do not know how it was spelt.
It was made of eggs and sugar and brandy whipped up into a
firm cream. Then we went to the cabin of the lady who had
translated my speech and there we made more speeches, oddly
enough most of them in French.

I woke up feeling a little ill after Independence Day, and found
that we had arrived in Algiers, and that the deck was already
covered with stalls as though for a charity bazaar. They were
selling filigree gold jewellery, binoculars, and carpets. The water
in the harbour was dense with floating refuse; young men swam
about, butting and churning back with their arms the scum of
empty bottles, sodden paper, grape-fruit skins, and kitchen waste,
and calling for coins to be thrown to them.

After luncheon I climbed rather heavily up to the Kasbar.

There is a fine view from there over the town and harbour and the whole Bay of Algiers; the houses are very old and the alleys narrow and precipitous; it has that vivid street life that one sees in every old town which has a slum quarter inaccessible to traffic; there was one street and a little terrace given up to houses of ill-fame – all very gay with bright paint and tiles, and crowded thick at every door and window with plain, obese young women in gaudy clothes. If I had come there fresh from England I should have found it amusing enough, but as a spectacle of Oriental life it was less exciting than Cairo on Bajiram night, and as an example of medieval town-planning less formidable than the Manderaggio at Valletta.

There was very little begging or street hawking except the inevitable swarm of boot-cleaners, and no native dragomans. Except on the harbour front one could walk about unmolested; there, however, one had to run the gauntlet of a great number of guides – nasty, jaunty young men for the most part, dressed in European suits and straw hats, bow ties, and Charlie Chaplin moustaches; their particular trade was organizing parties to see native dances – *fêtes Mauresques* – and an intolerable nuisance they were over it. Many of the passengers from the *Stella* went off with them and came back with very different reports of the entertainment. Some appeared to have seen decorous and perfectly genuine performances in the courtyards of one or other of the medieval Moorish houses; they described a native band with drums and wind instruments and a troupe of veiled dancing girls who went through the figures of various traditional tribal dances; they said it was a little monotonous, but they seemed quite satisfied with their evening. Another party, including two English-women, were led to the top floor of a house of ill-fame, where they were sat round the walls of a tiny room. Here they waited for some time in the light of a small oil lamp, becoming more and more uneasy, until the curtains of the door were suddenly thrust aside and a very large, elderly Jewess pranced in among them, quite naked except for a little cheap jewellery, and proceeded to a *danse de ventre* on the few yards of floor that separated them. The verdict of one of the Englishwomen on this experience was: 'Well, I am quite glad in a way to have seen it, but I should certainly never wish to go again.' Her companion refused to discuss the subject at all, from any angle, with anyone, and for the rest of the voyage entirely avoided the company of the gentlemen who had escorted her that evening.

But there was one party who had a still sadder time of it. They were five Scots people in early middle age, three women and two men, interrelated in some way that I never had occasion to define. These were caught by a very shady guide who took them up to the Kasbar in a taxi-cab. He charged them 200 francs for this drive, which they politely paid without question. He then took them to a house in a blind alley, knocked on the door three times, and excited their uneasiness by saying, 'This is very dangerous. You are safe as long as you are with me, but on no account get separated or I cannot answer for the consequences.' They were admitted one at a time and charged 100 francs each. The door was shut behind them and they were led down to a cellar. The guide explained to them that they must order coffee, which they did at the cost of 20 francs a head. Before they had tasted it a revolver shot sounded just outside the door.

'Run for your lives,' said the guide.

They scampered out and found their taxi, which, by apparent good fortune, was waiting for them.

'No doubt the ladies are feeling unsettled by their experience. Would they like a little cognac?'

He then directed the car, which cost another 200 francs, to one of the ordinary cafés of the town and gave them each a tot of *eau-de-vie*. He settled the bill for them and explained that it had come to 25 francs a head and 10 francs for the tip.

'That is the advantage of coming with me,' he explained. 'I do the tips for you and you are not put upon. There are many cheats in this town who would take advantage of your inexperience if you were alone.'

He then saw them back to the ship, reminding them discreetly that the fees for his evening's services were 100 francs or whatever they liked to make it. They were still so bewildered and agitated that they gave him a hundred and fifty, thanking him very much and congratulating themselves on the narrow escape they had had.

It did them credit that they did not conceal this dismal story, but told it to everyone on board, half resentfully but half humorously.

'I'd like to go back and have a few words with that merchant,' remarked the men of the party, but, alas, by that time we had left Algiers.

All over the world there are rock formations in which people profess to see the likeness of natural objects – heads of crusaders, dogs, cattle, petrified beldams, etc. There is an idea, started, I believe, by Thackeray, that the Rock of Gibraltar looks like a lion. 'It is the very image,' he said, 'of an enormous lion, crouched between the Atlantic and the Mediterranean, and set there to guard the passage for its British mistress.' Everyone else on board was instantly struck by the felicity of this image, so I suppose that it must be due to some deficiency in my powers of observation that to me it appeared like a great slab of cheese and like nothing else.

An English policeman with helmet, whistle, truncheon, and rolled mackintosh cape was on duty at the landing-stage. I think this man pleased the English passengers more than anything they had seen in their travels. 'It makes one feel so safe inside,' said one of the ladies.

I walked for some time about those very clean streets, feeling that there could be no town in the world without something of interest somewhere. The shop windows displayed little except seedy shaving brushes and tarnished cutlery and indefinable objects stitched on to cards; there were chemists' shops selling English aperients and patent pills; a paper-shop selling three-penny novelettes and twopenny weeklies; a few curiosity shops with a stock oddly composed of little Victorian and Edwardian knick-knacks – descended presumably from officers' villas – and flaring modern embroideries and beaten metal from Tangier. There was a tobacconist selling Dunhill pipes and tobacco-jars ornamented with regimental and naval devices. I passed some sailors' wives standing near a milliner's window; they shrank as I passed as though I had brought with me some of the polluted air of Málaga. Most of them, I learned later, keep strictly to their houses when there are 'trippers about', like Hampstead residents on bank-holidays.

As I was walking along very disconsolately I found a notice which said, 'To Brighter 'Bralter. ☞' I followed it for some way until I came to another, similar announcement, and so, in pursuit of pleasure, I began a kind of lugubrious treasure hunt, following these clues through the length of that town. At last I came to the South Port Gate and a neat little cemetery, where are buried a number of men who fell at Trafalgar. Many of the graves were of pretty, Wedgwood pattern, with urns and delicate carved plaques. Somewhat farther ahead, in a kind of recreation ground, preparations were being made with tents and awnings for some kind of gymkhana. I felt, however, that the posters had at least led me to the one tolerable spot on the Rock.

At the time of our visit, Seville was illuminated in the evenings by flood-lights, in honour of the Spanish-American Exposition. This exhibition had only just opened, and many of the buildings were still unfinished. It must not be supposed, however, that the project had been hurriedly or frivolously undertaken. The 1913 edition of Baedeker's *Spain and Portugal* mentions that large portions of the park were at that time closed for the preparations. We were presented on landing with a prettily decorated prospectus written in English, which remarked: 'Five hundred years from now the descendants of those who visit this Exposition will see with their own eyes these very same buildings, mellowed by the passing ages, but equal to their present grandeur in lines and in massive construction.' Some of the buildings certainly will profit by mellowing, being at present very gay indeed in a bright patterned brickwork and coloured tiles; a little too gay, perhaps, for their 'massive construction' and the academic future ordained for them. Their contents, however, were magnificent. I spent a delightful afternoon quite alone in the two great art galleries. So far from suffering the bargain-sale scramble of a loan collection in London, one was able to walk round these superb galleries absolutely alone.

But the whole exhibition was like that. Tourists had so far not arrived in any appreciable quantities, and the Sevillians after sixteen years' preparation were bored with the whole business. There were elements of ill-feeling in their neglect. They considered that the price of admission was too high and that they had been unrighteously defrauded of the use of their favourite park. There was no organized boycott, but it just so happened that no Sevillians went to their exhibition. There was a model railway, with a miniature steam-engine, which took an empty train round and round the ground; there was an *Atracción* Park in which a great wheel revolved, empty; there were switch-backs and scenic railways on which empty cars swooped and swerved through breath-taking descents; there were silent rifle ranges with heaps of ammunition lying undischarged and mountains of bottles unbroken; in the evening the gardens were brilliantly illuminated; the trees were filled with electric-light bulbs in the shape of apples, oranges, and clusters of bananas; ingeniously concealed flood-lamps made the lawns luminous and many-coloured; electric lights were hidden under the water-lilies on the lake; illuminated fountains sparkled high in the air, like soundless and inexhaustible fireworks. It would have been a fascinating scene even in a Wembley crowd; on the night of my visit there was not another figure stirring anywhere; I felt as if I had achieved the Nonconformist ideal of being the only righteous soul saved in the universe; quite, quite alone in the whole of paradise. I suppose it really is not wholly gracious to emphasize this particular feature of the exhibition, as it can clearly not have come about by any deliberate intention of the organizers. To compliment them on it is somewhat like the polite painter who I once overheard, while being shown round the infinitely nurtured and tended garden of an acquaintance, congratulate his host on the excellence of his 'soft, mossy lawns'. Rather a touching paragraph in the prospectus said: 'In view of the large number of visitors expected at Seville throughout the Exposition, several new hotels and two garden-cities have been constructed ... suited equally, in their variety, to the millionaire and to the most moderate purses ... Seville will accommodate some 25,000 visitors simultaneously throughout the Exposition.' It certainly merited the concurrence of 250,000, but I was very thankful that I saw it as I did, before anyone else arrived.

In Sao Roque at Lisbon I reflected: It is only since the

discovery of photography that perspective has ceased to be an art.

We sailed late that evening. Next day we were in a choppy sea, with a cold wind blowing from the shore, and that night we came into the Bay of Biscay; the ship developed a slow roll which caused serious discomfort to many. A great number of the passengers remained on deck during luncheon, nourishing themselves with dry biscuits and quarter-bottles of champagne. The roll went on undiminished until we rounded Cape Finisterre late in the afternoon.

The sea was quite calm now that we were out of the Bay of Biscay, but we ran into recurrent banks of fog which held up our progress; there was talk of our not getting in until late the next afternoon.

That evening there was a small party in the Captain's cabin, consisting of the officers off duty and two or three of the Scandinavian passengers and myself; we drank each other's health and exchanged invitations to visit each other in our countries. After a time I went out from the brightly lighted cabin on to the dark boat-deck. For the moment the night was clear and starry. I was carrying my champagne glass in my hand, and, for no good reason that I can now think of, I threw it out over the side, watched it hover for a moment in the air as it lost momentum and was caught by the wind, then saw it flutter and tumble into the swirl of water. This gesture, partly, I suppose, because it was of its own moment, spontaneous and made quite alone, in the dark, has become oddly important to me, and bound up with the turgid, indefinite feelings of home-coming.

For to return to one's own country, even after the shortest absence, is, in its way, an emotional business. I had left in the depth of winter and was coming back to late spring; then, if ever, England is still a lovely country.

While I still stood on the boat-deck we ran into another belt of mist. The engines changed to slow and then to dead slow, and the fog-horn began dolefully sounding the half-minutes.

In twenty minutes we were clear again, and running under the stars at full speed.

I woke up several times in the night to hear the horn again

sounding through the wet night air. It was a very dismal sound, premonitory, perhaps, of coming trouble, for Fortune is the least capricious of deities, and arranges things on the just and rigid system that no one shall be very happy for very long.

CHAPTER TWO

A Coronation in 1930

(From *Remote People*)

THEY were still dancing when, just before dawn on 19th October, 1930, the *Azay le Rideau* came into harbour at Djibouti. The band – a pitiably hot quartet in alpaca dinner-jackets – had long ago packed up their instruments and retired to their remote and stifling cabin. An Annamite boy was swabbing the deck and pushing into the scuppers sodden masses of paper streamers. Two or three stewards were at work pulling down the flags and festoons of coloured lights with which the ship had been decorated. One couple remained: a girl of mixed blood, second-class passenger to Mauritius; and an officer in the French Foreign Legion. Their feet moved slowly over the wet boards to the music of a portable gramophone; at intervals they stopped, and unclasped each other, to rewind the instrument and reverse the single record.

For two days of gross heat the ship had been *en fête*. There had been deck games, races for the children, a tombola with two-franc tickets and such prizes as could be procured on board – bottles of vermouth and eau-de-Cologne, tins of tobacco, sweets, lumps of coral, and ornamental cigarette-holders from Port Said. An autographed photograph of Marshal d'Esperez had been put up to auction and sold, amid wild applause, to a Press photographer for 900 francs; a cinema film had been exhibited by one of the passengers, with a faltering light on a screen that flapped restlessly in the hot breeze; there had been a horse-race decided by throw of dice, with a pari-mutuel and many hotly disputed results; at the deck bar there had been frequent orders for champagne, shared among families of French officials, six or eight of them to a bottle. Finally, on the last evening of the voyage, the fête had culminated in a fancy-dress dinner, a concert, and a ball.

It was a diverse company who had been thus indulged. There

sat at my table a red-headed American on his way to Saigon, where he hoped to sell agricultural machinery; his watch-chain was loaded with Masonic insignia, he wore a ring of the interlaced initials of some other commercial secret society, he had Froth Blowers' cuff-links, and a Rotarian wheel in his buttonhole; the Italian proprietor of the third-best hotel in Madras. There was a large number of French colonial officials, their wives and disorderly children, who make up the bulk of a normal Messageries Maritimes passenger list, on this occasion reinforced by a draft of the Foreign Legion on their way to preserve discipline in Indo-China. The men travelled fourth class, sprawling about the lower deck by day, battened down in the hold at night. They were mostly Germans and Russians; in the evening they formed into little groups and sang songs. They had a band of drums and mouth-organs which came up to play in the first-class saloon on the evening of the concert. The drum was painted, with the device 'Mon Jazz'. Two of them climbed through a porthole one night in the Suez Canal and escaped. Next day a third tried to follow their example. We were all on deck drinking our morning apéritifs when we heard a splash and saw a shaven-headed figure in shirt-sleeves scrambling up the bank behind us. He had no hat and the sun was at its strongest. He ran through the sand, away from the ship, with gradually slackening speed. When he realized that no one was pursuing him he stopped and turned round. The ship went on. The last we saw of him was a figure stumbling after us and waving his arms. No one seemed the least put out by the occurrence. My cabin steward usually had some story to tell me of daily life on the lower deck. One day two of the legionaries began fighting and were put in the cells; another day a Chinaman went mad in the night and tried to commit suicide; another day there had been a theft on board, and so on. I think he used to invent a great deal to amuse me.

Besides this normal traffic of the line, there were about twenty of us bound for Djibouti on our way to Abyssinia for the Emperor's coronation. Six weeks before, I had barely heard Ras Tafari's name. I was in Ireland, staying in a house where chinoiserie and Victorian gothic contend for mastery over a Georgian structure. We were in the library, discussing over the atlas a journey I proposed to make to China and Japan. We began talking of other journeys, and so of Abyssinia. One of the party was on leave from Cairo; he knew something of Abyssinian politics and the coming coronation. Further information was contributed from less reliable sources; that the Abyssinian Church had canonized Pontius Pilate, and consecrated their bishops by spitting on their heads; that the real heir to the throne was hidden in the mountains, fettered with chains of solid gold; that the people lived on raw meat and mead; we looked up the royal family in the *Almanach de Gotha* and traced their descent from Solomon and the Queen of Sheba; we found a history which began: 'The first certain knowledge which we have of Ethiopian history is when Cush ascended the throne immediately after the Deluge'; an obsolete encyclopaedia informed us that, 'though nominally Christian, the Abyssinians are deplorably lax in their morals, polygamy and drunkenness being common even among the highest classes and in the monasteries.' Everything I heard added to the glamour of this astonishing country. A fortnight later I was back in London and had booked my passage to Djibouti. Five days later I was on board the *Azay le Rideau* at Marseilles, and ten days after that I was standing on deck in my pyjamas watching the dawn break over the low coast-line of French Somaliland and over the haggard couple dancing to the gramophone.

Sleep had been impossible for some time, as the servants of the Egyptian delegation had been at work assembling their masters' luggage immediately opposite the door of my cabin. Tin trunk after tin trunk was dragged out with loud military commands from the sergeant in charge and loud unmilitary remonstrances from his subordinates. It seemed hardly conceivable that five men could have so many clothes. And after the tin trunks came the great crates which contained the King of Egypt's present to the Emperor. These had appeared on board at Port Said under escort of an armed patrol, and throughout the voyage had been guarded with some ostentation; their contents had been the object of wild speculation among the passengers, our imaginations wallowing in a profusion of Biblical opulence – frankincense, sardonyx, madrepore, and porphyry. In point of fact, as appeared later, they contained a handsome but unexceptional suite of bedroom furniture.

There were three other delegations on board, from France, Holland, and Poland; a fourth, the Japanese, was awaiting our arrival at Djibouti. When not exchanging ceremonious introductions, or pacing the decks at great speed, these envoys occupied themselves with finely emblazoned despatch-cases, writing, typing and annotating their complimentary addresses.

At first sight there is something a little surprising in this sudden convergence on Abyssinia of the envoys of the civilized world, and I think that the Abyssinians were as surprised as anyone. After the sudden death of the Empress Zauditu in the spring of the year, immediately subsequent to the defeat of her husband Ras Gougsa, Ras Tafari notified the Powers that he proposed, as soon as he decently could, to assume the title of Emperor of Ethiopia, and included in this announcement, in the case of those few nations who maintained diplomatic representatives at his Court, an invitation to attend the ceremonies. A few years before, he had been crowned Negus; on that occasion his immediate neighbours had taken a few days' holiday to visit him, and there had been a mild exchange of courtesies by telegram. Something a little more conspicuous was expected of the imperial coronation, but the response of the world Powers exceeded Ethiopian expectation in a manner that was both gratifying and embarrassing. Two Governments sent members of their royal families; the United States of America sent a gentleman of experience in the electric installation trade; the Governors of British Somaliland, the Sudan, Eritrea, the Resident at Aden, a marshal of France, an admiral, three airmen, and a marine band all appeared in various uniforms and orders. Substantial sums of public money were diverted to the purchase of suitable gifts; the Germans brought a signed photograph of General von Hindenburg and eight hundred bottles of hock; the Greeks a modern bronze statuette; the Italians an aeroplane; the British a pair of elegant sceptres with an inscription composed, almost correctly, in Amharic.

The simpler Abyssinians interpreted it as a suitable tribute to Abyssinian greatness; the kings of the world were doing homage. Others, a little more versed in world affairs, saw in it some plot against Abyssinian integrity – the *ferangi* had come to spy out the land.

One need not explore any deep political causes for a plausible explanation. Addis Ababa is not a place where great diplomatic reputations are easily won, and the potentates of the Foreign Office do not keep any very keen scrutiny to see how their cadets are shaping in that rare altitude. Who could blame these officials if occasionally there crept into their despatches phrases tending to estimate with some generosity the importance of the land of their exile? Is Abyssinia not the source of the Blue Nile? May there not be vast mineral wealth in those unprospected hills? And if, in the trivial course of compound life, that unvarying round of modest entertainment, there suddenly came to the women of the diplomatic corps – poor half-sisters of the great ladies of Washington or Rome – the possibility of sudden splendour, of royalty and gold braid, curtsies and champagne and handsome A.D.C.s, who can blame them if they strengthened their menfolk in urging the importance of really imposing special representation at the festivities?

And need one wonder if States very remote from Africa – sledded Polaks and blond Swedes – decided to join in the party? If the glamour of Abyssinia had drawn me there from a life of comparative variety and freedom, why not them from their grey chanceries? Gun-cases among their trunks of uniform showed that they intended to make the most of their jaunt, and several of them, I know, had paid their own fares. 'Nous avons quatre citoyens ici, mais deux sont juifs,' one attaché explained to me, and proceeded to demonstrate the apparatus with which, during his sojourn in Africa, he hoped to add to his already extensive collection of butterflies.

Day broadened rapidly and the dancers finally separated and went off to bed. Lighters came out from shore and coaling began. Planks stretched between the ship and the barges. One of them broke, throwing the Somali coolies heavily on to the coal – a drop of ten feet or more. One lay on his back groaning after the others had got up. The foreman threw a lump of coal at him. He groaned and turned on to his face; another lump, and he staggered to his feet and resumed work. Somali boys came swimming

77

round the ship calling for money to be thrown them. Passengers appeared on deck.

Soon it began to rain.

Great uncertainty prevailed as to how or when we should get to Addis Ababa.

We waited our turn to go ashore with some anxiety. The coolies droned dismally up and down the unstable planks; the little boys in the water cried for francs, or appeared shivering on deck, offering to amuse us by jumping back again; guns on shore boomed the salutes as the Government launch fetched each delegation in turn. The warm rain poured down steadily.

Eventually we were free to land. There was another Englishman travelling to Addis Ababa, an elderly gentleman on his way to the legation as a private visitor. Throughout the voyage he had studied a formidable little book about tropical hygiene, and passed on to me much disquieting information about malaria and blackwater, cholera and elephantiasis; he used, over his cigar in the evenings, to explain how hook-worms ate their way from the soles of the feet to the internal organs, how jiggers laid their eggs under the toe-nails, and retailed the symptoms of slow paralysis with which the spirillum tick might infect us.

Together we put our luggage in charge of the French-speaking native porter of the Hôtel des Arcades and went to the English vice-consul who told us that there were in fact two trains that evening, but both of them were reserved for delegations; the next train was three days later; that was reserved for the Duke of Gloucester; there was another one three days after that – reserved for Prince Udine. He could hold out very little hope of our getting up to Addis. In a state of mind born of this information we drove to the Hôtel des Arcades. Our topees were soft on our heads, our white suits clinging about our shoulders. The porter said I must go with him to the customs. We arrived there to find a damp native soldier on guard with water running down his rifle. The customs officer was at the reception at Government House, he said. He could not tell what time he would return or whether he would return at all that day. I pointed out that we must have our luggage to change into dry clothes. Nothing could be moved until the officer returned, he said. The porter, without more ado, picked up the nearest pieces and began piling them into the taxi. The guard remonstrated, but the porter continued undeterred. Then we drove back to the hotel.

This was a two-storeyed building with an arcaded front of shabby stucco; at the back a wooden staircase led to two broad verandahs on to which the two or three bedrooms opened. There was a lemon-tree in the yard inhabited by a misanthropic black monkey. The proprietress, a handsome Frenchwoman abounding in commercial good nature, made light of our troubles. It was her peculiar fortune to subsist upon the inadequacies of the Franco–Ethiopian railway service, for no one voluntarily spends long in Djibouti.

This fact, sufficiently clear from our earliest impression, became clearer when, after luncheon, the rain having stopped, we drove for a tour of the town. We bumped and rocked along in a one-horse cab through pools of steaming mud. The streets, described by the official guide-book as 'elegant and smiling', were mere stretches of waste land between blocks of houses. These, in the European quarter, were mostly built on the same plan as the hotel, arcaded and decaying.

'They look as though they might fall down any minute,' remarked my companion as we drove past one more than usually dissolute block of offices, and while we looked they actually did begin to fall. Great flakes of stucco crumbled from the front; a brick or two, toppling from the coping, splashed into the mud below. Some scared Indian clerks scampered into the open, a Greek in shirt-sleeves appeared from the house opposite, a group of half-naked natives rose from their haunches and, still scouring their teeth with sticks of wood, gazed apprehensively about them. Our driver pointed excitedly with his whip and admonished us in Somali. It had been an earthquake which, in the more sensible motion of the cab, had escaped our notice.

We jolted on past a whitewashed mosque to the camel-market and native quarter. The Somalis are a race of exceptional beauty, very slender and erect, with delicate features and fine, wide-set eyes. Most of them wore a strip of rag round their waists and a few coils of copper wire on wrists and ankles. Their heads were either shaven or dyed with ochre. Eight or nine harlots besieged our carriage until whipped away by the driver; innumerable naked children splashed through the mud after us, screaming for bakshish. Some splendid fellows with spears, in from the country, spat contemptuously as we passed. We came to the outskirts of the town, where the huts, formerly grass-thatched, mud-built squares, became little domed structures like inverted birds' nests, made out of twigs, grass, rags, and flattened tins, with one hole through which a man might crawl on his belly. When we returned to the hotel we found the vice-consul there with the good news that he had obtained a carriage for us in the first special train that evening. Elated though we felt, the heat was still overpowering; we went to sleep.

At evening, with the knowledge of our imminent departure, Djibouti suddenly became more tolerable. We visited the shops, bought a French novel with an inflammatory wrapper, some Burma cheroots, and changed money, getting, in return for our scattered and grimy notes of the Banque d'Indo-Chine, massive silver dollars of superb design.

Most recent books about Abyssinia – and I had read many between Westmeath and Marseilles – contain graphic descriptions of the train journey between Djibouti and Addis Ababa. Normally there is a weekly service which does the journey in three days; the two nights are spent in hotels at Dirre-Dowa and Hawash. There are several good reasons for not travelling at night; one is that the lights in the train are liable to frequent failure; another that during the rainy season it is not unusual for parts of the line to get washed away; another that the Galla and Danakil, through whose country the line passes, are still primarily homicidal in their interests, and in the early days of the railway formed a habit, not yet wholly eradicated, of taking up steel sleepers here and there to forge into spear-heads. During coronation week, however, it was found necessary, if the rolling-stock was to be adequate to the additional traffic, to run through trains. We left Djibouti after dinner on Friday and arrived at Addis on Sunday morning. It was a fairly comfortable journey.

We passed in the darkness the intolerable desolation of French Somaliland – a country of dust and boulders, utterly devoid of any sign of life, and arrived at Dirre-Dowa at dawn. This orderly little township sprang up during the construction of the railway on the land conceded to the French company, and has lived on the railway ever since with slightly diminishing prosperity. It contains two hotels, a café, and a billiard-saloon, a few shops and offices, a bank, a flour-mill, one or two villas, and the residence of an Abyssinian governor. Bougainvillea and acacia-trees border the streets. Twice a week the arrival of a train stirs up a few hours' activity; travellers arrive for the hotels; luggage is carried about the street; postal officials sort out the mail; commercial agents put on their sun-helmets and saunter down with their invoices to the goods office; then, like a small island when the mail-boat steams out of harbour, Dirre-Dowa relapses into its large siesta.

This, however, was no ordinary week. Not since 1916 – the civil war before the last – when Lej Yasu's Mohammedan followers were massacred just over the hills at Harar, had Dirre-Dowa known so many radically disturbing events as this succession of special trains bringing the Emperor's visitors to the coronation. Flagstaffs painted with the Abyssinian colours had been planted down the main streets, and lines of yellow, red, and green flags strung between them; motor-cars had been brought by train from the capital – for there are no roads outside the town – to convey the delegates to breakfast; the irregular troops of the whole province had been mobilized to line the way.

It was a grand and startling spectacle. My companion and I waited behind for some minutes in our carriage until the formal greetings were at an end and the delegates were clear of the station. Then we crossed the platform into the square. It was quite empty and quite silent. On three sides stood the Abyssinian soldiers; in front, where the main avenue led up to the governor's house, the last of the cars was just disappearing; as far as one could see stood the ranks of motionless, white-clothed tribesmen, bareheaded, barefooted, with guns on their shoulders; some had olive skins and keen, aquiline features; others were darker, with thick lips and flat noses showing the infection of slave blood; all wore curly black beards. Their dress was the invariable costume of the country – a long white shirt, white linen breeches loose above the knee and tight at the calves like jodhpurs, and the *chamma*, a white shawl worn like the toga over one shoulder, and a

81

bandolier of cartridges prominently displayed. In front of each section stood their chief in the gala dress so frequently photographed for the European Press. This, varying in grandeur with the wearer's wealth, consisted of a head-dress of lion's mane and gold ornament, a lion's skin, a brilliantly striped shirt, and a long sword curving out behind for some three feet or more; in some cases the lion's skin was represented by a garment of embroidered satin, like a chasuble, slit in front and behind in conventionalized tail and legs. It was a memorable experience to emerge, after the Latin holiday-making on the *Azay le Rideau*, the scramble at Djibouti, and the unquiet night in the train, into the sweet early morning air and the peace cast by these motionless warriors; they seemed at once so savage and so docile; great shaggy dogs of uncertain temper held for the moment firmly at leash.

We breakfasted at the hotel, and smoked a pipe on the terrace, awaiting the return of the delegates. Presently the soldiers who had been squatting on their haunches were called to attention; the cars came down the hill bearing diplomats handsomely refreshed by a banquet of porridge, kippers, eggs, and champagne. We returned to the train and resumed our journey.

From now until Hawash, where we arrived at sundown, the line ran through mile upon mile of featureless bush country – thorn, scrub, and flat, brownish mimosa-trees, and dust, ant-hills, a few vultures, now and then a dry watercourse or outcrop of stone, nothing else, hour upon hour. At noon we lunched in a tent at Afdem; luncheon consisted of four courses of meat variously prepared. We waited four hours at Hawash, from six until ten, while mechanics experimented with the lighting of the train; an armed guard squatted at the door of each coach. There are several sheds at Hawash, two or three bungalows of railway officials, a concrete platform, and an inn. After dinner we sat in the yard of the inn on hard little chairs, or paced about the platform or stumbled between the steel sleepers of the permanent way; there was no village or street; it was better to keep in the open as there were fewer mosquitoes; the lights in the carriage windows flashed feverishly on and off. Presently a group of ragged Gallas appeared and began a dance; two performed in the centre of the circle; the others stood round singing, stamping their feet and clapping their hands; they acted a lion hunt in dumb show. The guards wanted to drive them away, but the Egyptian Minister restrained them and gave a handful of dollars to the dancers; this set them going more eagerly and they spun about in the dust like tops; they were extremely fierce men, their long hair matted with butter and mud, and their thin, black bodies hung with scraps of skin and sacking.

At last the lighting was put right and we started again. Hawash lies at the foot of the highlands; throughout the night we climbed steadily. Each time we were jolted into consciousness between intermittent periods of sleep, we found the air fresher and the temperature lower, and by early morning we had wrapped ourselves in rugs and overcoats. We breakfasted before dawn at Mojo and resumed our journey just as the first light began to break. It revealed a profound change in the landscape; the bush and plain had disappeared, and in its place there extended crests of undulating downland with a horizon of blue mountains. Wherever one looked were rich little farms, groups of circular thatched huts inside high stockades, herds of fine humped cattle browsing in deep pastures, fields of corn and maize being worked by families; camel caravans swayed along the track by the railway, carrying fodder and fuel. The line still mounted, and presently, between nine and ten, we came in sight, far ahead of us, of the eucalyptus-woods that surround Addis Ababa. Here, at a station named Akaki, we stopped again to allow the delegates time to shave and put on their uniforms. Tin trunks and dressing-cases appeared again, valets ran between the luggage-van and the sleeping-cars. The Dutch Minister soon appeared at the side of the line in cocked hat and gold braid, the Egyptian in tarboosh and epaulettes, the Japanese in evening coats and white waistcoats and top hats; then all got into the train again and proceeded. We puffed up the winding track for another half-hour and at last arrived at Addis Ababa.

Red carpet had been put out, and before the carpet were drawn up a very different body of troops from those we had passed on the way. These were squat, coal-black boys from the Sudanese border. They wore brand-new, well-cut, khaki uniforms; the lion of Judah shone in polished brass on cap badges and buttons; with bayonets fixed and rifles of recent pattern. Beside them a band of bugle and drums, with a little black drummer poising crossed sticks above the big drum. But for the bare feet below their puttees, they might have been the prize platoon of some public school O.T.C. In front of them with drawn sword stood a European officer. This was a squad of Tafari's own guard.

As the train stopped, the guard presented arms; the head chamberlain advanced in a blue satin cloak to greet the delegations, and the band struck up. There was no skimping of difficulties, every anthem was played through thoroughly verse by verse. The Poles came out easy winners in prolixity. Finally, the Ethiopian anthem was played; we heard this so often during the next ten days that it became vaguely familiar, even to me.

Eventually the last delegation disappeared. The Minister's daughters had come from the British Legation to meet the train. They asked me what arrangements had been made for my accommodation, and I replied, to the best of my knowledge, none. Consternation. They said the town was completely full. It would be impossible to get a room now. There might be a tent somewhere at the legation; it was conceivable that one of the hotels would let me pitch it in their yard. We got into the car and mounted the hill into the town. Half-way up we passed the Hôtel de France. At the entrance stood the Western figure of a friend named Irene Ravensdale in riding habit. We stopped to greet her. I ran indoors and asked the manager whether there was, by any chance, a vacant room. Why, yes, certainly. It was not a very good room, it was in an outhouse behind the hotel; but, if I cared to take it, it was mine for two pounds a day. I accepted eagerly, signed the register, and rejoined Irene. The legation car and the luggage had disappeared. Instead, the street was full of Abyssinians arriving from the country on mules, slaves trotting all round them, clearing and obstructing the way. The preposterous *Alice in Wonderland* fortnight had begun.

It is to *Alice in Wonderland* that my thoughts recur in seeking some historical parallel for life in Addis Ababa. There are others: Israel in the time of Saul, the Scotland of Shakespeare's *Macbeth*,

84

the Sublime Porte as one sees it revealed in the despatches of the late eighteenth century, but it is in *Alice* only that one finds the peculiar flavour of galvanized and translated reality, where animals carry watches in their waistcoat pockets, royalty paces the croquet lawn beside the chief executioner, and litigation ends in a flutter of playing-cards. How to recapture, how retail, the crazy enchantment of these Ethiopian days?

Addis Ababa is a new town; so new, indeed, that not a single piece of it appears to be really finished.

The first, obvious, inescapable impression was that nothing was ready or could possibly be made ready in time for the official opening of the celebrations six days hence. It was not that one here and there observed traces of imperfect completion, occasional scaffolding or patches of unset concrete; the whole town seemed still in a rudimentary stage of construction. At every corner were half-finished buildings; some had been already abandoned; on others, gangs of ragged Guraghi were at work. One afternoon I watched a number of them, twenty or thirty in all, under the surveillance of an Armenian contractor, at work clearing away the heaps of rubble and stone which encumbered the courtyard before the main door of the palace. The stuff had to be packed into wooden boxes swung between two poles, and emptied on a pile fifty yards away. Two men carried each load, which must have weighed very little more than an ordinary hod of bricks. A foreman circulated among them, carrying a long cane. When he was engaged elsewhere the work stopped altogether. The men did not sit down, chat, or relax in any way; they simply stood stock-still where they were, motionless as cows in a field, sometimes arrested with one small stone in their hands. When the foreman turned his attention towards them they began to move again, very deliberately, like figures in a slow-motion film; when he beat them they did not look round or remonstrate, but quickened their movements just perceptibly; when the blows ceased they lapsed into their original pace until, the foreman's back being turned, they again stopped completely. (I wondered whether the Pyramids were built in this way.) Work of this nature was in progress in every street and square of the town.

Addis Ababa extends five or six miles in diameter. The station is at the southern extremity of the town, and from it a broad road leads up to the post office and principal commercial buildings. Two deep watercourses traverse the town, and round their slopes, and in small groves of eucalyptus scattered between the more permanent buildings, lie little clusters of *tukals*, round native huts, thatched and windowless. Down the centre of the main thoroughfares run metalled tracks for motor-traffic, bordered on either side by dust and loose stones for mules and pedestrians; at frequent intervals are sentry-boxes of corrugated iron, inhabited by drowsy, armed policemen. Attempts are even made with canes to regulate the foot-traffic, a fad which proves wholly unintelligible to the inhabitants. The usual way for an Abyssinian gentleman to travel is straight down the middle of the road on mule-back with ten or twenty armed retainers trotting all round him; there are continual conflicts between the town police and the followers of the country gentlemen, from which the police often come out the worse.

Every man in Abyssinia carries arms; that is to say, he wears a dagger and bandolier of cartridges round his waist and has a slave-boy walking behind with a rifle. Cartridges are a symbol of wealth and, in the interior, a recognized medium of exchange; their propriety for any particular brand of firearm is a matter of secondary importance.

The streets are always a lively scene; the universal white costume being here and there relieved by the brilliant blues and violets of mourning or the cloaks of the upper classes. The men walk about hand in hand in pairs and little groups; quite often they are supporting some insensible drunkard. Women appear in the markets, but take no part in the general street-lounging of their men. Occasionally a woman of high degree passes on a mule; under a vast felt hat her face is completely bandaged over with white silk, so that only the two eyes appear, like those of a hooded rider of the Ku Klux Klan. There are numerous priests, distinguished by long gowns and high turbans. Sometimes the Emperor passes in a great red car surrounded by cantering lancers. A page sits behind holding over his head an umbrella of crimson silk embroidered with sequins and gold tassels. A guard sits in front nursing a machine-gun under a plush shawl; the chauffeur is a European wearing powder-blue livery and the star of Ethiopia.

As part of the general policy for tidying up the town for the arrival of the visitors, high stockades have been erected, or are being erected, down all the streets, screening from possibly critical eyes the homes of the poorer inhabitants. Half-way up the hill stands the Hôtel de France, a place of primitive but cordial hospitality, kept by a young Frenchman and his wife who have seen better days as traders in hides and coffee at Djibouti.

There is another large hotel kept by a Greek, the Imperial, most of which has been requisitioned for the Egyptian delegation. There are two or three small hotels, cafés, and bars, kept either by Greeks or Armenians. There is another large hotel under construction. It was being made specially for the coronation, but is still hopelessly unready. It is here that the Marine band of H.M.S. *Effingham* are put up.

The Gebbi is a great jumble of buildings on a hill to the east of the town. At night, during coronation week, it was lit up with rows of electric bulbs, but by day it presented a slightly dingy appearance. High walls encircle the whole, and the only approach, through which came alike butchers and ambassadors, is through two heavily guarded doors. In spite of this, the precincts seemed to be always full of loafers, squatting and squabbling, or gaping at the visitors.

It is now possible to reach the British Legation by car; until quite lately guests rode out to dinner on mules, a boy running in front with a lantern. Indeed, as further preparation for the visitors, the road from the town had been strewn with stones, and a motor-roller of the latest pattern brought from Europe; this machine was sometimes seen heading for the legations, but some untoward event always interposed, and the greater part of the way was left to be rolled by the tyres of private cars. It was an expensive and bumpy journey.

The legation stands in a small park, and on either side of the drive a little garden city has sprung up of pretty thatched bungalows which accommodate the officials. During the coronation a camp was pitched in the paddock for the staffs of the various visitors, and periodic bugling, reminiscent of an ocean liner, added a fresh incongruity to the bizarre life of the little community.

Outside the legations was a personnel of supreme diversity. There was the Caucasian manager of the Haile Selassie Casino; the French editor of the *Courier d'Éthiopie*, an infinitely helpful man, genial, punctilious, sceptical; an Englishman in the employ of the Abyssinian Government; a French architect married to an Abyssinian; a bankrupt German planter obsessed by grievances; a tipsy old Australian prospector, winking over his whisky and hinting at the mountains full of platinum he could tell you about if he cared to. There was Mr Hall, in whose office I spent many frantic hours; he was a trader, of mixed German and Abyssinian descent, extremely handsome, well dressed, and monocled, a man of imperturbable courtesy, an exceptional linguist. During the coronation he had been put in a little tin house next to the Casino and constituted chief, and, as far as one could see sole, member, of a *bureau d'étrangers*. It was his week's task to listen to all the troubles of all the foreigners, official or unofficial, to distribute news to the Press, issue tickets and make out lists for the Abyssinian functions; if the Italian telegraph company took an hour's rest, it was Mr Hall who heard the complaints; if an officious police-officer refused someone admittance to some grand stand, Mr Hall must see to it that the officer was reprimanded; if His Majesty's Stationery Office forgot to issue the text of the coronation service, Mr Hall promised everyone a copy; if a charabanc had not arrived to take the band to the racecourse, if there had not been enough coronation medals to go round the church, if, for any reason or no reason, anyone in Addis Ababa was in a bad temper – and at that altitude the most equable natures become unaccountably upset – off he went to Mr Hall. And whatever language he cared to speak, Mr Hall would understand and sympathize; with almost feminine delicacy he would calm him and compliment him; with masculine decision he would make a bold note of the affair on his pad; he would rise, bow, and smile his pacified visitor out with every graceful assurance of goodwill – and do absolutely nothing about it.

Of the Abyssinians we saw very little except as grave, rather stolid figures at the official receptions. There was Ras Hailu, owner of the rich province of Gojam, reputed wealthier than the Emperor himself; a commanding figure, dark complexioned, with his little pointed beard dyed black, and slightly insolent eyes. Among his many great possessions was a night-club two miles out on the Addis Alem road. He had planned this himself and, wishing to be up-to-date, had given it an English name. It was called 'Robinson'. There was the venerable Ras Kassa and Moulungetta, the commander-in-chief of the army, a mountain of a man with grey beard and bloodshot eyes; in full-dress uniform with scarlet-and-gold cloak and lion's-mane busby, he looked hardly human.

Apart from the officials and journalists who pullulated at every corner, there were surprisingly few visitors.

There was a slightly class-conscious lady with a French title and an American accent, who left the town suddenly after a luncheon-party at which she was not accorded her proper precedence. There was the American professor, who will appear later in this narrative, and two formidable ladies in knitted suits and topees; though unrelated by blood, long companionship had made them almost indistinguishable, square-jawed, tight-lipped, with hard, discontented eyes. For them the whole coronation was a profound disappointment. What did it matter that they were witnesses of a unique stage of the interpenetration of two cultures? They were out for Vice. They were collecting material, in fact, for a little book on the subject, an African *Mother India*, and every minute devoted to Coptic ritual or displays of horsemanship was a minute wasted. Prostitution and drug traffic comprised their modest interests, and they were too dense to find evidence of either.

But perhaps the most remarkable visitors were the Marine band. They arrived on the same day as the Duke of Gloucester, under the command of Major Sinclair, strengthened by a diet of champagne at breakfast, luncheon, tea, and dinner throughout their journey, and much sage advice about the propriety of their behaviour in a foreign capital. At Addis they were quartered in a large, unfinished hotel; each man had his own bedroom, furnished by his thoughtful hosts with hairbrushes, clothes-hangers, and brand-new enamelled spittoons.

Perhaps no one did more to deserve his star of Ethiopia than Major Sinclair. Eschewing the glitter and dignity of the legation camp, he loyally remained with his men in the town, and spent anxious days arranging appointments that were never kept; his diary, which some of us were privileged to see, was a stark chronicle of successive disappointments patiently endured. '*Appointment 9.30 emperor's private secretary to arrange for this evening's banquet; he did not come. 11. Went as arranged to see master of the king's music; he was not there. 12. Went to see Mr Hall to obtain score of Ethiopian national anthem – not procurable. 2.30 Car should have come to take men to aerodrome – did not arrive ...*' and so on. But, in spite of every discouragement, the band was always present on time, irreproachably dressed, and provided with the correct music.

One morning in particular, on which the band played a conspicuous part, remains vividly in my memory as typical of the whole week. It was the first day of the official celebrations, to be inaugurated by the unveiling of the new Menelik memorial. The ceremony was announced for ten o'clock. Half an hour before the time, Irene Ravensdale and I drove to the spot. Here, on the site of the old execution-tree, stood the monument, shrouded in brilliant green silk. Round it was a little ornamental garden with paving, a balustrade, and regular plots, from which, here and there, emerged delicate shoots of newly-sown grass. While some workmen were laying carpets on the terrace and spreading yellow sunshades of the kind which cover the tables at open-air restaurants, others were still chipping at the surrounding masonry and planting drooping palm-trees in the arid beds. A heap of gilt armchairs lay on one side; on the other a mob of photographers and movietone men were fighting for places. Opposite the carpeted terrace rose a stand of several unstable tiers. A detachment of policemen were engaged furiously laying about them with canes in the attempt to keep these seats clear of natives. Four or five Europeans were already established there. Irene and I joined them. Every ten minutes or so a police officer would appear and order us all off; we produced our *laissez-passer*; he saluted and went away, to be succeeded at a short interval by a colleague, when the performance was repeated.

The square and half a mile of the avenue approaching it were lined with royal guards; there was a band formed up in front of them; the Belgian colonel curvetted about on an uneasy chestnut horse. Presently, punctual to the minute, appeared Major Sinclair and his band. They had had to march from their hotel, as the charabanc ordered for them had failed to appear. They halted, and Major Sinclair approached the Belgian colonel for instructions. The colonel knew no English, and the major no French; an embarrassing interview followed, complicated by the caprices of the horse, which plunged backwards and sideways over the square. In this way the two officers covered a large area of ground, conversing inconclusively the while with extravagant gestures. Eventually Irene heroically stepped out to interpret for them. It appeared that the Belgian colonel had had no orders about the English band. He had his own band there and did not want another. The major explained he had had direct instructions to appear in the square at ten. The colonel said the major could not possibly stay in the square; there was no room for him, and anyway he would have no opportunity of playing, since the native band had a programme of music fully adequate for the whole proceedings. At last the colonel conceded that the English band might take up a position at the extreme end of his troops at the bottom of the hill. The officers parted, and the band marched away out of sight. A long wait followed, while the battle between police and populace raged round the stand. At last the delegations began to arrive; the soldiers presented arms; the native band played the appropriate music; the Belgian colonel was borne momentarily backwards through the ranks, capered heroically among the crowd, and reappeared at another corner of the square. The delegations took up their places on the gilt chairs under the umbrellas. A long pause preceded the Emperor's arrival; the soldiers still stood stiff. Suddenly up that imposing avenue there appeared a slave, trotting unconcernedly with a gilt chair on his head. He put it among the others, looked round with interest at the glittering uniforms, and then retired. At last the Emperor came; first a troop of lancers, then the crimson car and silk umbrella. He took up his place in the centre of the Court under a blue canopy; the band played the Ethiopian national anthem. A secretary presented him with the text of his speech; the camera-men began snapping and turning. But there was a fresh delay. Something had gone wrong. Messages passed from mouth to mouth; a runner disappeared down the hill.

One photographer, bolder than the rest, advanced out of the crowd and planted his camera within a few yards of the royal party; he wore a violet suit of plus-fours, a green shirt open at the neck, tartan stockings, and parti-coloured shoes. After a few happy shots of the Emperor he walked slowly along the line, looking the party critically up and down. When he found anyone who attracted his attention, he took a photograph of him. Then, expressing his satisfaction with a slight inclination of the head, he rejoined his colleagues.

Still a delay. Then up the avenue came Major Sinclair and the Marine band. They halted in the middle of the square, arranged their music, and played the national anthem. Things were then allowed to proceed according to plan. The Emperor advanced, read his speech, and pulled the cord. There was a rending of silk and a vast equestrian figure in gilt bronze was partially revealed. Men appeared with poles and poked away the clinging folds. One piece, out of reach of their efforts, obstinately fluttered over the horse's ears and eyes. The Greek contractor mounted a ladder and dislodged the rag.

The Marine band continued to play; the delegations and cour-tiers made for their cars; the Emperor paused, and listened attentively to the music, then smiled his approval to the major before driving away. As the last of the visitors disappeared, the people broke through the soldiers, and the square became a dazzle of white tunics and black heads. For many days to come, numbers of them might be seen clustering round the memorial and gazing with puzzled awe at this new ornament to their city.

Until late on the preceding afternoon, wild uncertainty pre-vailed about the allocation of tickets for the coronation. The legations knew nothing. Mr Hall knew nothing, and his office was continuously besieged by anxious journalists whose only hope of getting their reports back in time for Monday's papers was to write and despatch them well before the event. What could they say when they did not even know where the ceremony would take place?

With little disguised irritation they set to work making the best of their meagre material. Gorgis and its precincts were impenetrably closed; a huge tent could be discerned through the railings, built against one wall of the church. Some described the actual coronation as taking place there; others used it as the scene of a state reception and drew fanciful pictures of the ceremony in the interior of the cathedral, '*murky, almost suffocating with incense and the thick, stifling smoke of tallow candles*' (Associated Press); authorities on Coptic ritual remarked that as the coronation proper must take place in the inner sanctuary, which no layman might glimpse, much less enter, there was small hope of anyone seeing anything at all. The cinema-men, whose companies had spent very large sums in importing them and their talking apparatus, began to show signs of restlessness, and some correspondents became almost menacing. Mr Hall, however, remained his own serene self. Everything, he assured us, was being arranged for their particular convenience; only, he admitted, the exact details were still unsettled.

Eventually, about fourteen hours before the ceremony was due to start, numbered tickets were issued through the legations; there was plenty of room for all, except, as it happened, for the Abyssinians themselves. The rases and Court officials were provided with gilt chairs, but the local chiefs seemed to be wholly neglected; most of them remained outside, gazing wistfully at the ex-Kaiser's coach and the tall hats of the European and American visitors; those that succeeded in pushing their way inside were kept far at the back, where they squatted together on their haunches, or, in all the magnificent trappings of their gala dress, dozed simply in distant corners of the great tent.

For it was there, in the end, that the service took place. It was light and lofty, supported by two colonnades of draped scaffold-poles; the seat end was hung with silk curtains, behind which a sanctuary had been improvised to hold the tabor from the cathedral. A carpeted dais ran half the length of the floor. On it stood the silk-covered table that bore the regalia and the crown neatly concealed in a cardboard hat-box; on either side were double rows of gilt chairs for the Court and the diplomatic corps, and at the end, with their backs to the body of the hall, two canopied thrones.

Their Majesties had spent the night in vigil, surrounded inside the cathedral by clergy, and outside by troops. One enterprising journalist headed his report '*Meditation Behind Machine-Guns*', and had the gratifying experience, when he was at last admitted into the precincts, of finding his guess fully justified; a machine-gun section was posted on the steps covering each approach.

It was highly interesting to me, when the papers began to arrive from Europe and America, to compare my own experiences with those of the correspondents. It seemed to me that we had been witnesses of a quite different series of events.

This is what I saw at the coronation:

The Emperor and Empress were due to appear from their vigil at seven in the morning. We were warned to arrive at the tent about an hour before that time. Accordingly, having dressed by candlelight, Irene and I proceeded there at about six. For many hours before dawn the roads into the town had been filled with tribesmen coming in from the surrounding camps. We could see them passing the hotel (the street lamps were working that night) in dense white crowds, some riding mules, some walking, some moving at a slow trot beside their masters. All, as always, were armed. Our car moved slowly to Gorgis, hooting continuously. There were many other cars; some carrying Europeans; others, Abyssinian officials. Eventually we reached the church and were admitted after a narrow scrutiny of our tickets and ourselves. The square inside the gates was comparatively clear; from the top of the steps the machine-guns compromised with ecclesiastical calm. From inside the cathedral came the voices of the priests singing the last phase of the service that had lasted all night. Eluding the numerous soldiers, policemen, and officials who directed us towards the tent, we slipped into the outer ambulatory of the church, where the choir of bearded and vested deacons were dancing to the music of hand drums and little silver rattles. The drummers squatted round them; but they carried the rattles themselves and in their other hand waved praying-sticks. Some carried nothing, but merely clapped their empty palms. They

94

shuffled in and out, singing and swaying; the dance was performed with body and arms rather than with the feet. Their faces expressed the keenest enjoyment – almost, in some cases, ecstasy. The brilliant morning sun streamed in on them from the windows, on their silver crosses, silver-headed rods, and on the large, illuminated manuscript from which one of them, undeterred by the music, was reciting the Gospels; the clouds of incense mounted and bellied in the shafts of light.

Presently we went on to the tent. This was already well filled. The clothes of the congregation varied considerably. Most of the men were wearing morning coats, but some had appeared in evening dress and one or two in dinner-jackets. One lady had stuck an American flag in the top of her sun-helmet. The junior members of the legations were there already, in uniform, fussing among the seats to see that everything was in order. By seven o'clock the delegations arrived.

It was long after the last delegate had taken his place that the Emperor and Empress appeared from the church. We could hear the singing going on behind the curtains. Photographers, amateur and professional, employed the time in taking furtive snapshots. Reporters despatched their boys to the telegraph office with supplementary accounts of the preliminaries. By some misunderstanding of the instructions of the responsible official, the office was closed for the day. After the manner of native servants, the messengers, instead of reporting the matter to their masters, sat, grateful for the rest, on the steps gossiping until it should open. It was late in the day that the truth became known, and then there was more trouble for Mr Hall.

The ceremony was immensely long, even according to the original schedule, and the clergy succeeded in prolonging it by at least an hour and a half beyond the allotted time. The six succeeding days of celebration were to be predominantly military, but the coronation day itself was in the hands of the Church, and they were going to make the most of it. Psalms, canticles, and prayers succeeded each other, long passages of Scripture were read, all in the extinct ecclesiastical tongue, Ghiz. Candles were lit one by one; the coronation oaths were proposed and sworn; the diplomats shifted uncomfortably in their gilt chairs, noisy squabbles broke out round the entrance between the imperial guard and the retainers of the local chiefs. Professor W., who was an expert of high transatlantic reputation on Coptic ritual, occasionally remarked: 'They are beginning the Mass now,' 'That was the offertory,' 'No, I was wrong; it was the consecration,' 'No, I was wrong; I think it is the secret Gospel,' 'No, I think it must be the Epistle,' 'How very curious; I don't believe it was a Mass at all,' '*Now* they *are* beginning the Mass ...' and so on. Presently the bishops began to fumble among the band-boxes, and investiture began. At long intervals the Emperor was presented with robe, orb, spurs, spear, and finally with the crown. A salute of guns was fired, and the crowds outside, scattered all over the surrounding waste spaces, began to cheer; the imperial horses reared up, plunged on top of each other, kicked the gilding off the front of the coach, and broke their traces. The coachman sprang from the box and whipped them from a safe distance. Inside the pavilion there was a general sense of relief; it had all been very fine and impressive, now for a cigarette, a drink, and a change into less formal costume. Not a bit of it. The next thing was to crown the Empress and the heir apparent; another salvo of guns followed, during which an Abyssinian groom had two ribs broken in an attempt to unharness a pair of the imperial horses. Again we felt for our hats and gloves. But the Coptic choir still sang; the bishops then proceeded to take back the regalia with proper prayers, lections, and canticles.

'I have noticed some very curious variations in the Canon of the Mass,' remarked the professor, 'particularly with regard to the kiss of peace.'

Then the Mass began.

For the first time throughout the morning the Emperor and Empress left their thrones; they disappeared behind the curtains into the improvised sanctuary; most of the clergy went too. The stage was empty save for the diplomats; their faces were set and strained, their attitudes inelegant. I have seen just that look in crowded railway carriages, at dawn, between Avignon and Marseilles. Their clothes made them funnier still. Marshal d'Esperez alone preserved his dignity, his chest thrown out his baton poised on his knee, rigid as a war memorial, and, as far as one could judge, wide awake.

It was now about eleven o'clock, the time at which the emperor was due to leave the pavilion. Punctually to plan, three Abyssinian aeroplanes rose to greet him. They circled round and round over the tent, eagerly demonstrating their newly acquired art by swooping and curvetting within a few feet of the canvas roof. The noise was appalling; the local chiefs stirred in their sleep and rolled on to their faces; only by the opening and closing of their lips and the turning of their music could we discern that the Coptic deacons were still singing.

'A most unfortunate interruption. I missed many of the verses,' said the professor.

Eventually, at about half past twelve, the Mass came to an end, and the Emperor and Empress, crowned, shuffling along under a red and gold canopy and looking, as Irene remarked, exactly like the processional statues of Seville, crossed to a grand stand, from which the Emperor delivered a royal proclamation; an aeroplane scattered copies of the text and, through loud speakers, the Court heralds re-read it to the populace.

There was a slightly ill-tempered scramble among the photographers and cinema-men – I received a heavy blow in the middle of the back from a large camera, and a hoarse rebuke, 'Come along there now – let the eyes of the world see.'

Dancing broke out once more among the clergy, and there is no knowing how long things might not have gone on, had not the photographers so embarrassed and jostled them, and outraged their sense of reverence, that they withdrew to finish their devotions alone in the cathedral.

Then at last the Emperor and Empress were conducted to their coach and borne off to luncheon by its depleted but still demonstratively neurasthenic team of horses.

My Indian chauffeur had got bored and gone home. Luncheon at the hotel was odious. All food supplies had been commandeered by the Government, M. Hallot told us; it was rather doubtful whether the market would open again until the end of the week. Meanwhile there were tinned chunks of pineapple and three courses of salt beef, one cut in small cubes with chopped onion, one left in a slab with tomato ketchup, one in slices with hot water and Worcestershire sauce; the waiters had gone out the night before to get drunk and had not yet woken up.

We were all in a bad temper that night.

Six days followed of intensive celebration. On Monday morning the delegations were required to leave wreaths at the mausoleum of Menelik and Zauditu. This is a circular, domed building of vaguely Byzantine affinities, standing in the Gebbi grounds. Its interior is furnished with oil-paintings and enlarged photographs of the royal family, a fumed oak grandfather clock, and a few occasional tables; their splay legs protruded from under embroidered linen tablecloths, laid diagonally; on them stood little conical silver vases of catkins boldly counterfeited in wire and magenta wool. Steps led down to the vault where lay the white marble sarcophagi of the two potentates. It is uncertain whether either contains the body attributed to it, or indeed any body at all. The date and place of Menelik's death are a palace secret, but it is generally supposed to have taken place about two years before its formal announcement to the people; the Empress probably lies out under the hill at Debra Lebanos. At various hours that morning, however, the delegations of the Great Powers dutifully appeared, and, not to be outdone in reverence, Professor W. came tripping gravely in with a little bunch of white carnations.

There was a cheerful, friendly tea-party that afternoon at the American Legation and a ball and firework display at the Italian, but the party which excited the keenest interest was the *gebbur* given by the Emperor to his tribesmen. These banquets are a regular feature of Ethiopian life, constituting, in fact, a vital bond between the people and their overlords, whose prestige in time of peace varies directly with their frequency and abundance. Until a few years ago attendance at a *gebbur* was part of the entertainment offered to every visitor in Abyssinia. Copious first-hand accounts can be found in almost every book about the country, describing the packed, squatting ranks of the diners; the slaves carrying the warm quarters of newly slaughtered, uncooked beef; the despatch with which each guest carves for himself; the upward slice of his dagger with which he severs each mouthful from the dripping lump; the flat, damp platters of local bread; the great draughts of *tedj* and *talla* from the horn drinking-pots; the butchers outside felling and dividing the oxen; the Emperor and notables at the high table, exchanging highly seasoned morsels of more elaborate fare. These are the traditional features of the *gebbur* and, no doubt, of this occasion also. It was thus that the journalists described their impressions in glowing paraphrases of Rhey and Kingsford. When the time came, however, we found that particular precautions had been taken to exclude all Europeans from the spectacle. Mr Hall loyally undertook to exercise his influence for each of us personally, but in the end no one gained admission except two resolute ladies and, by what was felt to be a very base exploitation of racial advantage, the coloured correspondent of a syndicate of Negro newspapers.

All that I saw was the last relay of guests shambling out of the Gebbi gates late that afternoon. They were a very enviable company, quite stupefied with food and drink. Policemen attempted to herd them on, kicking their insensible backs and whacking them with canes, but nothing disturbed their serene good temper. The chiefs were hoisted on to mules by their retainers and remained there blinking and smiling; one very old man, mounted back to front, felt feebly about the crupper for his reins; some stood clasped together in silent, swaying groups; others, lacking support, rolled contentedly in the dust. I remembered them that evening as I sat in the supper-room at the Italian Legation gravely discussing the slight disturbance of diplomatic propriety caused by the Emperor's capricious distribution of honours.

There were several parties that week, of more or less identical composition. At three there were fireworks, resulting in at least one nasty accident; at one, a cinema which failed to work; at one, Galla dancers who seemed to dislocate their shoulders, and sweated so heartily that our host was able to plaster their foreheads with banknotes; at another, Somali dancers shivered with cold on a lawn illuminated with coloured flares. There was a race meeting; the royal enclosure was packed and the rest of the course empty of spectators; a totalisator paid out four dollars on every winning three-dollar ticket; both bands played; Prince Udine presented an enormous cup and the Emperor a magnificent kind of urn whose purpose no one could discover; it had several silver taps and little silver stands, and a great tray covered with silver cups of the kind from which grape-fruit is eaten in cinema-films. This fine trophy was won by a gentleman, in gilt riding-boots, attached to the French Legation, and was used later at their party for champagne. There was a certain amount of whispering against French sportsmanship, however, as they had sent back their books of sweepstake tickets with scarcely one sold. This showed a very bad club spirit, the other legations maintained.

There was a procession of all the troops, uniformed and irregular, in the middle of which Irene appeared in a taxi-cab surprisingly surrounded by a band of mounted musicians playing six-foot pipes and banging on saddle drums of ox-hide and wood. The people all shrilled their applause, as the Emperor passed, in a high, wailing whistle.

There was the opening of a museum of souvenirs, containing examples of native craftsmanship, the crown captured by General Napier at Magdala and returned by the Victoria and Albert Museum, and a huge, hollow stone which an Abyssinian saint had worn as a hat.

There was a review of the troops on the plain outside the railway station.

But no catalogue of events can convey any real idea of these astounding days, of an atmosphere utterly unique, elusive, unforgettable. If I have seemed to give emphasis to the irregularity of the proceedings, to their unpunctuality, and their occasional failure, it is because this was an essential part of their character and charm. In Addis Ababa everything was haphazard and incongruous; one learned always to expect the unusual and yet was always surprised.

Every morning we awoke to a day of brilliant summer sunshine; every evening fell cool, limpid, charged with hidden vitality, fragrant with the thin smoke of the *tukal* fires, pulsing, like a live body, with the beat of the tom-toms that drummed incessantly somewhere out of sight among the eucalyptus-trees. In this rich African setting were jumbled together, for a few days, people of every race and temper, a company shot through with every degree of animosity and suspicion. There were continual rumours born of the general uncertainty; rumours about the date and place of every ceremony; rumours of dissension in high places; rumours that, in the absence at Addis Ababa of all the responsible officials, the interior was seething with brigandage; that the Ethiopian Minister to Paris had been refused admittance to Addis Ababa; that the royal coach-man had not had his wages for two months and had given in his notice; that one of the legations had refused to receive the Empress's first lady-in-waiting.

One morning Irene and I were sitting outside the hotel drinking apéritifs and waiting for luncheon; we were entertained by the way in which the various visitors treated a pedlar who diffidently approached them with a bundle of bootlaces in one hand and an enamelled *pot de chambre* in the other. Suddenly a taxi drove up, and a servant wearing the palace livery jumped out and emptied a large pile of envelopes into Irene's lap. Two were addressed to us. We took them and handed back the rest, which the man presented, to be sorted in the same way, at the next table.

The envelopes contained an invitation to lunch with the Emperor that day at one o'clock; as it was then after half past twelve we disregarded the request for an answer and hurried off to change.

Professor W. had spoken to me of this party some days before, saying with restrained relish, 'On Saturday I am lunching with the Emperor. There are several things I shall be interested to discuss with him.' But, as it turned out, he had little opportunity for conversation. There were about eighty guests and many empty places, showing that the messenger had not been able to finish his round in time. At first we stood in the glazed corridor which ran down one side of the main building. Then we were ushered into the throne-room, bowed and curtsied, and ranged ourselves round the walls while *byrrh* and vermouth and cigars were carried round. There was something slightly ecclesiastical in the atmosphere.

The Emperor then led the way into the dining-room. We tramped in behind him in no particular order. He seated himself at the centre of the top table; three tables ran at right angles to

101

him, resplendent with gold plate and white-and-gold china. Typewritten name-cards lay on each plate. Ten minutes or so followed of some confusion as we jostled round and round looking for our places; there was no plan of the table, and as most of us were complete strangers we were unable to help each other. The Emperor sat watching us with a placid little smile. We must have looked very amusing. Naturally no one cared to look at the places next to the Emperor, so that when at last we were all seated the two most honoured guests were left to sidle forlornly into the nearest empty places. Eventually they were fetched. Irene sat one one side and the French wife of the Egyptian consul on his other. I sat between an English airman and a Belgian photographer. A long meal followed, of many courses of fair French cooking and good European wines. There was also *tedj* and the national beverage made from fermented honey. We had sent out for some, one evening at the hotel, and found it an opaque yellowish liquid, mild and rather characterless. The Emperor's *tedj* was a very different drink, quite clear, slightly brown, heavy, rich, and dry. After luncheon, at Irene's request, we were given some of the liqueur distilled from it – a colourless spirit of fine flavour and disconcerting potency.

Only one odd thing happened at luncheon. Just as we were finishing, a stout young woman rose from a seat near the back and made her way resolutely between the tables until she planted herself within a few yards of the Emperor. I understand that she was a Syrian Jewess employed in some educational capacity in the town. She carried a sheaf of papers which she held close to her pince-nez with one plump hand while she raised the other above her head in a Fascist salute. Conversation faltered and ceased. The Emperor looked at her with kindly enquiry. Then, in a voice of peculiar strength and stridency, she began to recite an ode. It was a very long complimentary ode, composed by herself in Arabic, a language wholly unintelligible to His Majesty. Between verses she made a long pause during which she fluttered her manuscript, then she began again. We had just begun to feel that the performance would really prove interminable, when, just as suddenly as she had begun, she stopped, bobbed, turned about, and, with glistening forehead and slightly labouring breath, strode back to her place to receive the congratulations of her immediate neighbours. The Emperor rose and led the way back to the throne-room. Here we stood round the walls for a quarter of an hour while liqueurs were served. Then we bowed in turn and filed out into the sunshine.

One moment of that week is particularly vivid in my memory. It was late at night and we had just returned from a party. My room, as I have said, was in an outhouse at a little distance from the hotel; a grey horse, some goats, and the hotel guard, his head wrapped in a blanket, were sleeping in the yard as I went across. Behind my room, separated from the hotel grounds by wooden palings, lay a cluster of native *tukals*. That evening there was a party in one of them. The door faced my way and I could see a glimmer of lamplight in the interior. They were singing a monotonous song, clapping in time and drumming with their hands on petrol-tins. I suppose there were about ten or fifteen of them there. I stood for some time listening. I was wearing a tall hat, evening clothes and white gloves. Presently the guard woke up and blew a little trumpet; the sound was taken up by other guards at neighbouring houses (it is in this way that they assure their employers of their vigilance); then he wrapped himself once more in his blanket and relapsed into sleep.

The song continued unvarying in the still night. The absurdity of the whole week became suddenly typified for me in that situation – my preposterous clothes, the sleeping animals, and the wakeful party on the other side of the stockade.

It was during our third week in Addis Ababa, when the official celebrations were over and the delegations were being packed off to the coast as fast as the Franco-Ethiopian Railway's supply of sleeping cars would allow, that Professor W. suggested to me that we should make an expedition together to Debra Lebanos.

This monastery has for four centuries been the centre of Abyssinian spiritual life. It is built round a spring where the waters of Jordan, conveyed subterraneously down the Red Sea, are believed to well up endowed with curative properties; pilgrims go there from all parts of the country, and it is a popular burial-ground for those who can afford it, since all found there at the Last Trump are assured of unimpeded entry into Paradise.

It was the dry season, so that the road could be attempted by car. Professor Mercer had recently made the journey and had come back with photographs of a hitherto unknown version of Ecclesiastes. Ras Kassa had driven from Fiche only two weeks before and renewed the bridges for the occasion, so that we had little difficulty in finding a driver willing to take us. Permission had first to be obtained from Kassa to use the road. Professor W. obtained this and also a letter of commendation from the Abuna. An escort of soldiers was offered us, but refused. The expedition consisted simply of ourselves, a bullet-headed Armenian chauffeur, and a small native boy, who attached himself to us without invitation. At first we were a little resentful of this, but he firmly refused to understand our attempts at dismissal, and later we were grateful for his presence. The car, which did things I should have thought no car could possibly do, was an American make which is rarely seen in Europe. When we had packed it with our overcoats, rugs, tins of petrol, and provisions, there was just room for ourselves. The hotel supplied beer and sandwiches and olives and oranges, and Irene gave us a hamper of tinned and truffled foods from Fortnum & Mason. We were just starting, rather later than we had hoped, when Professor W. remembered something. 'Do you mind if we go back to my hotel for a minute? There's just one thing I've forgotten.' We drove round to the Imperial.

The thing he had forgotten was a dozen empty Vichy bottles. 'I thought it would be courteous,' he explained, 'to take some holy water back to Ras Kassa and the Abuna. I'm sure they would appreciate it.'

'Yes, but need we take quite so much?'

'Well, there's the patriarchal legate, I should like to give him some, and Belatingeta Herui, and the Coptic patriarch at Cairo.... I thought it was a nice opportunity to repay some of the kindness I have received.'

I suggested that this purpose could be more conveniently achieved by giving them *tedj*, and that from what I had seen of Abyssinians they would much prefer it. Professor W. gave a little nervous laugh and looked anxiously out of the window.

'Well, why not fill my empty beer-bottles?'

'No, no, I don't think that would be quite suitable. I don't really like using Vichy bottles. I wish I had had time to scrape off the labels,' he mused. 'I don't *quite* like the idea of holy water in Vichy bottles. Perhaps the boy could do it tomorrow – before they are filled, of course.'

A new aspect of the professor's character was thus revealed. My acquaintance with him until that day was limited to half a dozen more or less casual encounters at the various parties and shows. I had found him full of agreeably ironical criticism of our companions, very punctilious, and very enthusiastic about things which seemed to me unexceptionable. 'Look,' he would say with purest Boston intonation, 'look at the exquisite grace of the basket that woman is carrying. There is the whole character of the people in that plaited straw. Ah, why do we waste our time looking at crowns and canons? I could study that basket all day.' And a wistful, far-away look would come into his eyes as he spoke.

Remarks of that kind went down very well with some people, and I regarded them as being, perhaps, one of the normal manifestations of American scholarship. They were compensated for by such sound maxims as 'Never carry binoculars; you only have to hand them over to some wretched woman as soon as there is anything worth seeing.' But this worldly good sense was a mere mask over the essentially mystical nature of the professor's mind; one touch of church furniture, and he became suddenly transfused with reverence, with an impulsive and demonstrative devotion, that added a great deal to the glamour of our expedition together.

Those bottles, however, were an infernal nuisance. They clinked about the floor, making all the difference between tolerable ease and acute discomfort. There was nowhere to rest our feet except on their unstable, rolling surface. We drew up our knees and resigned ourselves to cramp and pins and needles.

Debra Lebanos is practically due north of Addis Ababa. For the first mile or two there was a clearly marked track which led out of the town, right over the summit of Entoto. It was extremely steep and narrow, composed of loose stones and boulders; on the top of the hill was a little church and parsonage, the ground all round them broken by deep ravines and outcrops of stone.

'Whatever happens,' we decided, 'we must make quite certain of coming over here by daylight.'

From Entoto the way led down to a wide plain, watered by six or seven shallow streams which flowed between deep banks at right angles to our road. Caravans of mules were coming into the town laden with skins. Professor W. saluted them with bows and blessings; the hillmen answered him with blank stares or broad incredulous grins. A few, more sophisticated than their companions, bellowed, 'Bakshish!' Professor W. shook his head sadly and remarked that the people were already getting spoiled by foreign intrusion.

It took two or three hours to cross the plain; we drove, for the most part, parallel to the track, rather than on it, finding the rough ground more comfortable than the prepared surface. We crossed numerous dry watercourses and several streams. At some of these there had been rough attempts at bridge-building, usually a heap of rocks and a few pieces of timber; in rare cases a culvert ran underneath. It was in negotiating these that we first realized the astonishing powers of our car. It would plunge nose first into a precipitous gully, shiver and stagger a little, churn up dust and stones, roar, and skid, bump and sway until we began to climb out, and then it would suddenly start forward and mount very deliberately up the other side as though endowed with some peculiar prehensile quality in its tyres. Occasionally, in conditions of scarcely conceivable asperity, the engine would stop. Professor W. would sigh, and open the door, allowing two or three of his empty bottles to roll out on to the running-board.

'Ah, ça n'a pas d'importance,' said the driver, prodding the boy, who jumped out, restored the bottles, and then leant his shoulder against the back of the car. This infinitesimal contribution of weight seemed to be all the car needed; up it would go out of the river-bed, and over the crest of the bank, gaining speed as it reached level ground; the child would race after us and clamber in as we bumped along, a triumphant smile on his little black face.

At about eleven we stopped for luncheon by the side of the last stream. The boy busied himself by filling up the radiator by the use of a small cup. I ate sandwiches and drank beer rendered volatile by the motion of the car. The professor turned out to be a vegetarian; he unwrapped a little segment of cheese from its silver paper and nibbled it delicately and made a very neat job of an orange. The sun was very powerful, and the professor advanced what seemed, and still seems, to me the radically unsound theory that you must wear thick woollen underclothes if you wish to keep cool in the tropics.

After leaving the plain we drove for three hours or so across grassy downland. There was now no track of any kind, but occasional boundary-stones hinted at the way we should follow. There were herds grazing, usually in charge of small naked children. At first the professor politely raised his hat and bowed to them, but the effect was so disturbing that after he had sent three or four out of sight, wailing in terror, he remarked that it was agreeable to find people who had a proper sense of the menace of motor transport, and relapsed into meditation, pondering, perhaps, the advisability of presenting a little holy water to the Emperor. The route was uneventful, broken only by occasional clusters of *tukals*, surrounded by high hedges of euphorbia. It was very hot, and after a time, in spite of the jangle of the bottles and the constriction of space, I fell into a light doze.

I awoke as we stopped on the top of a hill; all around us were empty undulations of grass. 'Nous sommes perdus?' asked the professor. 'Ça n'a pas d'importance,' replied the driver, lighting a cigarette. The boy was despatched, like the dove from Noah's ark, to find direction in the void. We waited for half an hour before he returned. Meanwhile three native women appeared from nowhere, peering at us from under straw sunshades. The professor took off his hat and bowed. The women huddled together and giggled. Presently fascination overcame their shyness and they approached closer; one touched the radiator and burned her fingers. They asked for cigarettes and were repelled, with some very forceful language, by the driver.

At last the child returned and made some explanations. We turned off at right angles and drove on, and the professor and I fell asleep once more.

When I next woke, the landscape had changed dramatically. About half a mile from us, and obliquely to the line of our path, the ground fell away suddenly into a great canyon, descending abruptly in tiers of sheer cliff, broken by strips and patches of timber. At the bottom a river ran between green banks, to swell the Blue Nile; it was practically dry at this season except for a few shining channels of water which split and reunited on the sandy bed in delicate threads of light. Poised among trees, two-thirds of the way down on a semi-circular shelf of land, we could discern the roofs of Debra Lebanos. A cleft path led down the face of the cliff and it was for this that we were clearly making. It looked hopelessly unsafe, but our Armenian plunged down with fine intrepidity.

Sometimes we lurched along a narrow track with cliffs rising on one side and a precipice falling away on the other; sometimes we picked our way on broad ledges among great boulders; sometimes we grated between narrow rock walls. At last we reached a defile which even our driver admitted to be impassable. We climbed out along the running-boards and finished the descent on foot. Professor W. was clearly already enchanted by the sanctity of the place.

'Look,' he said, pointing to some columns of smoke that rose from the cliffs above us, 'the cells of the solitary anchorites.'

'Are you sure there are solitary anchorites here? I never heard of any.'

'It would be a good place for them,' he said wistfully.

The Armenian strode on in front of us, a gallant little figure with his cropped head and rotund, gaitered legs; the boy staggered behind, carrying overcoats, blankets, provisions, and a good half-dozen of the empty bottles. Suddenly the Armenian stopped and, with his finger on his lips, drew our attention to the rocks just below us. Twenty or thirty baboons of both sexes and all ages were huddled in the shade.

'Ah,' said Professor W., 'sacred monkeys. How very interesting!'

'Why do you think they are sacred? They seem perfectly wild.'

'It is a common thing to find sacred monkeys in monasteries,' he explained gently. 'I have seen them in Ceylon and in many parts of India.... Oh, why did he do that? How very thoughtless!'

For our driver had thrown a stone into their midst and scattered them barking in all directions, to the great delight of the small boy behind us.

It was hot walking. We passed one or two *tukals* with women and children staring curiously at us, and eventually emerged on an open green ledge littered with enormous rocks and a variety of unimposing buildings. A mob of ragged boys, mostly infected with skin diseases, surrounded us and were repelled by the Armenian. (These, we learned later, were the deacons.) We sent the boy forward to find someone more responsible, and soon a fine-looking, bearded monk, carrying a yellow sunshade, came out of the shadow of a tree and advanced to greet us. We gave him our letter of introduction from the Abuna, and after he had scrutinized both sides of the envelope, with some closeness, he agreed, through our Armenian, who from now on acted as interpreter, to fetch the head of the monastery. He was away some time and eventually returned with an old priest, who wore a brown cloak, a very large white turban, steel-rimmed spectacles, and carried in one hand an old black umbrella and in the other a horsehair fly-whisk. Professor W. darted forward and kissed the cross which swung from the old man's neck. This was received rather well, but I felt too shy to follow his lead and contented myself with shaking hands. The monk then handed his superior our letter, which was tucked away in his pocket unopened. They then explained that they would be ready to receive us shortly, and went off to wake up the other priests and prepare the chapter house.

We waited about half an hour, sitting in the shade near the church, and gradually forming round us a circle of inquisitive ecclesiastics of all ages. The Armenian went off to see about his car. Professor W. replied to the questions that were put to us, with bows, shakes of the head, and little sympathetic moans. Presently one monk came up and, squatting beside us, began to write on the back of his hand with a white pencil in a regular, finely-formed Amharic script. One of the letters was in the form of a cross. Professor W., anxious to inform them all that we were good Christians, pointed to this mark, then to me and to himself, bowed in the direction of the church, and crossed himself. This time he made a less happy impression. Everyone looked bewildered and rather scared; the scribe spat on his hand and, hastily erasing the text, fell back some paces. There was an air of tension and embarrassment, which was fortunately disturbed by our Armenian with the announcement that the council of the monastery were now ready to receive us.

Apart from the two churches, the most prominent building was a tall, square house of stone, with a thatched roof and a single row of windows set high up under the eaves; it was here that we were led. A small crowd had collected round the door, which was covered with a double curtain of heavy sackcloth. The windows also were heavily screened, so that we stepped from the brilliant sunshine into a gloom which was at first completely baffling. One of the priests raised the door-curtain a little to show us our way. A single lofty room constituted the entire house; the walls were of undisguised stone and rubble, no ceiling covered the rafters and thatch. Preparations had clearly been made for us; carpets had been spread on the earthen floor, and in the centre stood two low stools covered with rugs; twelve priests stood ranged against the wall, the head of the monastery in their centre; between them and our seats stood a table covered with a shawl; the only other furniture was a cupboard in the far corner, roughly built of irregularly-stained white wood, the doors secured with a staple and padlock. We sat down and our chauffeur-interpreter stood beside us jauntily twirling his cap. When we were settled, the head of the monastery, who apparently also bore the title of abuna, brought our letter of introduction out of his pocket and, for the first time, opened it. He read it first to himself and then aloud to the company, who scratched their beards, nodded, and grunted. Then he addressed us, asking us what we wanted. Professor W. explained that we had heard from afar of the sanctity of the place and the wisdom and piety of the monks, and that we had come to do reverence at their shrine, pay our duty and respects to them, and take away some account of the glories of the monastery of which all the world stood in awe. This pretty speech was condensed by our chauffeur into three or four harsh vocables, and greeted with further nods and grunts from the assembly.

One of them then asked whether we were Mohammedans. It seemed sad that this question was necessary after all Professor

W.'s protestations. We assured him that we were not. Another asked where we had come from. Addis Ababa? They asked about the coronation, and Professor W. began a graphic outline of the liturgical significance of the ceremony. I do not think, however, that our chauffeur was at very great pains to translate this faithfully. The response, anyway, was a general outburst of chuckling, and from then onwards, for about ten minutes, he took the burden of conversation from our shoulders and speedily established relations of the utmost geniality. Presently he began shaking hands with them all and explained that they would like us to do the same, a social duty which Professor W. decorated with many graceful genuflexions and reverences.

The professor then asked whether we might visit the library of which the world stood in awe. Why, certainly; there it was in the corner. The abuna produced a small key from his pocket and directed one of the priests to open the cupboard. They brought out five or six bundles wrapped in silk shawls, and, placing them with great care on the table, drew back the door-curtain to admit a shaft of white light. The abuna lifted the corners of the shawl on the topmost bundle and revealed two pieces of board clumsily hinged together in the form of a diptych. Professor W. kissed them eagerly; they were then opened, revealing two coloured lithographs, apparently cut from a religious almanac printed in Germany some time towards the end of the last century, representing the Crucifixion and the Assumption, pasted on to the inner surfaces of the wood. The professor was clearly a little taken aback. 'Dear, dear, how remarkably ugly they are,' he remarked as he bent down to kiss them.

The other bundles contained manuscripts of the Gospels, lives of the saints, and missals, written in Ghiz and brightly illuminated. The painting was of the same kind as the frescoes, reduced to miniature. Sometimes faces and figures had been cut out of prints and stuck into the page with a discomposing effect on their highly stylized surroundings. They told us with great pride that the artist had been employed at Addis Ababa on some work for the late Empress. Professor W. asked whether there were not some older manuscripts we might see, but they affected not to understand. No doubt there were still reserves hidden from us.

It was then suggested that we should visit the sacred spring. Professor W. and I set out with a guide up the hillside. It was a stiff climb; the sun was still strong and the stones all radiated a fierce heat. 'I think, perhaps, we ought to take off our hats,' said the professor; 'we are on very holy ground.'

I removed my topee and exposed myself to sunstroke, trusting in divine protection; but, just as he spoke, it so happened that our guide stopped on the path and accommodated himself in a way which made me think that his reverence for the spot was far from fanatical.

On our way we passed a place where overhanging cliffs formed a shallow cave. Water oozed and dripped all round, and the path was soft and slippery. It is here that the bodies of the faithful are brought; they lay all about, some in packing cases, others in hollow tree-trunks, battened down with planks, piled and tumbled on top of each other without order; many were partly submerged in falls of damp earth, a few of these rough coffins had broken apart, revealing their contents. There were similar heaps, we were told, on other parts of the hillside.

We had a fine view of the valley; our guide pointed out a group of buildings on the far side. 'That is the convent for the women,' he explained. 'You see it is quite untrue that we live together. The houses are entirely separate. We do not cross the valley to them, and they do not cross to us. Never. It is all a lie.' He wanted to make this point quite clear.

At last we reached the spring, which fell in a pretty cascade to join the river far below at the bottom of the valley. Most of the water, however, had been tapped, and was conveyed in two iron pipes to bathing-places near the monastery. We climbed down again to see them. One, built especially for Menelik, was a little brick house with a corrugated iron roof. The old Empress had frequently come here, and since her death it had not been used. We peered through the window and saw a plain kitchen-chair. There was a rusty spout in the ceiling from which a trickle of water fell on the brick floor and drained away through the waste-pipe in one corner. The other bath was for public use. The pipe was fitted with a double spout, directing two streams of water on to either side of a brick wall. One side was for men and the other for women, and a three-sided screen was built round each. The floor was made of cement. A boy was in there at the time of our visit, swilling himself down with as much puffing and spluttering as if he were under any purely secular shower-bath.

As we turned back, our Armenian and a monk met us with a message from the abuna – should they kill a goat, a sheep, or a calf for our dinner? We explained that we had full provision for our food. All we required was shelter for the night and water to wash in. The Armenian explained that it was usual to accept something. We suggested some eggs, but were told that they had none. They urged a goat very strongly. Meat is a rare luxury in the monastery, and they were, no doubt, eager to take the opportunity of our visit for a feast. The professor's vegetarian scruples, however, were unconquerable. At last they suggested honey, which he accepted readily. The question of our accommodation was then discussed. There was a hut or a tent. The Armenian warned us that if we slept in the hut we should certainly contract some repulsive disease, and if in the tent, we might be killed by hyenas. He had already made up his own mind, he said, to sleep in the car. We returned to the monastery, and the abuna led us in person to see the hut. It was some time before the key could be found; when the door was at last wrenched open, an emaciated she-goat ran out. The interior was windowless and foetid. It appeared to have been used as a kind of lumber-room; heaps of old rags and broken furniture encumbered the floor. A swarm of bees buzzed in the roof. It was not quite ready, the abuna explained; he had not expected guests. It could, of course, be prepared, or would we think it inhospitable if he offered us the tent? We declared that the tent would be wholly satisfactory, and so, with evident relief, the abuna gave instructions for its erection. It was now nearly sunset. A spot of ground was chosen near the house where we had been received, and a very decent bell-tent pitched. (It was the property of the old Empress, we learned. She had often slept there on her visits to the spring.) The floor was covered with hay and the hay with rugs. A little boat-shaped oil-lamp was hung from the tent-pole; our rugs, provisions, and bottles were brought in and laid on one side. We were then invited to enter. We sat down cross-legged and the abuna sat beside us. He looked enormous in the tiny light; the shadow from his great turban seemed to fill the whole tent. The chauffeur squatted opposite us. The abuna smiled with the greatest geniality and expressed his best wishes for our comfort; we thanked him heartily. Conversation lapsed and we all three sat smiling rather vacantly. Presently the flap was lifted and a monk came in wearing a heavy brown burnous and carrying an antiquated rifle. He bowed to us and retired. He was a guard, the abuna explained, who would sleep outside across our door. Another smiling pause. At last supper arrived; first a basket containing half-a-dozen great rounds of native bread, a tough, clammy substance closely resembling crêpe rubber in appearance; then two earthenware jugs, one of water, the other of *talla* – a kind of thin, bitter beer, then two horns of honey, but not of honey as it is understood at Thame; this was the product of wild bees, scraped straight from the tree; it was a greyish colour, full of bits of stick and mud, bird dung, dead bees, and grubs. Everything was first carried to the abuna for his approval, then to us. We expressed our delight with nods and more extravagant smiles. The food was laid before us and the bearers retired. At this moment the Armenian shamelessly deserted us, saying that he must go and see after his boy.

The three of us were left alone, smiling over our food in the half darkness.

In the corner lay our hamper packed with Irene's European delicacies. We clearly could not approach them until our host left us. Gradually the frightful truth became evident that he was proposing to dine with us. I tore off a little rag of bread and attempted to eat it. 'This is a very difficult situation,' said the professor; 'I think, perhaps, it would be well to simulate ill-health,' and, holding his hands to his forehead, he began to rock gently from side to side, emitting painfully subdued moans. It was admirably done; the abuna watched him with the greatest concern; presently the professor held his stomach and retched a little; then he lay on his back, breathing heavily with closed eyes; then he sat up on his elbow and explained in eloquent dumb show that he wished to rest. The abuna understood perfectly, and, with every gesture of sympathy, rose to his feet and left us.

In five minutes, when I had opened a tinned grouse and a bottle of lager and the professor was happily mumbling a handful of ripe olives, the Armenian returned. With a comprehensive wink, he picked up the jug of native beer, threw back his head, and, without pausing to breathe, drank a quart or two. He then spread out two rounds of bread, emptied a large quantity of honey into each of them, wrapped them together, and put them in his pocket. 'Moi, je puis manger comme abyssin,' he remarked cheerfully, winked at the grouse, wished us good night, and left us.

'Now at last,' said the Professor, producing a tin of Keating's powder, 'I feel in the heart of Ethiopia.' He sprinkled the rugs and blankets, wrapped his head in a pale grey scarf, and prepared to settle down for the night. We had had a tiring day, and after smoking a pipe I decided to follow his example. The lamp was flickering and smoking badly and threatened at any moment to burn through its own string and set us on fire. I blew it out, and was just becoming drowsy when the abuna returned, carrying a lantern, to see whether the professor felt any better. We all smiled inarticulately for some time, and the professor pointed to the half-empty beer-jug and the horns of honey as proof of his recovery. The abuna noted them with evident satisfaction, and then his eye, travelling round the tent, was attracted by the Keating's powder which lay like thick dust over the floor and bedding. He called in the guard and rather crossly pointed out this evidence of neglect. The man hastily produced a broom and brushed out the tent. Then, when everything was again in order, and after many bows, smiles, and blessings, he left us to sleep.

But I, at any rate, slept very little. It was a deadly cold night and a bitter wind sprang up, sweeping the valley and driving under the tent and through our thin blankets, while outside the door the guard coughed and grunted. I was out before dawn and watched the monastery waking into life. There seemed very little order. The monks emerged from the huts in ones and twos and pottered off to work in the fields and woods. A certain number of them went down to the church, where the professor and I followed them. They sat about outside until a priest appeared with the keys; then a service began, apparently quite at haphazard. Two or three would start intoning some kind of psalm or litany, and others

115

seemed to join in as they thought fit; two or three were reading aloud from large manuscripts supported on folding rests; others leant on their praying-sticks or squatted in corners muttering. Now and then one would stop on his way to work, kiss the door on the inner wall, and pass on. The frescoes of the inner sanctuary were hung with green curtains; one of the priests pointed to them and explained in dumb show that they would be drawn for our inspection later in the day.

We returned to our tent for breakfast. Beer and anchovies seemed rather discouraging after our chilly night, but there was no alternative except tinned loganberries and *foie gras*. The guard came in, finished the beer, and ate some bread and honey. He showed great interest in our belongings, fingering everything in turn – the tin-opener, electric torch, a pocket-knife, a pair of hairbrushes. I let him play with the sword-stick I happened to have brought with me; he in exchange showed me his rifle and bandolier. About half the cartridges were empty shells; the weapon was in very poor condition. It could not possibly have been used with any accuracy, and probably not with safety. I asked whether he had ever killed anything with it; he shook his head, and produced a large, rather blunt dagger, which he stabbed into the earth.

Presently the chauffeur came to assure us that he had spent a very comfortable night and felt fairly confident that he would be able to extricate the car from its position on the path, where it blocked all approach to the monastery and was causing a good deal of trouble to the herdsmen in charge of the community's cattle. We told him to remain at hand to act as interpreter, and soon a priest came to conduct us to the churches. There were two of these; the main building, where we had already been, and a small shrine, containing a cross which had fallen from heaven. The professor thought this might be a piece of the true cross brought there from Alexandria after the Arab invasion, and displayed great veneration; we were not allowed to see it, but as a special concession we were shown the shawl in which it was wrapped.

In the main church we paid a fee of seven dollars to have the frescoes unveiled. They had lately been repainted in brilliant colours and the priest was justly proud of the renovation. On one wall were portraits of Ras Kassa, Menelik, and the late Empress. It was clear that these heads had been copied from photographs, with the curious result that they stood out solidly, in carefully articulated light and shade and great fidelity of detail, against a composition of purely conventional pre-Renaissance design. Another wall was filled with rider saints. The professor made a plan of it and took down their names. We were then shown some brass processional crosses and some illuminated missals, none of any great antiquity. It was, in fact, a curious feature of Debra Lebanos that, although the community had been the centre of Abyssinian spiritual life since the conversion of the country, and had been settled on this spot for several centuries, they seem to have preserved no single object from the past. It may be that their treasures have all been pillaged in the continual invasions and disorders of Abyssinian history, or that they have been sold from time to time in moments of financial need, or perhaps simply that they did not choose to show them to strangers.

One thing, however, we did see of the greatest interest. That was the sanctuary. We might not, of course, enter it, but the priest drew back the curtain for us and allowed a short glimpse of the dark interior. In the centre stood the tabor, which is both altar-stone and tabernacle, a wooden cupboard built like a miniature church in three tiers, square at the base, from which rose an octagonal story surmounted by a circular dome. Round the tabor, in deep dust – for the sanctuary is rarely, if ever, swept out – lay an astonishing confusion of litter. There was not time to take in everything but, in the brief inspection, I noticed a wicker chair, some heaps of clothes, two or three umbrellas, a suitcase of imitation leather, some newspapers, and a teapot and slop-pail of enamelled tin.

It was about ten o'clock when we left the church; there was a Mass at one o'clock, which we were both anxious to attend, which would not be over until half past two or three. We were thus undecided about our movements. We might spend another night there and start back early next day for Addis Ababa; we might go and see Fiche, Kassa's capital fifteen miles away, and spend a night in the car there, or we might start immediately after Mass

117

and try to get to Addis that night. The chauffeur favoured the last plan and was hopeful of his ability, now that he knew the way, of doing the journey in five or six hours. We had not provisions to last us in any comfort for two days, and I was reluctant to fall back on Abyssinian food. Together we persuaded the professor to attempt the journey; if the worst came to the worst we could spend the night on the plain; a prospect to which the chauffeur added romance with gloomy stories of wild beasts and brigands. As the sun mounted, it became intensely hot. We lay in the tent smoking and dozing until the abuna came to conduct us to Mass.

I will not attempt any description of the ritual; the liturgy was quite unintelligible to me, and, oddly enough, to the professor also. No doubt the canon of the Mass would have been in part familiar, but this was said in the sanctuary behind closed doors. We stood in the outer ambulatory. A carpet was placed for us to stand on and we were given praying-sticks, with the aid of which we stood throughout the two hours of service. There were twenty or thirty monks round us and some women and babies from the *tukals*. Communion was administered to the babies, but to no one else. Many of the monks were crippled or deformed in some way; presumably they were pilgrims who had originally come to the spring in the hope of a cure, and had become absorbed into the life of the place. There seemed to be very little system of testing vocations in the community. The priests and deacons wore long, white-and-gold cloaks and turbans, and had bare feet. Now and then they emerged from the sanctuary, and once they walked round in procession. The singing was monotonous and more or less continuous, accompanied by a drum and sistrums. For any-one accustomed to the western rite it was difficult to think of this as a Christian service, for it bore that secret and confused character associated with the non-Christian sects of the East.

I had sometimes thought it an odd thing that Western Christianity, alone of all the religions of the world, exposes its mysteries to every observer, but I was so accustomed to this open-ness that I had never before questioned whether it was an essential and natural feature of the Christian system. Indeed, so saturated are we in this spirit that many people regard the growth of the

Church as a process of elaboration – even of obfuscation; they visualize the Church of the first century as a little cluster of pious people reading the Gospels together, praying and admonishing each other with a simplicity to which the high ceremonies and subtle theology of later years would have been bewildering and unrecognizable. At Debra Lebanos I suddenly saw the classic basilica and open altar as a great positive achievement, a triumph of light over darkness consciously accomplished, and I saw theology as the science of simplification by which nebulous and elusive ideas are formalized and made intelligible and exact. I saw the Church of the first century as a dark and hidden thing; as dark and hidden as the seed germinating in the womb; legionaries off duty slipping furtively out of barracks, greeting each other by signs and passwords in a locked upper room in the side street of some Mediterranean seaport; slaves at dawn creeping from the grey twilight into the candle-lit, smoky chapels of the catacombs. The priests hid their office, practising trades; their identity was known only to initiates; they were criminals against the law of their country. And the pure nucleus of the truth lay in the minds of the people, encumbered with superstitions, gross survivals of the paganism in which they had been brought up; hazy and obscene nonsense seeping through from the other esoteric cults of the Near East, magical infections from the conquered barbarian. And I began to see how these obscure sanctuaries had grown, with the clarity of the Western reason, into the great open altars of Catholic Europe, where Mass is said in a flood of light, high in the sight of all, while tourists can clatter round with their Baedekers, incurious of the mystery.

By the time Mass was over, our chauffeur had succeeded in the remarkable and hazardous feat of backing the car up the path. We said good-bye to the abuna and climbed the ravine, attended by a troop of small deacons. When we at last reached the top the professor took from his pocket a handful of half-piastre pieces with which he had secretly provided himself. He ordered the children to line up, and our boy cuffed and jostled them into some kind of order. Then he presented them with a coin apiece. They had clearly not expected any such donation, but they quickly got the hang of the business, and, as soon as they were paid, queued up again at the back. Our boy detected this simple deception and drove away the second-comers. When each had received his half-piastre, and some had grabbed two, there were still a number of coins left over. 'Do you think,' asked the professor rather timdily, 'that it would be very vulgar and tripperish to make them scramble for them?'

'Yes,' I said.

'Of course it would,' said the professor decidedly. 'Quite out of the question.'

The deacons, however, continued to caper round us, crying for more and clinging to the car, so that it became impossible to start without endangering several lives. 'Ça n'a pas d'importance,' said the chauffeur inevitably, cranking up the engine. The professor, however, preferred a more humane release. 'Perhaps, after all ...' he said, and threw his handful of money among the children. The last we saw of Debra Lebanos was a scrambling heap of naked black limbs and a cloud of dust. It was interesting to be in at the birth of a tradition. Whoever in future goes to Debra Lebanos will, without doubt, find himself beset by these rapacious children; Professor W. had taught them the first easy lesson of civilization.

Our journey back for the first three hours was uneventful. We made good time on the downs, and darkness found us at the beginning of the plain. From then onwards progress was slow and uncertain. Four or five times we lost the track and continued out of our way until a patch of bush or marsh brought us up short. Twice we got stuck and had to push our way out; two or three times we were nearly overturned by sudden subsidences into the watercourses. It was these channels that enabled us to find our way, for they all ran at right angles to our route. When we reached one the Armenian and the boy would take opposite sides and follow the bank down until one of them reached the crossing; there would then be whistles and signals and we resumed the right road.

At each check, the professor made up his mind to stop. 'It is quite impossible. We shall never find the road until daylight. We may be going miles out of our way. It is dangerous and futile. We had far better spend the night here and go back at dawn.'

Then the driver would return with news of success. 'J'ai décidé; nous arrêtons ici,' the professor would say.

'Ah,' came the invariable response, 'Vous savez, monsieur, ça n'a pas d'importance.'

Throughout the journey the boy sat on the mudguard in front, picking out the rare stones and hoof-marks which directed us. Once, however, the Armenian despaired. We had all walked round and round for half an hour in widening circles, searching the completely blank earth with electric torches. We came back defeated. It was now about ten o'clock and bitterly cold. We were just discussing how we could possibly keep ourselves warm during the coming eight hours, when the boy saw lights ahead. We drove on and ran straight into a caravan bivouacked round a camp-fire. Our arrival caused great consternation in the camp. Men and women ran out of the tents or sprang out of the ground from huddled heaps of blankets; the animals sprang up and strained at their tethers or tumbled about with hobbled legs. Rifles were levelled at us. The Armenian strode into their midst, however, and, after distributing minute sums of money as a sign of goodwill, elicited directions.

Our worst check was within sight of Addis, on the top of Entoto. This part of the journey had seemed perilous enough by daylight, but by now we were so stiff and cold as to be indifferent to any other consideration. Twice we pulled up within a few feet of the precipice, the boy having fallen asleep on the mudguard where he sat. We got stuck again with two wheels in the air and two in a deep gully, but eventually we found the road and at that moment ran out of petrol. Two minutes earlier this disaster would have been insuperable. From now on, however, it was all downhill and we ran into the town without the engine. When at last we reached the professor's hotel we were too tired to say good night. He silently picked up his bottles of holy water and, with a little nod, went up to his room, and I had fallen asleep before he was out of sight. A sulky night-porter found us a can of petrol and we drove on to the Hôtel de France. The manager was sitting up for me with a boiling kettle and a bottle of rum. I slept well that night.

In London, full of ingenuous eagerness to get aboard, I had booked my ticket through to Zanzibar, between which island and Djibouti the Messageries Maritimes maintain a fortnightly service. Now, with everyone else going home, I began rather to regret the arrangement and think wistfully of an Irish Christmas. The next ship, the *General Voyson*, was not due for ten days and the prospect of spending the time either at Addis Ababa or Djibouti was unattractive. I was on the point of forfeiting my ticket and joining the Italian ship by which Irene was sailing north, when Mr Plowman, the British consul at Harar, who with his family was visiting the capital for the coronation, very kindly suggested that I should return with him and break my journey at his home for a few days. No suggestion could have been more delightful. There was glamour in all the associations of Harar, the Arab city-state which stood first among the fruits of Ethiopian imperialism, the scene of Sir Richard Burton's *First Steps in Africa*, the market where the caravans met between coast and highlands; where Galla, Somali, and Arab interbred to produce women whose beauty was renowned throughout East Africa. There is talk of a motor-road that is to connect it with the railway, but at present it must still be approached by the tortuous hill-pass and small track along which Arthur Rimbaud had sent rifles to Menelik.

On the morning of November 15th, we left by the last of the special trains. The departures took place with far less formality than the arrivals. There was no band, but the platform was crowded with the whole European population. Even our Armenian chauffeur came to see us off; the carriage in which I travelled was filled with little bunches of flowers hung there by the servants of one of the British officials who was going home on leave. Mr Hall was there with eye-glass and top hat.

Next day at dawn we arrived at Dirre-Dowa, and the Plowmans and I took leave of our fellow passengers. We had all spent a practically sleepless night, and for the greater part of that hot Sunday we remained in our rooms at Bollolakos' hotel. I went to Mass at a church full of odious French children, washed in a sandy bath, slept.

We dined that evening in a pleasant little party consisting of the

Plowmans and their governess, the Cypriot manager of the local bank, Mr Hall's brother, who was in business at Dirre-Dowa, and his wife, an English lady who wore a large enamelled brooch made in commemoration of the opening of Epping Forest to the public and presented to her father who was, at the time, an alderman of the City of London. We sat in the open under an orange-tree and drank chianti and gossiped about the coronation, while many hundreds of small red ants overran the table and fell on to our heads from above.

The Plowmans' horses had not arrived that day, so that their start would have to be delayed until Tuesday morning and their arrival at Harar until Thursday. The director of the railway had wired to the station-master at Dirre-Dowa to reserve mules and servants for me, and I decided to avail myself of them next day and reach Harar a day ahead of my hosts. I felt that it was, in a way, more suitable to enter the town alone and unofficially.

Accordingly, I set out early next morning, riding a lethargic grey mule, accompanied by a mounted Abyssinian guide who spoke French, an aged groom who attached himself to me against my express orders, and a Galla porter, of singularly villainous expression, to carry my luggage. We had not been going long before this man, easily outdistancing our beasts, disappeared into the hills with great lurching strides, the bag containing my passport, letter of credit, and all of my essential clothes balanced negligently on his head. I became apprehensive, and the guide was anything but reassuring. All Gallas were dishonest, he explained, and this one was a particularly dirty type. He disclaimed all responsibility for engaging him; that had been done by the station-master; he himself would never have chosen a man of such obvious criminal characteristics. It was not unusual for porters to desert with the luggage; there was no catching them once they got over the hills among their own people; they had murdered an Indian not long ago in circumstances of peculiar atrocity. But it was possible, he added, that the man had merely hurried on to take his *khat*.

This was, in fact, what had happened. We came upon him again some hours later, squatting by the roadside with his lap full of the leaves and his teeth and mouth green with chewing; his

123

expression had softened considerably under the influence of the drug, and for the rest of the journey he was docile enough trailing along behind us in a slightly bemused condition.

For the first few miles we followed the river-bed, a broad stretch of sand which for a few hours in the year is flooded from bank to bank with a turgid mountain torrent, which sweeps down timber and boulders and carries away the accumulated refuse of the town. It was now nearing the end of the dry season and the way was soft and powdery; it was heavy going until we reached the foot of the caravan route. There is a short cut over the hills which is used by foot passengers and riders who are much pressed for time; on the guide's advice we chose the longer more leisurely road which winds in a detour round the spur and joins the rock path at the summit. It is about four hours from the hotel to the uplands by this road. The mules took things easily; it was neces-sary to beat them more or less continually to keep them moving at all. At the top we paused for a rest.

Behind us, as far as we could see, the country was utterly desolate; the hillside up which we had climbed was covered with colourless sand and rock, and beyond, on the other side of the valley, rose other hills equally bare of dwelling or cultivation. The only sign of life was a caravan of camels, roped nose to tail, following us a mile or so below. In front of us everything was changed. This was Galla country, full of little villages and roughly demarcated arable plots. The road in places was bordered with cactus and flowering euphorbia-trees; the air was fresh and vital.

Another three hours brought us to a native inn, where the boys hoped to get some food. The landlord, however, told us that the local governor had recently cancelled his licence, an injustice which he attributed to the rivalry of the Greek who kept the rest house at Haramaya. He provided them with a tin can full of *talla*, which the two Christians drank, the Mohammedan religiously contenting himself with another handful of *khat*. Then we went on. In another hour we were in sight of the lake of Haramaya, a welcoming sheet of light between two green hills. It was here that we proposed to break the journey for a night, for the gates of the city are shut at sundown and it is difficult to obtain admission after that time. I was tired out, and at the sight of water the mules for the first time showed some sign of interest. Indeed, it became impossible to keep them to the path, so I left the boys to water them and walked the last mile round the lake to the rest house.

The accommodation was very simple; there was, of course, no bath or sanitation and no glass in the windows. There was, however, a most delightfully amiable young Greek in charge of it, who got me a meal and talked incessantly in very obscure English. It was now about three o'clock. Seeing that I was tired, he said he would make me a cocktail. He took a large glass and poured into it whisky, crème de menthe, and Fernet Branca, and filled up with soda-water. He made himself a glass of the same mixture, clinked glasses, and said, 'Cheerioh, damned sorry no ice.' After luncheon I went to my room and slept until late in the evening.

We dined together on tinned spaghetti and exceedingly tough fried chicken. He prattled on about his home in Alexandria and his sister who was taking a secretarial course and his rich uncle who lived at Dirre-Dowa and had set him up in the inn. I asked what the uncle did, and he said he had a 'monopole'; this seemed to be a perfectly adequate description of almost all commercial ventures in Abyssinia. I could not gather what he monopolized; whatever it was seemed extremely profitable and involved frequent excursions to Aden. The nephew hoped to succeed to the business on his uncle's retirement.

While we were dining, two heavily armed soldiers appeared with a message for my host. He seemed mildly put out by their arrival, explaining with great simplicity that he was involved in a love-affair with an elderly Abyssinian lady of high birth; she was not very attractive, but what choice had he in a remote place like this? She was generous, but very exacting. Only that afternoon he had been with her and here were her retainers come to fetch him again. He gave them each a cigarette and told them to wait. When they had finished smoking, they returned; he offered them more cigarettes, but they refused; apparently their mistress was impatient; the young man shrugged and, excusing himself with the phrase 'You won't allow me, won't you?' went away with them into the darkness. I returned to my bed and slept.

Next morning we rode into Harar. The way was full of traffic, caravans of camels, mules and asses, horsemen, and teams of women bent double under prodigious loads of wood. There were no carts of any kind; indeed, I think that they are quite unknown in Abyssinia, and that the railway engine was the first wheeled vehicle to appear there. After three hours' gentle ride we came in sight of the town. Approached from Haramaya it presents a quite different aspect from the drawing in Burton's *First Steps in Africa*; there it appears as he saw it coming from the Somali coast, perched on a commanding hill; we found it lying below us, an irregular brown patch at the foot of the hills. In the distance rose the flat-topped mountain which the Abyssinians have chosen for their refuge in the event of the country rising against them; there is a lake of fresh water at the summit, and a naturally fortified camp which they hope to hold against the Galla until relief arrives from their own highlands. No one may visit the place without a permit from the local dedejmatch.

A few buildings – the British consulate, Lej Yasu's deserted palace, a Capuchin leper settlement, a church, and the villas of one or two Indian merchants – have spread beyond the walls; outsidé the main gate a few women squatting beside little heaps of grain and peppers constituted a market; there was a temporary and rather unstable arch of triumph presented to the town by the firm of Mohammed-Ali in honour of the coronation. A guard was posted at the gate; there was also an octroi, where we had to leave the luggage until the officer should return from his luncheon some hours later.

As in most medieval towns, there was no direct street in Harar leading from the gates to the central square. A very narrow lane ran under the walls round numerous corners before it turned inwards and broadened into the main street. On either side of this passage stood ruined houses, desolate heaps of stone and rubble, some of them empty, others patched up with tin to accommodate goats or poultry. The town, like the numerous lepers who inhabit it, seemed to be dying at its extremities; the interior, however, was full of vitality and animation.

There are two inns in Harar, boasting the names of Lion d'Or and Bellevue; both universally condemned as unsuitable for European habitation. Any doubt I might have had about which to patronize was resolved, as soon as we turned into the main

126

street, by a stout little man in a black skull-cap, who threw himself at my bridle and led me to the Lion d'Or. During my brief visit I became attached to this man. He was an Armenian of rare character, named Bergebedgian; he spoke a queer kind of French with remarkable volubility, and I found great delight in all his opinions; I do not think I have ever met a more tolerant man; he had no prejudice or scruples of race, creed, or morals of any kind whatever; there were in his mind none of those opaque patches of principle; it was a single translucent pool of placid doubt; whatever splashes of precept had disturbed its surface from time to time had left no ripple; reflexions flitted to and fro and left it unchanged.

Unfortunately his hotel was less admirable. Most of his business was done in the bar, where he sold great quantities of a colourless and highly inflammatory spirit distilled by a fellow countryman of his and labelled, capriciously, 'Very Olde Scotts Whiskey', 'Fine Champayne', or 'Hollands Gin' as the taste of his clients dictated. Next to the bar was a little dining-room where two or three regular customers (also fellow countrymen) took their greasy and pungent meals. The bedrooms were built round a little courtyard, where some pathetic survivals of a garden were discernible amid the heaps of kitchen refuse with which it was littered. This building had formerly been the town house of an Abyssinian official. It was rarely that anyone came to stay; usually not more than one in any three weeks, he said; but, as it happened, there was a second guest at that moment, a French clerk on business from the Banque d'Indo-Chine at Djibouti. I lunched with this young man, who was a punctilious, mannerly person; the hot wind had chapped his lips so that he was unable to smile – an affliction which made him seem a little menacing in light conversation. It was he who first put into my head the deplorable notion of returning to Europe across the Congo by the west coast. The proprietor waited on us in person, and made it hard to escape the forbidding dishes; we both felt moderately ill after every meal.

That afternoon I went for a walk round the town and saw that a large part of it was in decay. The most prominent buildings were the modern Government House, the French hospital,

127

Mohammed Ali's offices, a Capuchin mission cathedral, and an ancient mosque with two whitewashed minarets; the rest of the place was made up of a bunch of small shops, a few Armenian, Greek, and Indian stores, single-roomed dwelling-houses, mostly standing back behind grubby little yards, and numerous *tedj* houses, combined brothels and public houses which advertise themselves with a red cross over the door – a traditional sign which caused some misunderstanding when the Swedish medical mission first established itself in the country.

The appearance of the buildings and the people was wholly foreign to Abyssinia; a difference which was emphasized on this particular afternoon by the fact that all the Abyssinians were indoors at a party at Government House, so that the streets were peopled almost exclusively by turbaned Harari. The beauty of the women was dazzling – far exceeding anything I had expected. The native women at Addis Ababa had been far from attractive; their faces had been plump and smug, their hair unbecomingly heaped up in a black, fuzzy mass, glittering with melted butter, their figures swollen grotesquely with a surfeit of petticoats. The women of Harar are slender and very upright; they carry themselves with all the grace of the Somalis, but, instead of their monkey-like faces and sooty complexions, they had golden-brown skins and features of the utmost fineness. Moreover, there was a delicacy about their clothes and ornaments which the Somalis entirely lacked; their hair was plaited into innumerable tight little ropes and covered with bright silk shawls; they wore long trousers and silk shawls wound under their arms, leaving their shoulders bare. Most of them had bright gold ornaments. Burton admits their beauty, but condemns their voices as harsh and outstandingly displeasing. I cannot conceive what prompted this statement; indeed, compared with those of Arab women, they seemed soft and sweet. (No sound made by mankind is quite so painful as the voices of two Arab women at variance.) An alliance might be formed with any of these exquisite people, the Armenian informed me later, for four thalers a month and board. That it was possible that the parents might expect more in the case of a foreigner. This sum, however, covered the girl's services in the house, so that it was a perfectly sound investment if I

128

intended making a stay of any length in the town. I explained that I was only there for three days. In that case, he said, it was obviously more convenient to confine myself to married women. There were certain preliminary formalities to be gone through with an unmarried girl which cost time and money.

I visited the leper settlement; a little collection of *tukals* outside the walls, in the charge of a French priest. Four or five sleep in each hut, an arrangement which the old priest explained in what seems to me a very terrible phrase, 'You understand, monsieur, that it takes several lepers to make one man.'

I went to the cathedral and there met the Bishop of Harar, the famous Monsignor Jerome, of whom I had heard many reports in Addis Ababa. He has been in the country for forty-eight years, suffering, at first, every kind of discouragement and persecution, and attaining, towards the middle of his career, a position of great influence at Court. He acted as Tafari's tutor, and many people attributed to him, often in harsh terms, the Emperor's outstanding skill as a political tactician. Lately, as his pupil's ambitions have become realized, the bishop's advice has been less devotedly canvassed. Indeed, it is doubtful whether it would still be of great value, for he is a very old man now and his mind is losing something of its former grasp of public affairs.

It is his practice to greet all visitors to his church, but I did not know this at the time and was greatly startled when he suddenly swooped in upon me. He was tall and emaciated, like an El Greco saint, with very long white hair and beard, great roving eyes, and a nervous, almost ecstatic smile; he advanced at a kind of shuffling jog-trot, fluttering his hands and uttering little moans. After we had been round the church, which was shabby and unremarkable enough, he invited me into his divan to talk. I steered the conversation as delicately as I could from church expenses to Arthur Rimbaud. At first we were at cross purposes because the bishop, being a little deaf, mistook my '*poète*' for '*prêtre*', and inflexibly maintained that no Father Rimbaud had ever, to his knowledge, ministered in Abyssinia. Later this difficulty was cleared up, and the bishop, turning the name over in his mind, remembered that he had, in fact, known Rimbaud quite well; a young man with a beard, who was in some trouble

129

with his leg; a very serious man who did not go out much; he was always worried about business; not a good Catholic, though he had died at peace with the Church, the bishop understood, at Marseilles. He used to live with a native woman in a little house, now demolished, in the square; he had no children; probably the woman was still alive; she was not a native of Harar, and after Rimbaud's death she had gone back to her own people in Tigre . . . a very, very serious young man, the bishop repeated. He seemed to find this epithet the most satisfactory – very serious and sad.

It was rather a disappointing interview. All the way to Harar I had nurtured the hope of finding something new about Rimbaud, perhaps even to encounter a half-caste son keeping a shop in some back street. The only significant thing I learned from the bishop was that, living in Harar, surrounded by so many radiant women, he should have chosen a mate from the stolid people of Tigre – a gross and perverse preference.

That evening, at about six o'clock, Mr Bergebedgian suggested that we might go to the Abyssinian party which had now finished luncheon and was settling down to an evening's music at Government House. He himself was an indispensable guest, as he had promised the loan of an Aladdin lamp, without which they would be left in complete darkness. Accordingly, we set out and were received with great warmth by the acting governor. A considerable sum had been granted to the municipality to be spent on rejoicings for the coronation, an object which was rightly interpreted as meaning a series of parties. They had been going on for a fortnight and would continue until the dedejmatch returned from the capital. As a symbol of the origin of the feast, a kind of altar had been built, at one end of the room, on which stood a large photograph of Tafari surrounded by flowers. About fifty Abyssinians in white *chammas* sat round on the floor, already fairly drunk. Green chairs of the kind one finds in public parks were set for us at a velvet-covered round table. The acting governor sat with us and poured out extravagant glasses of whisky. Slaves trotted about among the other guests, distributing bottles of German beer. With the appearance of our lamp the entertainment began. An orchestra emerged, furnished with three single-stringed fiddles.

The singer was an Abyssinian woman of startling girth. She sang in a harsh voice, panting for breath between each line, an immensely long ballad of patriotic sentiment. The name Haile Selassie recurred with great regularity. No one paid any more attention than they would have at a musical party in Europe, but she sang on cheerfully, through the buzz of conversation, with an expression of settled amiability. When a gatecrasher was detected and expelled with some disorder, she merely turned round and watched the proceedings, still singing lustily. At the end of her song she was given some beer and many friendly smacks on the behind. The whisky was reserved for us and for a few favoured guests; the host singled these out, called for their glasses, and poured it into their beer from the bottle on the table.

The second song was a great deal longer than the first; it was of the kind, popular in European cabarets, which introduces references to members of the audience. Each name was greeted with cheers and a good deal of boisterous back-smacking. The host asked our names and repeated them in her ear, but they came out so distorted, if they came out at all, as to be wholly unrecognizable. After about two hours, Mr Bergebedgian said he must return to the inn and see to the dinner. This was the signal for a general movement; three or four notables were invited to the table, wine-glasses were produced, a dish of sponge fingers, and finally a bottle of champagne. We drank each other's health, making graceful unintelligible little speeches in our own languages. Then, after much handshaking, we returned to the inn, leaving our Aladdin lamp at the party.

After a profoundly indigestible dinner, Mr Bergebedgian joined us – the unsmiling clerk and myself – in a glass of a disturbing liqueur labelled 'Koniak'. Presently he said, would we like to go to another party? There was a wedding in the town. This time our expedition was attended with grave precautions. First, Mr Bergebedgian buckled on bandolier and revolver-holster; then he went to the cash-desk and produced a heavy automatic pistol, charged the magazine, and tucked it into place; then he reached under the bar and drew out four or five wooden clubs, which he dealt out to his servants; the bank-clerk showed a revolver, I my sword stick; he nodded approval. It was all very much like Rat's preparation for the attack on Toad Hall. Then he barred up the house, a process involving innumerable bolts and padlocks. At last, attended by three servants with staves and a storm lantern, we set out. Things were safer at Harar than they used to be, he explained, but it was wiser to take no risks. As we emerged into the street, a hyaena flashed red eyes at us and scuttled off. I do not know how hyaenas have got their reputation for laughing. Abyssinia is full of them; they come into the towns at night scavenging and performing the less valuable service of nosing up corpses in the cemeteries; they used to bay all round the hotel at Addis Ababa, and the next night, which I spent in a tent in the Plowmans' garden, was disturbed by a small pack of them crunching bones within a few yards of my bed, but not once did I hear anything approaching a laugh.

The streets were pitch black – not a lighted window showed anywhere – and, except for hyaenas, dogs, and cats fighting over the refuse, totally deserted. Our way led down a narrow passage, between high, crumbling walls, which was sometimes graded in steps and sometimes sloped steeply inwards to a dry gutter. Our first stop was at the house of a Greek grocer. We beat on the shutters, behind which a crack of light was immediately extinguished. Mr Bergebedgian called his name, and presently a little peep opened and a pair of eyes appeared. Some civilities were exchanged, and then, after much drawing of bolts, we were admitted. The grocer offered us 'koniak' and cigarettes. Mr Bergebedgian explained that we wanted him to accompany us to the party. He refused, explaining that he had to make up his books. Mr Bergebedgian, accordingly, borrowed some small silver (a loan which, I observed, was duly noted in the accounts) and we took our leave. More black, empty alleys. Suddenly a policeman rocketed up from the gutter where he had been taking a rest, and challenged us with some ferocity. Mr Bergebedgian replied with a mock flourish of his revolver; some light exchange of chaff and back-chat followed, in the course of which the policeman decided to join the party. After a few minutes we found another policeman, huddled in his blanket on the counter of a deserted greengrocer's stall; they shook him awake and brought him along with us. At last we reached a small courtyard, beyond which, from a lighted door, came the sound of singing.

No doubt we looked rather a formidable gang as we stalked in bristling with weapons, but it was probably the sight of the two policemen which caused most alarm. Anyway, whatever the reason, wild panic followed our entry. There was only one door, through which we had come, and a stream of Harari girls dashed past us, jostling, stumbling, and squealing; others cowered away under their shawls or attempted to climb the steps which led to a little loft. Mr Bergebedgian repeatedly explained our pacific intentions, but it was some time before confidence was restored. Then a young man appeared with chairs for us and the dance was resumed.

The house consisted of a single room with a gallery full of coffee sacks at one end. A large stove, built of clay and rubble, stood under the ladder, and two or three earthenware jars and pots lay on and around it. Opposite the door the floor was raised in a carpeted dais. The few men of the party lounged round the door; the girls squatted together on the dais; the dance took place in the well of the floor to the music of the girls' singing, and the beating of hand drums. It was a pretty scene, lit by a single oil-lamp; the walls were decorated with coloured wickerwork plates; a brazier of charcoal and incense stood in one corner; a wicker dish of sweets was passed from one delicate henna-stained hand to another among the girls on the dais.

The dance was of the simplest kind. One girl and two men stood opposite each other; the girl wore a shawl on her head and the men held their *chammas* over the lower part of their faces. They shuffled up to each other and shuffled back; after several repetitions of this movement they crossed over, revolving as they passed each other, and repeated the figure from opposite sides. As the girl came to our end, Mr Bergebedgian pulled her shawl off. 'Look,' he said, 'hasn't she got nice hair?' She recovered it crossly and Mr Bergebedgian began teasing her, twitching it back every time she passed. But he was a soft-hearted fellow and he desisted as soon as he realized that he was causing genuine distress.

133

This was the bride's house that we were in; a second party was in progress in another part of the town at the home of the bridegroom. We went to visit it and found it precisely similar in character, but very much larger and more splendid. Clearly the girl had made a good match. These parties are kept up every night for a week before the wedding; the bride's friends and relations in her home, the bridegroom's in his. They do not mix until the actual wedding-day. For some reason which I could not fathom they had lately come under ban of the law; hence the consternation at our arrival. We stayed for about an hour and then returned to the hotel. The policemen came in with us and hung about until they were given a tumblerful each of neat spirit. Sleep was difficult that night, for the pillows were hard as boards, and through the windows, devoid of glass and shutters, came the incessant barking of dogs and hyaenas and the occasional wailing of horns of the town guard.

Next morning the bank-clerk rode away and Mr Bergebedgian took me for a walk in the town. He was a remarkable guide. We went into the shops of all his friends and drank delicious coffee and smoked cigarettes; he seemed to have small financial transactions with all of them, paying out a thaler here, receiving another there. We went into the law-courts, where we saw a magistrate trying a case about real property; both litigants and all the witnesses were in chains; the plaintiff was a Galla who pleaded his own cause through an interpreter. He became so eager about his wrongs that the interpreter was unable to keep up with him, and after repeated admonishments left him to finish his case in his own tongue. Behind the court was a lion in a wooden cage so small that he could barely move in it, so foul that the air of the whole yard was insupportable. We saw the great hall used for the raw-beef banquets. A group of slave-boys were being instructed in squad drill by an older boy with a stick. The commands were recognizably of English origin – presumably imported by some old soldier from the K.A.R. We went into the prison, a place of frightful filth, comparable only to the lion's cage. Mr Bergebedgian, in whose character there was a marked strain of timidity, was very reluctant to enter, saying that three or four deaths occurred there every week from typhus; a flea from any one of the prisoners would kill us both. That evening in my bath I found myself covered with flea-bites, and remembered this information with some apprehension. The cells stood round a small yard; three or four men were tethered to the wall of each cell, with chains just long enough to allow of their crawling into the open. Those who were fed by their families never left the buildings; the others were allowed to earn their keep by working in gangs on the roads. The lot of the more neglected seemed by far preferable. Most of the prisoners were there for debt, often for quite trifling sums; they remained there until they paid or, more probably, died. There were no less than three prisons in Harar. My servant got locked up one day for a breach of the sanitary regulations and I had to pay five dollars to get him out. He remarked, with some justice, how could one tell that there were any sanitary regulations in Harar? In his opinion, it was a put-up job because he was a stranger.

We went into the two or three *tedj* houses. At this stage of the morning they were fairly empty, some had no customers at all, in others a few dissipated men, who had slept the night there, squatted holding their heads, quarrelling with the women about the reckoning; at only one did we find any gaiety, where a party just arrived from the country were starting to get drunk; each sat beside a decanter of cloudy *tedj*; one of them was playing a kind of banjo. The women were, without exception, grossly ugly. Mr Bergebedgian drew back a sleeve and exhibited a sore on the shoulder of one of them. 'A dirty lot,' he said, giving her an affectionate pat and a half-piastre bit.

We went through the bazaar, Mr Bergebedgian disparaging all the goods in the friendliest way possible, and I bought some silver bangles which he obtained for me at a negligible fraction of their original price. We went into several private houses, where Mr Bergebedgian examined and exhibited everything, pulling clothes out of the chests, bringing down bags of spice from the shelves, opening the oven and tasting the food, pinching the girls, and giving half-piastre pieces to the children. We went into a workshop where three or four girls of dazzling beauty were at work making tables and trays of fine, brilliantly-patterned basketwork. Everywhere he went he seemed to be welcome; everywhere he not only adapted, but completely transformed, his manners to the environment. When I came to consider the question I was surprised to realize that the two most accomplished men I met during this six months I was abroad, the chauffeur who took us to Debra Lebanos and Mr Bergebedgian, should both have been Armenians. A race of rare competence and the most delicate sensibility. They seem to me the only genuine 'men of the world'. I suppose everyone at times likes to picture himself as such a person. Sometimes, when I find that elusive ideal looming too attractively, when I envy among my friends this one's adaptability to diverse company, this one's cosmopolitan experience, this one's impenetrable armour against sentimentality and humbug, that one's freedom from conventional prejudices, this one's astute ordering of his finances and nicely calculated hospitality, and realize that, whatever happens to me and however I deplore it, I shall never in actual fact become a 'man of the world' of the kind I read about in novels – then I comfort myself a little by thinking that, perhaps, if I were an Armenian I should find things easier.

CHAPTER THREE

Globe-Trotting in 1930–31

(From *Remote People*)

PURE mischance had brought me to Aden, and I expected to dislike it, contrasting it angrily with the glamour and rich beauty I expected to find at Zanzibar. How wrong I was.

Zanzibar and the Congo, names pregnant with romantic suggestion, gave me nothing; Aden was full of interest.

On first acquaintance, however, there was much about the Settlement to justify my forebodings. It is, as every passenger down the Red Sea knows, an extinct volcano joined to the mainland by a flat and almost invisible neck of sand; not a tree or flower or blade of grass grows on it, the only vegetation is a meagre crop of colourless scrub which has broken out in patches among the cinders; there is no earth and no water, except what is dragged there in a ceaseless succession of camel-carts through the tunnelled road; the sanitation everywhere – in the hotels, the club, the mess, the private bungalows – is still that of a temporary camp. Architecture, except for a series of water-tanks of unknown age, does not exist. A haphazard jumble of bungalows has been spilt over the hillside, like the litter of picnic-parties after Bank Holiday. The hotel is as expensive as Torr's at Nairobi; the food has only two flavours – tomato ketchup and Worcestershire sauce; the bathroom consists of a cubicle in which a tin can is suspended on a rope; there is a nozzle at the bottom of the can encrusted with stalactites of green slime; the bather stands on the slippery cement floor and pulls a string releasing a jet of water over his head and back; for a heavy extra charge it is possible, with due notice, to have the water warmed; the hall-porter has marked criminal tendencies; the terrace is infested by money-changers. The only compensating luxury, a seedy, stuffed sea-animal, unmistakably male, which is kept in a chest and solemnly exhibited – on payment – as a mermaid. You would have to search a

137

long time before finding many such hotels in the whole of England.

There are other superficial disadvantages about Aden, notably the division of the Settlement into two towns. So far I have been speaking of the district known as Steamer Point; about three miles away lies Crater Town, the centre of such commerce as has survived. This was the original nucleus of the Settlement. It is surrounded on three sides by cliffs, and on the fourth by what was once a harbour, now silted up and for a long time closed to all traffic. The original Residency stands there, now a guest-house for visiting Arab chiefs; there is also a large derelict barracks, partially demolished, and an Anglican church, built in Victorian Gothic, which was once the garrison chapel, and is still provided with its own chaplain, who reads services there Sunday after Sunday in absolute void. This man, earnest and infinitely kind, had lately arrived from Bombay; he rescued me from the hotel, and took me to stay with him for a few days in his large, ramshackle house on the Crater beach, known to taxi-drivers as 'Padre sahib's bungalow'. A few of the political officers still have quarters round the Crater, and there are a half-dozen or so British commercial agents and clerks; the rest of the population are mixed Asiatics inhabiting a compact series of streets between the water and the hills.

The town affords a remarkable variety of race and costume. Arabs are represented in every grade of civilization, from courteous old gentlemen in Government service who wear gold-rimmed spectacles, silk turbans, and light frock coats and carry shabby umbrellas with highly decorated handles, to clusters of somewhat bemused Bedouin straight from the desert; these are, in appearance, very different from the noble savages of romance; their clothes consist of a strip of blanket round the waist, held up by a sash from which protrudes the hilt of a large dagger; their hair is straight, black, and greasy, lying on the back of the head in a loose bun and bound round the forehead with a piece of rag; they are of small stature and meagre muscular development; their faces are hairless or covered with a slight down, their expressions degenerate and slightly dotty, an impression which is accentuated by their loping, irregular gait.

The British political officer introduced me to a delightful Arab who acted as my interpreter and conducted me round Crater Town. He took me to his club, a large upper storey, where at the busy time of the commercial day we found the principal Arab citizens reclining on divans and chewing *khat*; later he took me to an Arab café where the lower class congregate; here, too, was the same decent respect for leisure; the patrons reclined round the walls in a gentle stupor, chewing *khat*. 'These simple people, too, have their little pleasures,' my companion remarked.

Later I received an invitation to tea from the president and committee of the club. This time the bundles of *khat* had been removed, and plates of sweet biscuits and dates and tins of cigarettes had taken their place. My friend and interpreter was there, but the president spoke enough English to make conversation very difficult.

I was introduced to about a dozen Arabs. We sat down in two rows opposite each other. A servant brought in a tray of tea and bottled lemonade. We talked about the distressing conditions of local trade.

Everything would be all right and everyone would be happy, said the Arabs, if only the bank would give longer and larger overdrafts. I remarked that in England we are embarrassed in exactly that way too. They laughed politely. Europeans, they said, could always get all the money they wanted. Even Indians, a race renowned for dishonour and instability, could get larger advances than the Arabs; how was one to live unless one borrowed the money? They had heard it said I was writing a book. Would I, in my book, persuade the bank to lend them more money? I promised that I would try. (Will any official of the Bank of India who reads this book please let the Aden Arabs have more money?)

We talked about London. They told me that the Sultan of Lahej had been there and had met the King-Emperor. We talked about the King-Emperor and pretty Princess Elizabeth. I confess I am pretty bad at carrying on this kind of conversation. There were several long pauses. One of them was broken by the president suddenly saying, 'We all take great sorrow at the loss of your R101.'

I agreed that it had been a terrible disaster, and remarked that I knew one of the victims fairly well.

'We think it very sad,' said the president, 'that so many of your well-educated men should have been killed.'

That seemed to me a new aspect of the tragedy.

Conversation again languished, until one of the company, who had hitherto taken no part in the conversation, rose to his feet and, tucking up his shirt, exhibited the scars in his side caused by a recent operation for gall-stone. This man was local correspondent to a London newspaper. He had lately, he told me, sent the foreign-news editor a complete genealogy of the Imam of Sana, compiled by himself with great labour. Did I know whether it had yet been printed, and, if not, could I put in a word for him in Fleet Street when I returned?

One evening there was a fair in Crater. There were stalls selling sweets and sherbet under naphtha flares, and tables with simple gambling-games. One of these was the simplest gambling-game I ever saw. The banker dealt five cards face downwards and the players placed a stake of an anna on one or other of them. When each card had found a backer – two players were not allowed to bet on the same card – they were turned up. The winning card was then paid even money and the banker pocketed three annas a time. Groups of men danced in circles between the stalls.

One unifying influence among the diverse cultures of the Crater was the Aden troop of Boy Scouts. It is true that Arabs cannot be induced to serve in the same patrol with Jews, but it is a remarkable enough spectacle to see the two races sitting amicably on opposite sides of a camp-fire, singing their songs in turn and occasionally joining each other in chorus. The scoutmaster, an English commercial agent, invited me to attend one of these meetings.

The quarters were a disused sergeants' mess and the former barrack square. My friend was chiefly responsible for the Arab patrol, the Jews having an independent organization. As I approached, rather late, I saw the latter drilling in their own quarter of the parade ground – a squad of lengthy, sallow boys in very smart uniforms furnished with every possible accessory by the benefaction of a still-wealthy local merchant. The Arabs –

with the exception of one resplendent little Persian, for 'Arab' in this connexion was held to include all Gentiles, Somali, Arab, and Mohammedan Indians – were less luxuriously equipped. There were also far fewer of them. This was explained by the fact that two of the second-class scouts were just at that time celebrating marriages.

Tests were in progress for the tenderfoot and other badges. The acquiring of various badges is a matter of primary concern in the Aden troop. Some of the children had their arms well covered with decorations. 'We generally let them pass after the third or fourth attempt,' the scoutmaster explained. 'It discourages them to fail too often.'

Two or three figures crouching against corners of masonry were engaged on lighting fires. This had to be done with two matches; they had been provided by their mothers with horrible messes of food in tin cans, which they intended to warm up and consume. I believe this qualified them for a cookery medal. 'Of course, it isn't like dealing with English boys,' said the scout-master, 'if one isn't pretty sharp they put paraffin on the sticks.'

The scoutmaster kept the matchbox, which was very quickly depleted. Breathless little creatures kept running up. 'Please, sahib, no burn. Please more matches.' Then we would walk across, scatter the assembled sticks and tinder, and watch them built up again. It was not a long process. A match was then struck, plunged into the centre of the little pile, and instantly extinguished. The second match followed. 'Please, sahib, no burn.' Then the business began again. Occasionally crows of delight would arise and we were hastily summoned to see a real conflagration. Now and then a sheet of flame would go up very suddenly, accompanied by a column of black smoke. 'Oil,' said the scoutmaster, and that fire would be disqualified.

Later a Somali boy presented himself for examination in scout law. He knew it all by heart perfectly. 'First scoot law a scoot's honour iss to be trust second scoot law . . .' et cetera, in one breath.

'Very good, Abdul. Now tell me what does "thrifty" mean?'

'Trifty min?'

'Yes, what do you mean, when you say a scout is thrifty?'

'I min a scoot hass no money.'

'Well, that's more or less right. What does "clean" mean?'

'Clin min?'

'You said just now a scout is clean in thought, word, and deed.'

'Yis, scoot iss clin.'

'Well, what do you mean by that?'

'I min tought, worden deed.'

'Yes, well, what do you *mean* by clean?'

Both parties in this dialogue seemed to be losing confidence in the other's intelligence.

'I min the tenth scoot law.'

A pause during which the boy stood first on one black leg, then on the other, gazing patiently into the sun.

'All right, Abdul. That'll do.'

'Pass, sahib?'

'Yes, yes.'

An enormous smile broke across his small face, and away he went capering across the parade ground, kicking up dust over the fire-makers and laughing with pleasure.

'Of course, it isn't quite like dealing with English boys,' said the scoutmaster again.

Presently the two bridegrooms arrived, identically dressed in gala clothes, brilliantly striped silk skirts, sashes, and turbans, little coats and ornamental daggers. They were cousins, about fourteen years of age. They had been married a week ago. Tonight they were going to see their brides for the first time. They were highly excited by their clothes, and anxious to show them to their fellow scouts and scoutmaster.

Meanwhile the Jews had made a huge bonfire on the beach. Both patrols assembled round it and a short concert was held. They sang local songs in their own languages. I asked what they meant, but the scoutmaster was not sure. From what I know of most Arabic songs, I expect that they were wholly incompatible with the tenth scout law.

I think that perhaps it was the predominance of bachelors at Steamer Point that made the English community there so unusually agreeable. At Aden the centres of social intercourse were in the club and the messes, not at bungalow 'sundowner'-parties. At Zanzibar the club was practically empty from eight o'clock onwards – everyone was at home with his wife; at Aden the bar and the card-room were full till midnight.

There was plenty of entertainment going on. During my brief visit – ten days only in Aden itself – there was a dance at the club, a ball at the Residency, and a very convivial party given by the Sappers. There was also a cinematograph performance.

This is a singular feature of Aden life which occurs every Thursday on the roof of the Seamen's Institute. I went with the flight-commander, who had been in charge of the Air Mission at Addis. We dined first at the club with two of his officers. There were parties at other tables, also bound for the cinema; there were also dinner-parties at many of the bungalows. People entertain for the cinema on Thursday nights as they do for dances in London. It is not a hundred yards from the club to the Seamen's Institute, but we drove there in two cars. Other parties were arriving; a few Somalis loitered round the entrance, watching the procession; the Residency car, flag flying on the bonnet, was already there. Upstairs the roof was covered with deep wicker chairs. The front row was reserved for the Resident's party. The other seats were already two-thirds full. Everyone, of course, was in evening dress. It was a warm night, brilliant with stars.

The first film was a Pathé Gazette, showing the King leaving London for Bognor Regis twenty months previously, and an undated Grand National, presumably of about the same antiquity. A fine old slapstick comedy followed. I turned to remark to my host how much superior the early comedies were to those of the present day, but discovered, to my surprise, that he was fast asleep. I turned to my neighbour on the other side; his head had fallen back, his eyes were shut, his mouth wide open. His cigarette was gradually burning towards his fingers. I took it from him and put it out. The movement disturbed him. He shut his mouth, and without opening his eyes, said, 'Jolly good, isn't it?' Then his mouth fell open again. I looked about me and saw in the half-light reflected from the screen that the entire audience were asleep. An abysmal British drama followed, called *The Woman Who Did*. It was about a feminist and an illegitimate child and a rich grand-

143

father. The roof remained wrapped in sleep. It is one of the odd characteristics of the Aden climate that it is practically impossible to remain both immobile and conscious.

Later, 'God Save the King' was played on the piano. Everyone sprang alertly to attention and, completely vivacious once more, adjourned to the club for beer, oysters, and bridge.

Everyone was hospitable, and between meals I made a serious attempt to grasp some of the intricacies of Arabian politics; an attempt which took the form of my spreading a table with maps, reports and notebooks, and then falling into a gentle and prolonged stupor. I spent only one really strenuous afternoon. That was in taking 'a little walk over the rocks', with Mr Leblanc and his 'young men'.

Nothing in my earlier acquaintance with Mr Leblanc had given me any reason to suspect what I was letting myself in for when I accepted his invitation to join him in his little walks over the rocks. He was a general merchant, commercial agent, and ship-owner of importance, the only European magnate in the Settle-ment; they said of him that he thrived on risk and had made and lost more than one considerable fortune in his time. I met him dining at the Residency, on my first evening in Aden. He talked of Abyssinia, where he had heavy business undertakings, with keen sarcasm; he expressed his contempt for the poetry of Rimbaud; he told me a great deal of very recent gossip about people in Europe; after dinner he played some very new gramo-phone records he had brought with him. To me, rubbed raw by those deadly four days at Dirre-Dowa and Djibouti, it was all particularly emollient and healing.

A day or two afterwards he invited me to dinner at his house in Crater. A smart car with a liveried Indian chauffeur came to fetch me. We dined on the roof; a delicious dinner; iced *vin rosé* – 'It is not a luxurious wine, but I am fond of it; it grows on a little estate of my own in the South of France' – and the finest Yemen coffee. With his very thin gold watch in his hand, Mr Leblanc predicted the rising of a star – I forget which. Punctual to the second, it appeared, green and malevolent, on the rim of the hills; cigars glowing under the night sky; from below the faint murmur of the native streets; all infinitely smooth and civilized.

144

At this party a new facet was revealed to me in the character of my host. Mr Leblanc the man of fashion I had seen. Here was Mr Leblanc the patriarch. The house where we sat was the top storey of his place of business; at the table sat his daughter, his secretary, and three of his 'young men'. The young men were his clerks, learning the business. One was French, the other two English lately down from Cambridge. They worked immensely hard – often, he told me, ten hours a day; often half way through the night, when a ship was in. They were not encouraged to go to the club or to mix in the society of Steamer Point. They lived together in a house near Mr Leblanc's; they lived very well and were on terms of patriarchal intimacy with Mr Leblanc's family. 'If they go up to Steamer Point, they start drinking, playing cards, and spending money. Here, they work so hard that they cannot help saving. When they want a holiday they go round the coast visiting my agencies. They learn to know the country and the people; they travel in my ships; at the end of a year or two they have saved nearly all their money and they have learned the business. For exercise we take little walks over the rocks together. Tennis and polo would cost them money. To walk in the hills is free. They get up out of the town into the cool air, the views are magnificent, the gentle exercise keeps them in condition for their work. It takes their minds, for a little, off business. You must come with us one day on one of our walks.'

I agreed readily. After the torpid atmosphere of Aden it would be delightful to take some gentle exercise in the cool air. And so it was arranged for the following Saturday afternoon. When I left, Mr Leblanc lent me a copy of Gide's *Voyage au Congo*.

Mr Leblanc the man of fashion I knew, and Mr Leblanc the patriarch. On Saturday I met Mr Leblanc the man of action, Mr Leblanc the gambler.

I was to lunch first with the young men at their 'mess' – as all communal *ménages* appear to be called in the East. I presented myself dressed as I had seen photographs of 'hikers', with shorts, open shirt, stout shoes, woollen stockings, and large walking-stick. We had an excellent luncheon, during which they told me how, one evening, they had climbed into the Parsees' death-house, and what a row there had been about it. Presently one of them said, 'Well, it's about time to change. We promised to be round at the old man's at half past.'

'Change?'

'Well, it's just as you like, but I think you'll find those things rather hot. We usually wear nothing except shoes and shorts. We leave our shirts in the cars. They meet us on the bathing-beach. And if you've got any rubber-soled shoes I should wear them. Some of the rocks are pretty slippery.' Luckily I happened to have some rubber shoes. I went back to the chaplain's house, where I was then living, and changed. I was beginning to be slightly apprehensive.

Mr Leblanc looked magnificent. He wore newly creased white shorts, a silk openwork vest, and white *espadrilles* laced like a ballet dancer's round his ankles. He held a tuberose, sniffing it delicately. 'They call it an Aden lily sometimes,' he said. 'I can't think why.'

There was with him another stranger, a guest of Mr Leblanc's on a commercial embassy from an oil firm. 'I say, you know,' he confided in me, 'I think this is going to be a bit stiff. I'm scarcely in training for anything very energetic.'

We set out in the cars and drove to a dead end at the face of the cliffs near the ancient reservoirs. I thought we must have taken the wrong road, but everyone got out and began stripping off his shirt. The Leblanc party went hatless; the stranger and I retained our topees.

'I should leave those sticks in the car,' said Mr Leblanc.

'But shan't we find them useful?' (I still nursed memories of happy scrambles in the Wicklow hills.)

'You will find them a great nuisance,' said Mr Leblanc.

We did as we were advised.

Then the little walk started. Mr Leblanc led the way with light, springing steps. He went right up to the face of the cliff, gaily but purposefully as Moses may have approached the rocks from which he was about to strike water. There was a little crack running like fork-lightning down the blank wall of stone. Mr Leblanc stood below it, gave one little skip, and suddenly, with

146

great rapidity and no apparent effort, proceeded to ascend the precipice. He did not climb; he rose. It was as if someone were hoisting him up from above and he had merely to prevent himself from swinging out of the perpendicular, by keeping contact with rocks in a few light touches of foot and hand.

In just the same way, one after another, the Leblanc party were whisked away out of sight. The stranger and I looked at each other. 'Are you all right?' came reverberating down from very far ahead. We began to climb. We climbed for about half an hour up the cleft in the rock. Not once during that time did we find a place where it was possible to rest or even to stand still in any normal attitude. We just went on from foothold to foothold; our topees made it impossible to see more than a foot or two above our heads. Suddenly we came to the Leblanc party sitting on a ledge.

'You look hot,' said Mr Leblanc. 'I see you are not in training. You will find this most beneficial.'

As soon as we stopped climbing, our knees began to tremble. We sat down. When the time came to start again, it was quite difficult to stand up. Our knees seemed to be behaving as they sometimes do in dreams, when they suddenly refuse support in moments of pursuit by bearded women broadcasters.

'We thought it best to wait for you,' continued Mr Leblanc, 'because there is rather a tricky bit here. It is easy enough when you know the way, but you need someone to show you. I discovered it myself. I often go out alone in the evenings finding tricky bits. Once I was out all night, quite stuck. I thought I should be able to find a way when the moon rose. Then I remembered there was no moon that night. It was a very cramped position.'

The tricky bit was a huge overhanging rock with a crumbling, flaky surface.

'It is really quite simple. Watch me and then follow. You put your right foot here ...' – a perfectly blank, highly polished surface of stone – '... then rather slowly you reach up with your left hand until you find a hold. You have to stretch rather far ... so. Then you cross your right leg under your left – this is the difficult part – and feel for a footing on the other side ... With your right hand you just steady yourself ... so.' Mr Leblanc hung over the abyss partly out of sight. His whole body seemed prehensile. He *stood* there like a fly on the ceiling. 'That is the position. It is best to trust more to the feet than the hands – push up rather than pull down ... you see the stone here is not always secure.' By way of demonstration he splintered off a handful of apparently solid rock from above his head and sent it tinkling down to the road below. 'Now all you do is to shift the weight from your left foot to your right, and swing yourself round ... so.' And Mr Leblanc disappeared from view.

Every detail of that expedition is kept fresh in my mind by recurrent nightmares. Eventually after about one hour's fearful climb we reached the rim of the crater. The next stage was a tramp across the great pit of loose cinders; then the ascent of the other rim to the highest point of the peninsula. Here we paused to admire the view, which was indeed most remarkable; then we climbed down to the sea. Variety was added to this last phase by the fact that we were now in the full glare of the sun, which had been beating on the cliffs from noon until they were blistering hot.

'It will hurt the hands if you hang on too long,' said Mr Leblanc. 'One must jump on the foot from rock to rock like the little goats.'

At last, after about three hours of it, we reached the beach. Cars and servants were waiting. Tea was already spread; bathing-dresses and towels laid out.

'We always bathe here, not at the club,' said Mr Leblanc. 'They have a screen there to keep out the sharks – while in this bay, only last month, two boys were devoured.'

We swam out into the warm sea. An Arab fisherman, hopeful of a tip, ran to the edge of the sea and began shouting to us that it was dangerous. Mr Leblanc laughed happily and, with easy, powerful strokes, made for the deep waters. We returned to shore and dressed. My shoes were completely worn through, and there was a large tear in my shorts where I had slipped among the cinders and slid some yards. Mr Leblanc had laid out for him in the car a clean white suit, a shirt of green crêpe-de-Chine, a bow tie, silk socks, buckskin shoes, ivory hairbrushes, scent spray, and hair lotion. We ate banana sandwiches and drank very rich China tea.

For a little additional thrill on the way back, Mr Leblanc took the wheel of his car. I am not sure that that was not the most hair-raising experience of all.

Next day – Sunday, December 14th – intolerably stiff in every muscle, bruised, scratched, blistered by the sun, I set out for Lahej, to spend two nights as the sultan's guest and see the assembly of the tributary chiefs on Tuesday.

We – Colonel Lake, the chief political officer, the driver, and I – bounced along in the sand, in a six-wheel army lorry, beside the remains of the track, which still clearly showed the corrugations where the sleepers had lain. It took us about two hours to reach the camp. The Aden Levy had arrived the day before. Great trouble had been taken with the alignment of the camp; an avenue of signalling-flags led up to its centre; the sites for the tents were symmetrically disposed round it. The tents themselves were causing some trouble, particularly a great cubic pavilion that was to be used for the Resident's durbar; there was a high, hot wind blowing; grass and reeds had been scattered about to lay the driving sand, but with little success. Clouds of grit eddied everywhere.

Just as we arrived they got the big tent fixed at last; they stood back to admire it. The subaltern in charge came to greet us. 'Thank heavens we've got that done. We've been at it since five this morning. Now we can have a drink.'

While he was still speaking, the tent bellied, sagged, and fell; the patient little Arabs began their work again, laying foundations of stones, three feet deep, to hold the pegs in the loose sand.

We lunched in the mess-tent, dozed, and then, mounted on camels, Colonel Lake and I rode the remaining two miles into the town. It was a typical Arab town of dun-coloured, flat-roofed houses and intricate alleyways. The palace was European in conception, smaller than the Gebbi at Addis, but better planned and better kept; there were pretty formal gardens in front, and all round the town lay bright green meadows and groves of coconut and date-palm.

A power station has lately been built and most of the principal

149

houses installed with electricity. This is naturally a matter for great pride and, to draw his visitors' attention more closely to the innovation, the sultan has conceived the rather unhappy plan of building the new guest-house immediately over the electric plant. Fortunately this was not yet finished, so that we were directed to the old guest-house, a pleasant, rather dilapidated villa of pseudo-European style, standing at the extremity of the town on the edge of the fields. Here Colonel Lake left me in the charge of the Arab butler, having elicited the fact that there were two other occupants of the house – German engineers in the sultan's employ. Except for these there were no Europeans of any kind in the town.

After about an hour they arrived. They were very young men – both twenty-two, I learned later – and they had come in overalls straight from work; they spoke English, one rather better than the other, but both very fluently, loudly, and unintelligibly. Their first concern was to apologize for their appearance. They would be ashamed to speak to me, they said, until they had washed and changed. They had fitted up a kind of shower-bath behind a curtain of sacking at the top of the stairs. Here they hid themselves and spluttered happily for some minutes, emerging later, naked, dripping, and better composed. They dried themselves, combed their hair, put on smart tropical suits, and called for dinner. They produced some bottled amstel from beneath their beds and put it under the shower-bath to cool, and opened a tin of green-gages in my honour. They were a most friendly, generous pair.

Dinner consisted of a highly pungent meat stew and salad. The cooking was not good, they explained, and they suspected the butler of cheating the sultan and themselves by confiscating their rations and substituting inferior purchases of his own; however, it did not do to complain; they were well paid and could afford to supplement their meals with biscuits and beer and tinned fruit; they would probably be the ultimate losers in any conflict with the butler. I should find, they said, that their food would make me rather ill. At first they suffered continuously from dysentery and nettle-rash; also the mosquito-curtains were too short and were full of holes. I should probably get a touch of malaria. The salad, they said, helping themselves profusely, was full of typhus.

I retail this information simply and concisely as though it had come to me in so many words. As a matter of fact, it took the whole of dinner in telling, and half an hour or so afterwards. Both spoke simultaneously all the time, and, when the issues became confused, louder and louder. 'We know English so well because we always speak it with our Dutch friends at Aden,' they explained (but again at far greater length and with many mis-understandings and cross purposes). 'It was largely from them that we learned it.'

There were interruptions. Fairly frequently the light turned orange, flickered, and went out, on one occasion for so long that we all set out to the power station to see what had happened. Just as we left the house, however, we saw the lights go up again, and returned to our conversation. 'Engineer,' I realized, was a title covering a variety of functions. Three times messages came from the palace; once, to say that the water-closet had broken and that they were to come and mend it first thing in the morning; again, to say that one of Sultan Achmed's (the Sultan of Lahej's brother) new tractors was stuck in a water-course; a third, to remark that the lights kept going out. All these things were duly noted down for their attention.

Next morning I had an audience with the sultan. His Highness was an impassive, middle-aged man, wearing semi-European clothes – turban, black frock coat, white linen trousers. As head of the Fadl family, the hereditary rulers of the Abdali tribe and, for a brief period, the former possessors of Aden, he holds by far the most influential position in the protectorate.

His is, in fact, the only really secure house in Southern Arabia. There is no resident adviser at Lahej and no attempt at domestic control. Within his own territory the sultan's power is limited only by the traditional law of his own people.

We drank delicious coffee on the balcony overlooking the palace gardens and, with the aid of an interpreter, asked politely after each other's health and the health of our relations. I commented on the striking modernity of his city – the electric light, the water-supply, the motor-buses; he remarked how much more modern these things were in London. He said that the Resident told him I wrote books; that he had not himself written a book, but that his

151

brother had written a very good one, which I must see before I left Lahej. He asked after my comfort at the guest-house; I replied that it was luxury itself; he said not so luxurious as London. I was at the moment, just as the Germans had predicted, tortured with nettle-rash. I said that the tranquillity was greater than in London. He said that soon he would have more motor-buses. Then we took leave of each other and I was conducted to Sultan Achmed Fadl.

His Highness's brother lived in a small, balconied house on the further side of the main square. He was already receiving company. A British political officer was there, the subaltern who had supervised the collapse of the Resident's durbar tent, and the Haushabi Sultan; a secretary was in attendance and numerous servants and guards sat about on the narrow staircase.

The Haushabi Sultan was an important young man finely dressed and very far from sane. He sat in a corner giggling with embarrassment, and furtively popping little twigs of *khat* into his mouth. It was not often that his womenfolk allowed him to leave his own district. Sultan Achmed was a good-looking man of forty, with high, intellectual forehead and exquisite manners; he spoke English well. His habit of life was pious and scholarly. He had private estates, almost as large as his brother's, whose cultivation he supervised himself, experimenting eagerly with new methods of irrigation, new tractors and fertilizers, new kinds of crops – a complete counterpart of the enlightened landed gentleman of eighteenth-century England.

He showed me his book: a history of the Fadl family from the remotest times until the death of his father (unfortunately shot by a British sentry during the evacuation of Lahej in 1915). It was written in exquisite script, illuminated with numerous genealogies in red and black. He hoped to have a few copies printed for distribution among his friends and relatives, but he did not think it was likely to command a wide sale.

He suggested a drive. When he gave orders, his servants kissed his knees, and, whenever we stopped during the drive, passers-by hurried to salute him in the same way. His car was not new – I think it must have been one of those devised by the German mechanics from the débris of former accidents – but it carried a crest of ostrich plumes on the bonnet and an armed guard beside the chauffeur. We drove to his country house a mile or two away and walked for some time in his gardens – shrubs flowering in the shade of coconut-palms by the bank of a stream. He ordered a bunch of flowers to be prepared for me, and the gardeners brought a vast bundle of small, sweet-smelling roses and some great spear-shaped white flowers, sheathed in barbed leaves, which gave out a scent of almost stifling richness, reputed throughout Arabia, so the Germans told me later, to act upon women as an aphrodisiac. He also gave me twelve gourds of Dhala honey, eight of which were subsequently stolen by the butler at the guest-house, who thus, with unconscious kindness, relieved me of a particularly unmanageable addition to my luggage, without my incurring any possible self-reproach on grounds of ingratitude.

That evening I sat with the Germans, gradually disentangling from their flow of sound an outline of their really remarkable careers. They had left school at Munich when they were eighteen and, together with a large number of boys of their year, had determined to seek their fortunes. Accordingly they had split up into pairs, made a solemn leavetaking, and scattered all over the globe. They had no money, their only assets being a sketchy knowledge of practical mechanics and, they said, a natural gift for languages. They had worked their way doing odd jobs at garages, through Spain and North Africa to Abyssinia, with the vague intention of some time reaching India. Two years before at Berbera they had heard that the Sultan of Lahej had just expelled his French engineer for dishonest practices; they had crossed the gulf on the chance of getting the job, had got it, and remained there ever since. They undertook every kind of work, from the mending of punctures in His Highness's tyres to the construction of a ferro-concrete dam on the wadi and the irrigation of his entire estates. They had charge of the electric plant and the water-supply of the town; they mended the firearms of the palace guard; they drew up the plans and supervised the construction of all new buildings; they advised on the choice of agricultural machinery; with their own hands they installed the palace water-closet – the only thing of its kind in the whole of Southern Arabia. When not otherwise engaged, they put in their time patching up abandoned army lorries and converting them into motor-buses. Their only fear was that the sultan might take it into his head to procure an aeroplane; that, they felt, would almost certainly lead to trouble. Meanwhile they were as happy as the day was long; they would have to move on soon, however; it would not do to risk Stagnation of the Spirit.

Sultan Achmed combined his gentler pursuits with the office of commander-in-chief of the army, and early next morning he was busy inspecting the guard of honour and inducing a high degree of uniformity in their equipment. Long before the Resident was due to arrive they were drawn up in the palace courtyard, arranged like strawberries on a coster's barrow, with the most presentable to the fore. The chiefs had been arriving on horses and camels throughout the preceding afternoon, and had been quartered according to their rank in various houses about the town. They formed a very remarkable spectacle as they assembled among the fumed-oak furniture and plush upholstery of the sultan's state drawing-room. No one except the Fadl family and their Ministers had attempted European dress. The chiefs from up-country wore their best and most brilliant robes, and in most cases jewelled swords of considerable antiquity. They talked very little to each other, but stood about awkwardly, waiting for the Resident's entry, mutually suspicious, like small boys during the first half-hour of a children's party. Most of them, in spite of interminable genealogies, lived, in their own homes, a life of almost squalid simplicity, and they were clearly overawed by the magnificence of Lahej; some from the remoter districts were barefooted and they trod the Brussels carpets with very uncertain steps; embarrassment gave them a pop-eyed look, quite unlike the keen, hawk faces of cinema sheiks. While we were waiting, I was introduced to each in turn, and through my interpreter had a few words with them, asking whether they had had a long journey and what the prospects were for the crops and grazing-land.

As soon as the Aden party arrived we took our places in the council-room, and the chiefs were formally announced one after another in order of precedence; each in turn shook hands with the Resident and then sat down in the chair assigned to him. Some were at first too shy to go the whole length of the room, and tried to get away with little bows from the door; their companions, however, prodded them on, and they came lolloping up with downcast eyes to give very hurried greeting and then shoot for a chair. It was all very much like the prize-giving after village sports, with Sir Stewart as the squire's wife and the Sultan of Lahej as the vicar, benevolently but firmly putting the tenants' children through their paces. It was hard to believe that each of them could lead a troop of fighting men into the field and administer an ancient and intricate law to a people of perhaps fifteen hundred, perhaps twenty thousand souls.

Speeches were made, a banquet was eaten; then, though the Durbar was only beginning, I drove back to Aden.

I wish I could have stayed longer, but my time at Aden was up. The *Explorateur Grandidier* was due next day, sailing for Zanzibar. It was six weeks since I had had any mail; I had arranged for everything to be sent to Zanzibar. My plans for the future were still vague, but that tight-lipped young man at Harar had set me considering the idea of crossing Africa to the west coast. And so, what with one thing and another, I decided to move on.

Everyone admitted that it was an unfortunate time to visit Zanzibar. Usually in the tropics, if one remarks on the temperature, the inhabitants assume an air of amused tolerance and say, 'You find *this* hot? You ought to see what it's like in such and such a month.' But December in Zanzibar is recognized as a bad season.

Throughout my stay I am obsessed by heat; I see everything through a mist, vilely distorted like those gross figures that loom at one through the steam of a Turkish bath.

I live at the English Club. Every day, soon after dawn, I am awakened by the heat; I lie there under my mosquito-net, streaming with sweat, utterly exhausted; I take time summoning enough resolution to turn the pillow dry side up; a boy comes in with tea and a mango; I lie there uncovered for a little while, dreading the day. Everything has to be done very slowly. Presently I sit limply in a hip-bath of cold water; I know that before I am dry of the water I shall again be damp with sweat. I dress gradually. One wears long trousers, coat, shirt, socks, suspenders, bow tie, buckskin shoes, everything, in this town. Halfway through dressing I cover my head with eau-de-cologne and sit under the electric fan. I do this several times during the day. They are the tolerable moments. I go up to breakfast. A Goan steward offers me bacon and eggs, fish, marmalade. I eat only *papai*. I go up to the library and read local history. I try to smoke. The fan blows fragments of burning tobacco over my clothes; the bowl of the pipe is too hot to hold. Through the window a very slight breeze carries up from the streets a reek of cloves, copra, and rotten fruit. A ship has been in the night before. I send a boy to the bank to inquire after my mail; there is still nothing. I make notes about the history of Zanzibar; the ink runs in little puddles of sweat that fall on to the page; I leave hot thumb-prints on the history-book. The plates have all come loose and the fan scatters them about the library. Luncheon is early. I usually sit with a young official who is living at the club during his wife's absence at home. I tease him by putting on an earnest manner and asking him for information which I know he will be unable to give me – 'Are there any reciprocal rights at law between French subjects in Zanzibar and British subjects in Madagascar? Where, in the protectorate Budget, do the rents appear, paid for the sultan's possessions on the mainland? What arrangement was made between the Italian Government and the sultan about the cession of the Somaliland littoral below the River Juba?' – or questions which I know will embarrass him – 'Were the commercial members of Council in favour of the loan from the Zanzibar Treasury to the Government of Kenya? Is it a fact that the sultan pays for his own postage account and the Resident does not; is it a fact that the sultan has money invested abroad which the administration want to trace?' He is very patient and promises to ring up the solicitor-general that afternoon and get the facts I want. After luncheon I go to bed. At two-forty exactly, every afternoon, the warm little wind that has been blowing from the sea drops. The sudden augmentation of heat wakes me up. I have another bath. I cover my head with eau-de-cologne and sit under the fan. Tea. Sometimes I go to Benediction in the Cathedral, where it is cool. Sometimes my official takes me for a drive into the country, through acres of copra-palm and clove-trees and tidy little villages, each with police station and clinic. Sometimes I receive a call from a Turk whom I met on the ship coming here; he talks of the pleasures of Nice and the glories of Constantinople before the war; he wears close-cropped hair and a fez; he cannot wear his fez in Nice, he tells me, because they take him for an Egyptian and charge him excessively for everything. We drink lemon squash together and plan a journey to the Hejaz. 'We will ride and ride,' he says, 'until our knees are cut and bleeding.' The warmth of my admiration for Armenians clearly shocks him, but he is too polite to say so. Instead, he tells me of splendid tortures inflicted on them by his relations.

Dinner on the club terrace; it is a little cooler now; one can eat almost with pleasure. Often, in the evening, we go out for a drive or visit a *ngoma*. Once I went to the cinema, where, quite unlike Aden, the audience was wide awake – mainly composed of natives, shrieking hysterically at the eccentricities of two drunken Americans. The *ngomas* are interesting. They are Swahili dances, originally, no doubt, of ritual significance, but nowadays performed purely for recreation. Like most activities, native or immigrant, in Zanzibar, they are legalized, controlled, and licensed. A list is kept in the police station of their place and date; anyone may attend. Once or twice, teams of fine Negroes from the mainland made their appearance, and gave a performance more varied and theatrical. One dance we attended took place in absolute darkness; we were even asked to put out our cigars. It was, as far as we could see, a kind of blind-man's-buff; a man stood in the centre enveloped in an enormous conical extinguisher made of thatched grass, while the rest of the company capered round him, making derisive cries, beating tins and challenging him to catch them. The tufted top of his hood could just be seen pitching and swaying across the sky. On another occasion a particularly good mainland party – from somewhere below Tanga I was told – brought a band of four or five tom-tom players. It was odd to see these men throwing back their heads and rolling their eyes and shoulders like trick drummers in a Paris orchestra.

The only thing which does not appear to be under the

157

benevolent eye of the administrator in Zanzibar is witchcraft, which is still practised surreptitiously on a very large scale. At one time, Zanzibar and Pemba – particularly the latter island – were the chief centres of black art on the whole coast, and novices would come from as far as the great lakes to graduate there. Even from Haiti, it is said, witch doctors will occasionally come to probe the deepest mysteries of voodoo. Nowadays everything is kept hidden from the Europeans, and even those who have spent most of their lives in the country have only now and then discovered hints of the wide, infinitely ramified cult which still flourishes below the surface. No one doubts, however, that it does flourish, and it seems appropriate that it should have its base here in this smug community.

There are no problems at all in Zanzibar; such difficulties as there are are mere matters of the suitable adjustment of routine. The sultan is the model of all that a figurehead should be; a man of dignified bearing and reputable private life. He has no exclusively valid claim to his office; the British Government put him there, and they pay him a sufficient proportion of his revenue to enable him to live in a modest degree of personal comfort. The two main industries of the islands, cloves and copra, are thoroughly prosperous compared with any other form of agriculture on the East African coast. Law and order are better preserved than in many towns in the British Isles. The medical and hygienic services are admirable; miles of excellent roads have been made. The administration is self-supporting. The British Government takes nothing out of the island. Instead, we import large numbers of well-informed, wholly honest members of our unemployed middle-class to work fairly hard in the islanders' interest for quite small wages. Gay, easily intelligible charts teach the Swahili peasants how best to avoid hookworm and elephantiasis. Instead of the cultured, rather decadent aristocracy of the Oman Arabs, we have given them a caste of just, soap-loving young men with public-school blazers. And these young men have made the place safe for the Indians.

We came to establish a Christian civilization and we have come very near to establishing a Hindu one.

The town is, I suppose, as good an example of Arabic eighteenth-century architecture as survives intact anywhere.

In the time of Burton it must have been a city of great beauty and completeness. Now there is not a single Arab in any of the great Arab houses; there are, instead, counting houses full of Indian clerks or flats inhabited by cosy British families.

I went to Pemba for two nights. It is all cloves, coconuts, and tarmac, very much like the interior of Zanzibar. On the night of my departure I witnessed a highly acrimonious dispute about the allotment of Christmas presents. My hosts were two elderly bachelors. They were giving a joint Christmas party to the European children of the island, and a fine heap of toys had arrived for them in the *Halifa* for distribution to their guests. They rehearsed the business with chairs for children. 'This will do for So-and-So's little boy,' and 'This for So-and-So's girl,' and 'Have the So-and-So's got two children or three?' At first it was all very harmonious and Dickensian. Then suspicion of favouritism arose over the allocation of a particularly large, brightly painted indiarubber ball. 'Mary — ought to have it; she's a sweet little thing.' 'Peter —'s brother has just gone to school in England. He's terribly lonely, poor kiddy.' The ball was put first on one dump, then on the other; sometimes it rolled off and bounced between them. 'Sweet little thing' and 'Lonely kiddy' became battle-cries as the big ball was snatched backwards and forwards. It was an odd sight to see these two hot men struggling over the toy. Presently came the inevitable 'All right. Do as you like. I wash my hands of the whole thing. I won't come to the party.' Renunciation was immediately mutual. There was a sudden reversal of the situation; each party tried to force the ball upon the other one's candidate. I cautiously eschewed any attempts at arbitration. Finally peace was made. I forget on what terms, but, as far as I remember, the ball was given to a third child and all the other heaps were despoiled to compensate Mary and Peter. They certainly came very well out of the business. Later that evening I went back to the *Halifa*. Some of my new friends came to see me off. We woke up the Goan steward and persuaded him to make lemon squash for us. Then we wished one another a happy Christmas, for it was past midnight, and parted. Early next morning we sailed for Zanzibar, arriving at tea-time. My mail had not yet come.

Christmas seemed very unreal, divorced from its usual Teutonic associations of yule logs, reindeer, and rum punch. A few of the Indian storekeepers in the main street had decked their windows with tinsel, crackers, and iridescent artificial snow; there was a homely crèche in the cathedral; beggars appeared with the commendation 'Me velly Clistian boy'; there was a complete cessation of the little club life that had flourished before.

Eventually the mail arrived, and I was able to leave for Kenya. I took an almost empty Italian liner. Her few passengers were nearly all restful people taking a few days' holiday on the water. The best thing about this ship was a nice old cinematograph; the worst was a plague of small blackbeetles which overran the cabins and died in vast numbers in the baths. An English lady declared that she had been severely stung by one in the back of the neck. She and her husband were from Nairobi. It was the first time they had seen the sea since their arrival in the country eleven years before. The husband was a manufacturer of bricks. The trouble about his bricks, he said, was that they did not last very long; sometimes they crumbled away before they had been laid; but he was hopeful of introducing a new method before long.

We stopped at Dar-es-Salaam. I visited the agent of the Belgian Congo and explained that I had an idea of returning to Europe by way of the west coast. He was sympathetic to the idea and told me of an air service running weekly between Albertville and Boma; the fare was negligible, the convenience extreme. He showed me a time-table of the flight. It was two years old. He had not yet received the new one, but, he assured me, I could be confident that any changes that might have been made would be changes for the better. I believed him.

On the last day of the year we arrived at Mombasa, where my whole time was occupied with the immigration officers.

But my ill temper gradually cooled as the train, with periodic derailments (three, to be exact, between Mombasa and Nairobi) climbed up from the coast into the highlands. In the restaurant

160

car that evening I sat opposite a young lady who was on her way to be married. She told me that she had worked for two years in Scotland Yard and that that had coarsened her mind; but since then she had refined it again in a bank at Dar-es-Salaam. She was glad to be getting married as it was impossible to obtain fresh butter in Dar-es-Salaam.

I awoke during the night to draw up my blanket. It was a novel sensation, after so many weeks, not to be sweating. Next morning I changed from white drill to grey flannel. We arrived in Nairobi a little before lunch time. I took a taxi out to Muthaiga Club. There was no room for me there, but the secretary had been told of my coming and I found I was already a temporary member. In the bar were several people I had met in the *Explorateur Grandidier*, and some I knew in London. They were drinking pink gin in impressive quantities. Someone said, 'You mustn't think Kenya is always like this.' I found myself involved in a luncheon party. We went on together to the Races. Someone gave me a cardboard disc to wear in my buttonhole; someone else, called Raymond, introduced me to a bookie and told me what horses to back. None of them won. When I offered the bookie some money he said in a rather sinister way, 'Any friend of Mr de Trafford's is a friend of mine. We'll settle up at the end of the meeting.'

Someone took me to a marquee where we drank champagne. When I wanted to pay for my round the barman gave me a little piece of paper to sign and a cigar.

We went back to Muthaiga and drank champagne out of a silver cup which someone had just won.

Someone said, 'You mustn't think Kenya is always like this.'

There was a young man in a sombrero hat, trimmed with snake skin. He stopped playing dice, at which he had just dropped twenty-five pounds, and asked me to come to a dinner party at Torrs. Raymond and I went back there to change.

On the way up we stopped in the bar to have a cocktail. A man in an orange shirt asked if we either of us wanted a fight. We both said we did. He said, 'Have a drink instead.'

That evening it was a very large dinner-party, taking up all one side of the ballroom at Torrs. The young lady next to me said, 'You mustn't think that Kenya is always like this.'

After some time we went on to Muthaiga.

There was a lovely American called Kiki, whom I had met before. She had just got up. She said, 'You'll like Kenya. It's always like this.'

Next morning I woke up in a very comfortable bedroom; the native boy who brought my orange juice said I was at Torrs.

I had forgotten all about Mombasa and the immigration officers.

At the end of Race Week, Raymond and I left Nairobi and drove through the Rift Valley to Lake Naivasha. A bad road; red earth cut into deep ruts; one of the best roads in the country. On the way we pass other settlers returning to their farms; they wear bright shirts and wide felt hats; they drive box-body cars, in most cases heaped with miscellaneous hardware they have been buying at the capital; groups of Kikuyu, the women with heavy luggage on their backs supported by a strap round their foreheads; their ears are slit and ornamented; their clothes of copper-coloured skins; the men have mostly made some effort at European dress in the form of discarded khaki shorts or an old hat. They attempt a clumsy kind of salute as we pass, smiling and saying 'Jambo bwana', rather as children in England still wave their pocket handkerchiefs to trains.

The scenery is tremendous, finer than anything I saw in Abyssinia; all round for immense distances successive crests of highland. In England we call it a good view if we can see a church spire across six fields; the phrase, made comic by the Frankaus of magazine fiction, 'Wide Open Spaces', really does mean something here. Brilliant sunshine quite unobscured, uninterrupted in its incidence; sunlight clearer than daylight; there is something of the moon about it, the coolness seems so unsuitable. Amber sunlight in Europe; diamond sunlight in Africa. The air fresh as an advertisement for toothpaste.

We are going to stay with Kiki. She lives in a single-storeyed, very luxurious house on the edge of the Lake. She came to Kenya for a short Christmas visit. Someone asked her why she did not stay longer. She explained that she had nowhere particular to go. So he gave her two or three miles of lake front for a Christmas

162

present. She has lived there off and on ever since. She has a husband who shoots most sorts of animals, and a billiard-room to accommodate their heads. She also has two children and a monkey, which sleeps on her pillow.

It was lovely at Naivasha; the grass ran down from the house to the water, where there was a bathing-place with a little jetty to take one clear of the rushes. We used to swim in the morning, eat huge luncheons and sleep in the afternoon. Kiki appeared soon after tea. There were small, hot sausages at cocktail time. Once Kiki and I went for a walk as far as some ants, fifty yards up the garden. She said 'You must just feel how they can sting,' and lifted a very large one on to the back of my hand with a leaf. It stung frightfully. More than that, several others ran up the leg of my trousers and began stinging there.

In Kenya it is easy to forget that one is in Africa; then one is reminded of it suddenly, and the awakening is agreeable. One day before luncheon we were sitting on the terrace with cocktails. Kiki's husband and a General were discussing someone they had blackballed for White's; Raymond was teaching chemin-de-fer to Kiki's little boy; there was a striped awning over our heads and a gramophone – all very much like the South of France. Suddenly a Kikuyu woman came lolloping over the lawn, leading a little boy by the hand. She said she wanted a pill for her son. She explained the sort of pain he had. Kiki's husband called his valet and translated the explanation of the pain. The valet advised soda-mint. When he brought it, the woman held out her hand but they – to the woman's obvious displeasure – insisted on giving it directly to the child. 'Otherwise she would eat it herself the moment she was round the corner.' The Kikuyu have a passion for pills equalled only in English Bohemia; they come at all hours to beg for them.

After a time Kiki made a sudden appearance before breakfast, wearing jodhpurs and carrying two heavy-bore guns. She had decided to go and kill some lions.

So Raymond and I went to his house at Njoro.

One does not – or at any rate I did not – look upon farming as the occupation of a bachelor. The large number of bachelor farmers was, to me, one of the surprising things about Kenya.

Raymond is one, though perhaps he is more typically bachelor than farmer. I spent about a fortnight with him off and on at Njoro; sometimes he was away for a day or two, sometimes I was. A delightful if rather irregular visit. His cook was away all the time. There was a head boy called Dunston who spent most of the day squatting outside cooking bath water on a wood fire. I learned some words of Swahili. When I woke up I said, 'Woppe chickule, Dunston?' which meant, 'Where is food, Dunston?' Dunston replied, 'Hapana chickule, bwana,' which meant, 'No food, my lord.' Sometimes I had no breakfast; sometimes I found Raymond, if he was at home, sitting up in bed with a tin of grouse paste and a bottle of soda water, and forced him to share these things with me; sometimes, if the telephone was working, I rang up Mrs Grant, the nearest neighbour, and had breakfast with her. We used to lunch and dine at the Njoro golf club or with the neighbours; very friendly dinner parties, Irish in character, to which we bounced over miles of cart track in a motor van which Raymond had just acquired in exchange for his car; it was full of gadgets designed to help him capture gorillas in the Eturi forest – a new idea of Raymond's, prompted by the information that they fetched two thousand pounds a head at the Berlin Zoo – but was less comfortable than the car for ordinary social use.

The houses of Kenya are mainly in that style of architecture which derives from intermittent prosperity. In many of them the living-rooms are in separate buildings from the bedrooms; their plan is usually complicated by a system of additions and annexes which have sprung up in past years as the result of a good crop, a sudden burst of optimism, the influx of guests from England, the birth of children, the arrival of pupil-farmers, or any of the chances of domestic life. In many houses there is sadder evidence of building begun and abandoned when the bad times came on. Inside they are, as a rule, surprisingly comfortable. Up an un-fenced cart-track, one approaches a shed made of concrete, matchboarding, and corrugated iron, and, on entering, finds oneself among old furniture, books, and framed miniatures.

There are very few gardens; we went to one a few miles outside Njoro where an exquisite hostess in golden slippers led us down grass paths bordered with clipped box, over Japanese bridges, pools of water-lilies, and towering tropical plants. But few settlers have time for these luxuries.

'Boy' and Genessie, with whom I spent a week-end, have one of the stately homes of Kenya; three massive stone buildings on the crest of a hill at Elmentaita overlooking Lake Nakuru, in the centre of an estate which includes almost every topographical feature – grass, bush forest, rock, river, waterfall, and a volcanic cleft down which we scrambled on the end of a rope.

On the borders a bush fire is raging, a low-lying cloud by day, at night a red glow along the horizon. The fire dominates the week-end. We watch anxiously for any change in the wind; cars are continually going out to report progress; extra labour is mustered and despatched to 'burn a brake'; will the flames 'jump' the railroad? The pasture of hundreds of head of cattle is threatened.

In the evening we go down to the lakeside to shoot duck; thousands of flamingo lie on the water; at the first shot they rise in a cloud, like dust from a beaten carpet; they are the colour of pink alabaster; they wheel round and settle farther out. The head of a hippopotamus emerges a hundred yards from shore and yawns at us. When it is dark the hippo comes out for his evening walk. We sit very still, huddled along the running-boards of the cars. We can hear heavy footsteps and the water dripping off him; then he scratches himself noisily. We turn the spotlight of the car on him and reveal a great mud-caked body and a pair of resentful little pink eyes; then he trots back into the water.

Again the enchanting contradictions of Kenya life; a baronial hall straight from Queen Victoria's Scottish Highlands – an open fire of logs and peat with carved-stone chimney-piece, heads of game, the portraits of prize cattle, guns, golf-clubs, fishing-tackle, and folded newspapers – sherry is brought in, but, instead of a waistcoated British footman, a bare-footed Kikuyu boy in white gown and red jacket. A typical English meadow of deep grass; model cowsheds in the background; a pedigree Ayrshire bull scratching his back on the gatepost; but, instead of rabbits, a company of monkeys scutter away at our approach; and, instead of a smocked yokel, a Masai herdsman draped in a blanket, his hair plaited into a dozen dyed pigtails.

I returned to Njoro to find Raymond deeply involved in preparations for his gorilla hunt; guns, cameras, telescopes, revolvers, tinned food, and medicine chests littered tables and floors. There was also a case of champagne. 'You have to have that to give to Belgian officials – and, anyway, it's always useful.'

That evening I dined with the Grants. They had an English-woman staying with them whose daughter had been in the party at Genessie's. It had been arranged that we should all climb Mount Kilimanjaro together; this plan, however, was modified, and, instead, we decided to go to Uganda. I wanted to visit Kisumu, so it was decided that they should pick me up there on the follow-ing Sunday. Next day I watched Raymond loading his van, and that evening we had a heavy evening at the Njoro club. Early the day after, I took the train for Kisumu.

I was going second class. My companion in the carriage was a ginger-haired young man a few years older than myself; he had an acquaintance with whom he discussed technicalities of local legislation; later this man got out and we were left alone. For some time we did not speak to each other. It was a tedious journey. I tried to read a copy of Burton's *Anatomy of Melancholy* which I had stolen from Raymond's shelves. Presently he said, 'Going far?'

'Kisumu.'

'What on earth for?'

'No particular reason. I thought I might like it.'

Pause. 'You're new in the country, aren't you?'

'Yes.'

'I thought you must be. Kisumu's bloody.'

Presently he said again: 'What have you seen so far?'

I told him briefly.

'Yes, that's all most visitors see. They're delightful people, mind you, but they aren't typical of Kenya.'

Two or three stations went by without any further conversation. Then he began getting together his luggage – a kit bag, some baskets, a small packing-case, and an iron stove-pipe. 'Look here. You won't like Kisumu. You'd far better stay with me the night.'

'All right.'

'Good.'

We got out at a station near the Nandi escarpment and trans-ferred his luggage to a Ford van that was waiting some distance away in charge of an Indian shopkeeper.

'I hope you don't mind; I've got to see my brother-in-law first. It isn't more than thirty miles out of the way.'

We drove a great distance along a rough track through country of supreme beauty. At cross roads the signposts simply bore the names of the settlers. Eventually we arrived at the house. There were several people there, among them a man I had been at school with. Until then my host and I did not know each other's names. There was an Italian garden, with trimmed yew hedges and grass, balustraded terrace, and a vista of cypresses; in the distance the noble horizon of the Nandi hills; after sundown these came alight with little points of fire from the native villages; the household was playing poker under a thatched shelter. My host transacted his business; we drank a glass of Bristol Cream and continued the journey. It was now quite dark. Another very long drive. At last we reached our destination. A boy came out to greet us with a lantern, followed by an elderly lady – my host's mother-in-law. 'I thought you were dead,' she said. 'And who is this?'

'He's come to stay. I've forgotten his name.'

'You'll be very uncomfortable; there's nothing in the home to eat and there are three swarms of bees in the dining-room.' Then, turning to her son-in-law: 'Belinda's hind-quarters are totally paralysed.'

This referred, not, as I assumed, to her daughter, but, I learned later, to a wolfhound bitch.

We went up to the house – a spacious, single-storeyed building typical of the colony. I made some polite comment on it.

'Glad you like it. I built most of it myself.'

'It is the third we have had in this spot,' remarked the old lady. 'The other two were destroyed. The first caught fire; the second was struck by lightning. All the furniture I brought out from England was demolished. I have had dinner prepared three nights running. Now there is nothing.'

There was, however, an excellent dinner waiting for us after

167

we had had baths and changed into pyjamas. We spent the evening dealing with the bees, who, at nightfall, had disposed themselves for sleep in various drawers and cupboards about the living-room. They lay in glutinous, fermenting masses, crawling over each other, like rotten cheese under the microscope; a fair number flew about the room stinging us as we dined, while a few abandoned outposts lurked among the embroidered linen sheets in the bedrooms. A subdued humming filled the entire house. Baths of boiling water were brought in, and the torpid insects were shovelled into them by a terrified native boy. Some of the furniture was carried out on to the lawn to await our attention in the morning.

Next day we walked round the farm – a coffee plantation. Later, a surveyor of roads arrived and we drove all over the countryside pointing out defective culverts. During the rains, the old lady told me, the farm was sometimes isolated from its neighbours for weeks at a time. We saw a bridge being built under the supervision, apparently, of a single small boy in gumboots. Poor Belinda lay in a basket on the verandah, while over her head a grey and crimson parrot heartlessly imitated her groans.

The surveyor took me to the station for the afternoon train to Kisumu – a town which proved as dreary as my host had predicted – numerous brand-new, nondescript houses, a small landing-stage and railway junction, a population entirely Indian or official. The hotel was full; I shared a bedroom with an Irish airman who was prospecting for the Imperial Airways route to the Cape. Next day, Sunday, I went to church and heard a rousing denunciation of birth-control by a young Mill Hill Father. The manager of the hotel took me for a drive in his car to a Kavirondo village where the people still wore no clothes except discarded Homburg hats. Then Mrs Grant arrived with her party.

We drove to Eldoret and stayed at one more house, the most English I had yet seen – old silver, family portraits, chintz-frilled dressing-tables – and next day crossed the frontier into Uganda.

There was nothing, however, to mark the frontiers of the two territories. We crossed sometime during the morning and arrived at Jinja in the late afternoon.

At Jinja there is both hotel and golf links. The latter is, I believe, the only course in the world which posts a special rule that the player may remove his ball by hand from hippopotamus footprints. For there is a very old hippopotamus who inhabits this corner of the lake. Long before the dedication of the Ripon Falls it was his practice to take an evening stroll over that part of the bank which now constitutes the town of Jinja. He has remained set in his habit, despite railway lines and bungalows. At first, attempts were made to shoot him, but lately he has come to be regarded as a local mascot, and people returning late from bridge parties not infrequently see him lurching home down the main street. Now and then he varies his walk by a detour across the golf links and it is then that the local rule is brought into force.

There were several big-game hunters staying in the hotel, so that there was not room for all of us. Accordingly I went off to the Government rest-house. These vary in range from small hotels to unfurnished shelters. At Jinja there was a bedstead and mattress, but no sheets or blankets. I had just made a collection of the overcoats of the party when we saw a black face grinning at us from below the hotel steps. It was Dunston, hat in hand, come to report the loss of Raymond. He and the neighbour who was joining his gorilla hunt had gone on in a car, leaving Dunston and the native driver to follow in the van. Somewhere they had missed the road. Anyway, here was the van with the rifles and provisions and 'Hapana bwana de Trafford'. Dunston wanted orders. We told him to take bwana de Trafford's blankets to the rest-house, make up the bed, and then wait for further instructions. Meanwhile we wired to Eldoret, Njoro, and Nairobi, reporting the position of Raymond's lorry. I do not know whether he ever found it, for we left next morning for Kampala.

Here I said good-bye to my companions and established myself at the hotel. I was becoming conscious of an inclination to return to Europe and wanted to get down to Albertville and the Belgian air service as soon as I could.

I left Kampala on the following Sunday afternoon. The

Rusinga, in which I travelled down the lake, was a comfortable little boat staffed with four smart officers who wore white and gold uniforms in the mornings and blue and gold at night. On Wednesday I disembarked at Mwanza, a deadly little town populated chiefly by Indians. I had to share a room at the inn with a C.M.S. chaplain. At meals I sat with him and an elderly 'tough-egg' from Manchester, engaged in the cotton trade. At least he was so engaged until Thursday morning. He had come down from the south to meet his local manager. When he returned from the interview I asked, with what I hoped would be acceptable jocularity, 'Well, did you get the sack?'

'Yes,' he answered, 'as a matter of fact, I did. How the devil did you know?'

An unfortunate episode.

Later at luncheon he got rather drunk and told some very unsuitable anecdotes about a baboon. The missionary went off immediately to write letters in the bedroom. That evening we took the train to Tabora and arrived at noon next day. I travelled with the missionary, a courteous man.

We also discussed the rite of female circumcision, which is one of the battlegrounds between missionaries and anthropologists. The missionary told me of an interesting experiment that was being made in his district. 'We found it impossible to eradicate the practice,' he said, 'but we have cleansed it of most of its objectionable features. The operation is now performed by my wife, in the wholesome atmosphere of the church hut.'

Perhaps it is by arrangement with the hotel proprietors that every change of train involves the delay of a night or two. It was not until late on Sunday evening that I could get my connexion to Kigoma. Even in Africa the hotel at Tabora is outstandingly desolate. It is very large and old. In the optimistic days of German imperialism it was built to provide the amusement of an important garrison. It is now rapidly falling to pieces under the management of a dispirited Greek.

The town is not without interest. It reflects the various stages of its history. Fine groves of mango remain to record the days of Arab occupation, when it was the principal clearing station for slaves and ivory on the caravan route to the coast. Acacia trees, a fort, and that sad hotel remain from the days of German East Africa. England's chief contribution is a large public school for the education of the sons of chiefs. It is a huge concrete building of two storeys, planted prominently on one of the most unsuitable sites in the territory for the agricultural demonstrations that are the principal feature of its training. At first it was intended exclusively for future chiefs, but now it has been opened to other promising natives. They wear crested blazers and little rugger caps; they have prefects and 'colours'; they have a brass band; they learn farming, typewriting, English, physical drill, and public-school *esprit de corps*. They have honour boards, on which the name of one boy is inscribed every year. Since there were no particular honours for which they could compete – Makerere was far above their wildest ambitions – it was originally the practice of the boys to elect their champion. Elections, however, proved so unaccountably capricious that nomination soon took their place. I was invited to attend a *sahri* (the local word for any kind of discussion). This was a meeting of the whole school, at which the prefects dealt with any misdemeanours. They sat in chairs on a dais; the school squatted on the floor of the great hall. Three boys were called up; two had smoked; one had refused to plough. They were sentenced to be caned. Resisting strongly, they were pinioned to the ground by their friends while the drill-sergeant, an old soldier from the K.A.R., delivered two or three strokes with a cane. It was a far lighter punishment than any at an English public school, but it had the effect of inducing yells of agony and the most extravagant writhings. Apparently this part of the public-school system had not been fully assimilated.

That evening an opinionated little Austrian sisal-farmer arrived at the hotel, full of ridicule of British administration. He had just returned to the farm he had worked before the war, as Germans and Austrians are now doing in large numbers. He was confident that after a few more years of British management the territory would have to be handed back to Germany. 'Before the war,' he said, 'every native had to salute every European or he knew the reason why. Now, with all this education ...'

On Saturday evening I went to an Indian cinema and saw an Indian film – a costume piece derived from a traditional fairy-story. A kindly Indian next to me helped me with the plot, explaining, 'That is a bad man', 'That is an elephant', etc. When he wished to tell me that the hero had fallen in love with the heroine – a situation sufficiently apparent from their extravagant gestures of passion – he said, 'He wants to take her into the bushes.'

Late in the evening I caught the train.

Kigoma is a haphazard spatter of bungalows differing very little from the other lakeside stations I had passed through, except in the size and apparent disorder of its wharfs and goods yard. The lake steamers belong to the Belgian Chemin de Fer des Grands Lacs; notices everywhere are in French and Flemish; there are the offices of Belgian immigration authorities, vice-consulate, and customs; a huge unfinished building of the Congo trading company. But the impression that I had already left British soil was dissipated almost at once by the spectacle of a pair of Tanganyika policemen who stood with the ticket collector at the station door and forcibly vaccinated the native passengers as they passed through.

It was now about noon and the heat was overpowering. I was anxious to get my luggage on board, but it had to be left at the customs sheds for examination when the official had finished his luncheon. A group of natives were squatting in the road, savages with filed teeth and long hair, very black, with broad shoulders and spindly legs, dressed in bits of skin and rag. A White Father of immense stature drove up in a box-body lorry containing crates, sacks, and nuns for transhipment; a red and wiry beard spread itself over his massive chest; clouds of dense, acrid smoke rose from his cheroot.

There was a little Greek restaurant in the main street, where I lunched and, after luncheon, sat on the verandah waiting for the customs office to open. A continual traffic of natives passed to and fro – most of them, in from the country, far less civilized than any I had seen since the Somalis; a few, in shirts, trousers, and hats, were obviously in European employment; one of them rode a bicycle and fell off it just in front of the restaurant; he looked very rueful when he got up, but when the passers-by laughed at him he began to laugh too and went off thoroughly pleased with himself as though he had made a good joke.

By about three I got my luggage clear, then after another long wait bought my ticket, and finally had my passport examined by British and Belgian officials. I was then able to go on board the *Duc de Brabant*. She was a shabby, wood-burning steamer, with passenger accommodation in the poop consisting of a stuffy little deck-saloon, with two or three cabins below and a padlocked lavatory. The short deck was largely taken up by the captain's quarters – an erection like a two-roomed bungalow, containing a brass double bedstead with mosquito-curtains, numerous tables and chairs, cushions, photograph frames, mirrors, clocks, china and metal ornaments, greasy cretonnes and torn muslin, seedy little satin bows and ribbons, pots of dried grasses, pin-cushions, every conceivable sort of cheap and unseamanlike knick-knack. Clearly there was a woman on board. I found her knitting on the shady side of the deckhouse. I asked her about cabins. She said her husband was asleep and was not to be disturbed until five. Gross snoring and grunting from the mosquito-curtains gave substance to her statement. There were three people asleep in the saloon. I went on shore again and visited the Congo agency, where I inquired about my aeroplane to Leopoldville. They were polite, but quite unhelpful. I must ask at Albertville.

Soon after five the captain appeared. No one, looking at him, would have connected him in any way with a ship; a very fat, very dirty man, a stained tunic open at his throat, unshaven, with a straggling moustache, crimson-faced, gummy-eyed, flat-footed. He would have seemed more at home as proprietor of an *estaminet*. A dozen or so passengers had now assembled – we were due to sail at six – and the captain lumbered round examining our tickets and passports. Everyone began claiming cabins. He would see to all that when we sailed, he said. When he came to me he said, 'Where is your medical certificate?'

I said I had not got one.

'It is forbidden to sail without a medical certificate.'

I explained that I had been given a visa, had bought a ticket, had had my passport examined twice by British and Belgian officials, but that no one had said anything to me about a medical certificate.

'I regret it is forbidden to travel. You must get one.'

'But a certificate of what? What do you want certified?'

'It is no matter to me what is certified. You must find a doctor and get him to sign. Otherwise you cannot sail.'

This was three-quarters of an hour before the advertised time of departure. I hurried on shore and inquired where I could find a doctor. I was directed to a hospital some distance from the town, at the top of the hill. I set out walking feverishly. Every now and then the steamer gave a whistle which set me going at a jog trot for a few paces. At last, streaming with sweat, I reached the hospital. It turned out to be a club house; the hospital was about two miles away on the other side of the town. Another whistle from the *Duc de Brabant*. I pictured her sailing away across the lake with all my baggage, money, and credentials. I explained my difficulty to a native servant; he did not at all understand what I wanted, but he caught the word doctor. I suppose he thought I was ill. Anyway, he lent me a boy to take me to a doctor's house. I set off again at high speed, to the disgust of my guide, and finally reached a bungalow where an Englishwoman was sitting in the garden with needlework and a book. No, her husband was not at home. Was it anything urgent?

I explained my predicament. She thought I might be able to find him on the shore; he might be there at work on his speed-boat, or else he might be playing tennis, or perhaps he had taken the car out to Ujiji. I had better try the shore first.

Down the hill again, this time across country over a golf course and expanses of scrub. Sure enough, at one of the landing stages about quarter of a mile from the *Duc de Brabant*, I found two Englishmen fiddling with a motor-boat. One of them was the doctor. I shouted down to him what I wanted. It took him some time to find any paper. In the end his friend gave him an old envelope. He sat down in the stern and wrote: '*I have examined Mr*' – 'What's your name?' – '*Waugh, and find him free from infectious disease, including omnis t.b. and trypanosomiasis. He has been vaccinated.*' – 'Five shillings, please.'

I handed down the money; he handed up the certificate. That was that.

It was ten past six when I reached the *Duc de Brabant*, but she was still there With a grateful heart I panted up the gangway and presented my certificate. When I had got my breath a little I explained to a sympathetic Greek the narrow escape I had had of being left behind. But I need not have hurried. It was a little after midnight before we sailed.

The boat was now very full. On our deck there were four or five Belgian officials and their wives, two mining engineers, and several Greek traders. There was also a plump young man with a pallid face and soft American voice. Unlike anyone I had seen for the past month, he wore a neat, dark suit, white collar and bow tie. He had a great deal of very neat luggage, including a typewriter and a bicycle. I offered him a drink and he said, 'Oh, no, thank you,' in a tone which in four monosyllables contrived to express first surprise, then pain, then reproof, and finally forgiveness. Later I found that he was a member of the Seventh Day Adventist mission, on his way to audit accounts at Bulawayo.

The waist and forecastle were heaped with mail-bags and freight over which sprawled and scurried a medley of animals and native passengers. There were goats and calves and chickens, naked Negro children, native soldiers, women suckling babies or carrying them slung between their shoulders, young girls with their hair plaited into pigtails, which divided their scalps into symmetrical patches, girls with shaven pates and with hair caked in red mud, old Negresses with bundles of bananas, overdressed women with yellow and red cotton shawls and brass bangles, Negro workmen in shorts, vests, and crumpled topees. There were several little stoves and innumerable pots of boiling banana. Bursts of singing and laughing.

They laid the tables in our saloon for dinner. We sat tightly packed at benches. There were three or four small children who were fed at the table. Two ragged servants cooked and served a very bad dinner. The captain collected the money. Presently he passed round a list of those to whom he had given cabins. I was not among them, nor was the American missionary nor any of the Greeks. We should have slipped him a tip with our tickets, I learned later. About a dozen of us were left without accommodation. Six wise men laid themselves out full length on the saloon benches immediately after dinner and established their claim for the night. The rest of us sat on our luggage on the deck. There were no seats or deck-chairs. Luckily it was a fine night, warm, unclouded, and windless. I spread an overcoat on the deck, placed a canvas grip under my head as a pillow and composed myself for sleep. The missionary found two little wooden chairs and sat stiff backed, wrapped in a rug, with his feet up supporting a book of Bible stories on his knees. As we got up steam, brilliant showers of wood sparks rose from the funnel; soon after midnight we sailed into the lake; a gentle murmur of singing came from the bows. In a few minutes I was asleep.

I woke up suddenly an hour later and found myself shivering with cold. I stood up to put on my overcoat and immediately found myself thrown against the rail. At the same moment I saw the missionary's two chairs tip over sideways and him sprawl on the deck. A large pile of hand luggage upset and slid towards the side. There was a tinkle of broken china from the captain's quarters. All this coincided with a torrential downpour of rain and a tearing wind. It was followed in a second or two by a blaze of lightning and shattering detonation. A chatter of alarm went up from the lower deck, and the various protests of disturbed livestock. In the half-minute which it took us to collect our luggage and get into the saloon we were soaked with rain. And here we were in scarcely better conditions, for the windows, when raised, proved not to be of glass, but of wire gauze. The wind tore through them, water poured in and slopped from side to side. Women passengers came up squealing from their cabins below, with colourless, queasy faces. The saloon became intolerably overcrowded. We sat as we had at dinner, packed in rows round the two tables. The wind was so strong that it was impossible, single-handed, to open the door. Those who were ill – the American missionary was the first to go under – were obliged to remain in their places. The shriek of the wind was so loud that conversation was impossible; we just clung there pitched and thrown, now out of our seats, now on top of one another; occasionally someone would fall asleep and wake up instantly with his head thumped hard against table or wall. It needed constant muscular effort to avoid injury. Vile retchings occurred on every side. Women whimpered at their husbands for support. The children yelled. We were all of us dripping and shivering. At last everyone grew quieter as alarm subsided and desperation took its place. They sat there, rigid and glum, gazing straight before them or supporting their heads in their hands until, a little before dawn, the wind dropped and rain ceased beating in; then some of them fell asleep and others slunk back to their cabins. I went out on deck. It was still extremely cold, and the little boat bobbed and wallowed hopelessly in a heavy sea, but the storm was clearly over. Soon a green and silver dawn broke over the lake; it was misty all round us, and the orange sparks from the funnel were just visible against the whiter sky. The two stewards emerged with chattering teeth and attempted to set things to order in the saloon, dragging out rolls of sodden matting and swabbing up the water-logged floor. Huddled groups on the lower deck began to disintegrate and a few cocks crowed; there was a clatter of breakfast cups and a welcome smell of coffee.

It was raining again before we reached harbour and moored against an unfinished concrete pier, where dripping convicts were working, chained together in gangs. Albertville was almost hidden in mist; a blur of white buildings against the obscurer background. Two rival hotel proprietors stood under umbrellas shouting for custom; one was Belgian, the other Greek. Officials came on board. We queued up and presented our papers one at a time. The inevitable questions: Why was I coming into the Congo? How much money had I? How long did I propose to stay there? Where was my medical certificate? the inevitable form to fill in – this time in duplicate: Date and place of father's birth? Mother's maiden name? Maiden name of divorced wife? Habitual domicile? By this time I had learned not to reveal the uncertainty of my plans. I told them I was going direct to Matadi and was given a certificate of entry which I was to present to the immigration officer at the frontier. It took two hours before we were allowed to land.

Quite suddenly the rain stopped and the sun came out. Everything began to steam.

I spent two nights at Albertville. It consists of a single street of offices, shops, and bungalows. There are two hotels catering for visitors in transit to and from Tanganyika; no cinemas or places of amusement. There are white people serving in the shops and white clerks at the railway station; no natives live in the town except a handful of dockers and domestic servants. I spend my time making inquiries about the air service. No one knows anything about it. One thing is certain, that there has never been an air service at Albertville. They think there was one once at Kabalo; that there still may be. Anyway, there is a train to Kabalo the day after tomorrow. There is no alternative; one can either take the train to Kabalo or the boat back to Kigoma; there are no other means of communication in any direction. With some apprehension of coming discomfort, I purchase a ticket to Kabalo.

The train left at seven in the morning and made the journey in a little under eleven hours, counting a halt for luncheon at the wayside. It is an uneven line; so uneven that at times I was hardly able to read. I travelled first class to avoid the American missionary, and had the carriage to myself. For half the day it rained. The scenery was attractive at first; we pitched and rocked through a wooded valley with a background of distant hills, and later along the edge of a river broken by islands of vivid swamp. Towards midday, however, we came into bush country, featureless and dismal; there was no game to be seen, only occasional clouds of white butterflies; in the afternoon we jolted over mile upon mile of track cut through high grass, which grew right up on either side of the single line to the height of the carriages, completely shutting out all view, but mercifully shading us from the afternoon sun.

It was just before sundown when we reached Kabalo, a place of forbidding aspect. There was no platform; a heap of wood-fuel and the abrupt termination of the line marked the station; there were other bits of line sprawling out to right and left; a few shabby trucks had been shunted on one of these, and apparently abandoned; there were two or three goods sheds of corrugated iron and a dirty little canteen; apart from these, no evidence of habitation. In front of us lay the Upper Congo – at this stage of its course undistinguished among the great rivers of the world for any beauty or interest; a broad flow of water, bounded by swamps; since we were in the rainy season, it was swollen and brown. A barge or two lay in to the bank, and a paddle steamer, rusted all over, which was like a flooded Thames bungalow more than a ship. A bit of the bank opposite the railway line had been buttressed up with concrete; on all sides lay rank swamp. Mercifully, night soon came on and hid this beastly place.

I hired a boy to sit on my luggage, and went into the canteen. There, through a haze of mosquitoes, I discerned a prominent advertisement of the Kabalo – Matadi air service; two or three railway officials were squatting about on stiff little chairs swilling tepid beer. There was a surly and dishevelled woman slopping round in bedroom slippers, with a tray of dirty glasses. In answer to my inquiry, she pointed out the patron, a torpid lump fanning himself in the only easy chair. I asked him when the next aeroplane left for the coast; everyone stopped talking and stared at me when I put this question. The patron giggled. He did not know when the *next* would leave; the *last* went about ten months ago. There were only two ways of leaving Kabalo; either by train back to Albertville or by river. The *Prince Leopold* was due that evening for Bukama.

At this stage one of the railway officials interposed helpfully. There were trains from Bukama to a place called Port Francqui. If I wired, and if the wire ever reached its destination, I could arrange for the Elisabethville–Matadi air service to pick me up there. Failing that, I could get from Bukama on to the newly-opened Benguela railway and come out on the coast at Lobita Bay in Portuguese West Africa. In any case, I had better go to Bukama. Kabalo, he remarked, was a dull place to stay in.

Two hours passed and there was no sign of the *Prince Leopold*. We ate a frightful (and very expensive) meal in the canteen. The Seventh Day Adventist came in from the railway line, where he had been sitting in the dark in order to avoid the sight and smell of beer-drinking. He was travelling by the *Prince Leopold*, too. Another two hours and she arrived. We went on board that night and sailed at dawn.

The journey took four days.

The *Prince Leopold* was a large paddle-steamer, twice the size

179

of the *Rusinga*, with half the staff. The captain and a Greek steward seemed to do all the work; the former young and neurotic, the latter middle-aged and imperturbable, both very grubby. It was a great contrast to all those dapper bachelors on Lake Victoria, with their white collars and changes of uniform. We stopped two or three times a day at desolate little stations. We delivered mail, took up cargo, and occasionally effected some change of passengers. These were all Greek or Belgian; either traders or officials; except for the inevitable round of handshaking each morning there was very little intercourse. The Seventh Day Adventist became slightly ill; he attributed his discomfort to the weakness of the tea. The scenery was utterly dreary, flat papyrus-swamps on either side broken by rare belts of palm. The captain employed his time in inflicting slight wounds on passing antelope with a miniature rifle. Occasionally he would be convinced that he had killed something; the boat would stop and all the native passengers disembark and scramble up the side with loud whoops and yodels. There was difficulty in getting them back. The captain would watch them, through binoculars, plunging and gambolling about in the high grass; at first he would take an interest in the quest, shouting directions to them; then he would grow impatient and summon them back; they would disappear further and further, thoroughly enjoying their romp. He would have the siren sounded for them – blast after blast. Eventually they would come back jolly, chattering, and invariably empty-handed.

We were due to arrive at Bukama on Sunday (February 8th). The train for Port Francqui did not leave until the following Tuesday night. It was customary for passengers to wait on board, an arrangement that was profitable to the company and comparatively comfortable for them. I was prevented from doing this by a violent and inglorious altercation with the captain, which occurred quite unexpectedly on the last afternoon of the journey.

I was sitting in my cabin, engrossed in the affairs of Abyssinia, when the captain popped in and, with wild eye and confused speech, demanded to be shown the ticket for my motor-bicycle. I replied that I had no motor-bicycle. 'What, *no* motor-bicycle?'

180

'No, *no* motor-bicycle.' He shook his head, clicked his tongue and popped out again. I went on writing.

In half an hour he was back again; this time with a fellow passenger who spoke English.

'The captain wishes me to tell you that he must see the ticket for your motor-bicycle.'

'But I have already told the captain that I have no motor-bicycle.'

'You do not understand. It is necessary to have a ticket for a motor-bicycle.'

'I have no motor-bicycle.'

They left me again.

Ten minutes later the captain was back. 'Will you kindly show me your motor-bicycle.'

'I have no motor-bicycle.'

'It is on my list that you have a motor-bicycle. Will you kindly show it to me.'

'I have no motor-bicycle.'

'But it is on my list.'

'I am sorry. I have no motor-bicycle.'

Again he went away; again he returned; now, beyond question, stark crazy. 'The motor-bicycle – the motor-bicycle! I must see the motor-bicycle.'

'I have no motor-bicycle.'

It is idle to pretend that I maintained a dignified calm. I was in a tearing rage, too. After all we were in the heart of the tropics where tempers are notoriously volatile.

'Very well, I will search your luggage. Show it to me.'

'It is in this cabin. Two suitcases under the bunk; one bag on the rack.'

'Show it to me.'

'Look for it yourself.' As I say, an inglorious, schoolboy brawl.

'I am the captain of this ship. Do you expect me to move luggage.'

'I am a passenger. Do you expect me to?'

He went to the door and roared for a boy. No one came. With a trembling hand I attempted to write. He roared again. Again.

181

At last a sleepy boy ambled up. 'Take those suitcases from under the bunk.'

I pretended to be writing. I could hear the captain puffing just behind me (it was a very small cabin).

'Well,' I said, 'have you found a motor-bicycle?'

'Sir, that is my affair,' said the captain.

He went away. I thought I had heard the last of the incident. In half an hour he was back. 'Pack your bag. Pack your bag instantly.'

'But I am staying on board until Tuesday.'

'You are leaving at once. I am the captain. I will not allow people of your kind to stay here another hour.'

In this way I found myself stranded on the wharf at Bukama with two days to wait for my train. A humiliating situation, embittered by the Seventh Day Adventist, who came to offer his sympathy. 'It doesn't do to argue,' he said, 'unless you understand the language.'

I thought I had touched bottom at Kabalo, but Bukama has it heavily beaten. An iron bridge spans the river leading from the European quarter to the desolated huts of the native navvies who built it. Two ruined bungalows stand by the waterside and the overgrown Government rest-house, whose use has been superseded by the *Prince Leopold*; it is still nominally open, and it was here that I should have to stay if I decided to wait for the Port Francqui train. It is unfurnished and infested with spirillum tick. Some distance from the landing-point lies the jumble of huts that serve as ticket and goods office of the Katanga railway. A road leads up the hill, where are two abandoned offices and a Greek bar and general store. At the top of the hill is the administrative post – a flagstaff, the bungalow of the resident official, and a small hospital round which squatted a group of dejected patients enveloped in bandages. A platoon of native soldiers shuffled past. The heat and damp were appalling, far worse than anything I had met in Zanzibar. At sundown, swarms of soundless, malarial mosquitoes appeared. I sat in the Greek bar, with sweat splashing down like rain-water from my face to the floor; the proprietor knew only a few words of French. In these few words he advised me to leave Bukama as soon as I could, before I went down with fever. He himself was ashen and shivering from a recent bout. There was a train some time that evening for Elisabethville. I decided to take it.

We had a long wait, for no one knew the time when the train was expected. The station was completely dark except for one window at which a vastly bearded old man sold the tickets. Little groups of natives sat about on the ground. Some of them carried lanterns, some had lighted little wood fires and were cooking food. There was a ceaseless drumming in the crowd – as difficult to locate as the song of a grasshopper – and now and again a burst of low singing. At ten o'clock the train came in. The carriage was full of mosquitoes; there was no netting; the windows were jammed; the seats hard and extremely narrow. Two Greeks ate oranges all through the night. In this way I went to Elisabethville.

There the air service proved definitely and finally to be useless to me. The 'newly opened' railway to Lobita Bay was closed again. It had been possible only in the dry season when motor-transport could bridge the unfinished gap at the Belgian end of the line. Paradoxically enough, the quickest way to Europe was hundreds of miles out of the way through the Rhodesias and the Union of South Africa. There I could get a fast mail-boat from Cape Town to Southampton.

I had some difficulty in explaining, to the satisfaction of the immigration officer whose permission was necessary before I could leave the Congo, why I diverged so much from the itinerary outlined in my certificate of entry. In the end, however, he understood my difficulties and gave me leave to depart. In the meantime I worked, rested, and enjoyed the comfort and tranquillity of Elisabethville.

Six days in the train. At Bulawayo I bought a novel called *A Muster of Vultures*, in which the villain burned away his victims' faces with 'the juice of a tropical cactus'; at Mafeking I bought peaches; once our windows were bedewed with spray from the Victoria Falls; once everything was powdered deep in dust from the great Karroo Desert; once we took in a crowd of bad men dismissed from the Rhodesian copper-mines; two were known to be without passports and there was a frantic search for them by bare-kneed police officers, up and down the corridors and under the seats; one of them stole nine shillings from the half-caste boy who made up the beds. When we changed on to a new train at Bulawayo there were white stewards in the dining-car; after so many months it seemed odd and slightly indecent to see white men waiting on each other.

At last we arrived in Cape Town.

I had about forty pounds left in my pocket. A boat was sailing that afternoon. For £20 I bought a third-class berth in a large and clean cabin. The stewards treated us with superiority, but good nature; the food was like that of an exceptionally good private school – large luncheons, substantial meat teas, biscuit suppers. There was a very fat Welsh clergyman travelling in the third class with us. His congregation came to see him off. They sang hymns on the quayside, which he conducted with extravagant waving of his arms until we were out of earshot. Chiefly they sang one whose refrain was 'I'm sailing home', but they had been a little deluded by the felicity of these words, for the general theme of the composition was less appropriate. It referred, in fact, not to the journey from Cape Town to England, but to death and the return of the soul to its Creator. However, no one seemed depressed by this prediction, and the clergyman's wife sang it with great feeling long after her husband had stopped beating the time.

It was a pleasant voyage. In the evenings we played 'pontoon'. In the mornings we boxed or played 'pontoon'. There were frequent sing-songs, led by a troop of disgruntled dirt-track racers whose season in South Africa had been a failure.

A sports committee was organized, and proved the occasion for much bad blood; the Welsh clergyman in particular came in for criticism, on the ground that a man with a child of his own had no business to organize the children's fancy-dress party. 'He'll give his own little boy the best prize,' they said. 'Who wouldn't?' He replied by saying that he would have them know that, when he came out, a special presentation had been made to him by his fellow passengers in thanks for his public-spirited management of the deck-games. They said, 'That's as may be.' He said he would sooner give up the whole thing than have his honour questioned. It was all most enjoyable.

Eventually, on March 10th, we berthed at Southampton.

On the night of my return I dined in London. After dinner we were in some doubt where to go. The names I suggested had long ceased to be popular. Eventually we decided, and drove to a recently opened supper-restaurant which, they said, was rather amusing at the moment.

It was underground. We stepped down into the blare of noise as into a hot swimming-pool, and immersed ourselves; the atmosphere caught our breath like the emanation in a brewery over the tanks where fermentation begins. Cigarette-smoke stung the eyes.

A waiter beckoned us to a small table, tight-packed among other tables, so that our chairs rubbed backs with their neighbours. Waiters elbowed their way in and out, muttering abuse in each others' ears. Some familiar faces leered through the haze: familiar voices shrilled above the din.

We chose some wine.

'You'll have to take something to eat with it.'

We ordered seven-and-sixpenny sandwiches.

Nothing came.

A Negro in fine evening-clothes was at the piano, singing. Afterwards, when he went away, people fluttered their hands at him and tried to catch his eye. He bestowed a few patronizing nods. Someone yelled, 'He's losing his figure.'

A waiter came and said, 'Any more orders for drinks before closing time?' We said we had had nothing yet. He made a face and pinched another waiter viciously in the arm, pointing at our table and whispering in Italian. That waiter pinched another. Eventually the last-pinched waiter brought a bottle and slopped out some wine into glasses. It frothed up and spilt on the table-cloth.

Someone shrilled in my ear: 'Why, Evelyn, where *have* you been? I haven't seen you about anywhere for days.'

The wine tasted like salt and soda water. Mercifully a waiter whisked it away before we had time to drink it. 'Time, if you please.'

I was back in the centre of the Empire, and in the spot where, at the moment, 'everyone' was going. Next day the gossip-writers would chronicle who were assembled in that rowdy cellar, hotter than Zanzibar, noisier than the market at Harar, more reckless of the decencies of hospitality than the taverns of Kabalo or Tabora. And a month later the wives of English officials would read about it, and stare out across the bush or jungle or desert or forest or golf links, and envy their sisters at home, and wish they had the money to marry rich men.

I paid the bill in yellow African gold. It seemed just tribute from the weaker races to their mentors.

CHAPTER FOUR

A Journey to Brazil in 1932

(From *Ninety-two Days*)

ONE does not travel, any more than one falls in love, to collect material. It is simply part of one's life. For myself and many better than me, there is a fascination in distant and barbarous places, and particularly in the borderlands of conflicting cultures and states of development, where ideas, uprooted from their traditions, become oddly changed in transplantation. It is there that I find the experiences vivid enough to demand translation into literary form.

Just as a carpenter, I suppose, seeing a piece of rough timber feels an inclination to plane it and square it and put it into shape, so a writer is not really content to leave any experience in the amorphous, haphazard condition in which life presents it; and putting an experience into shape means, for a writer, putting it into communicable form.

So for the next month or two I shall be reliving my journey in Guiana and Brazil. Not that it has ever been out of my memory. It has been there, ill digested, throughout a crowded and fretful summer, obtruding itself in a fragmentary way at incongruous moments. Now, in this seaside nursery, it will be all laid out, like the maps and photographs and drawings on the writing table, while falling leaves in the autumnal sunshine remind me that it will soon be time to start out again somewhere else.

December, 1932

Warm sun, calm water, a slight following wind; after a week of heavy seas it was at last possible to write. Passengers, hitherto invisible, appeared from below. The ship was small, old and slow, a cargo boat carrying a few passengers and not caring much about them. It was not until the sea became smooth that one saw how slow she was.

The company was, presumably, typical of the route; three or four planters returning to the islands, men of old-fashioned appearance, thin brown faces and bulky watchchains; two parsons, one white, one black, both affable; two English soaks doing the 'round trip' for the good of their health, both surly when sober; some nondescript women of various colours rejoining husbands or visiting brothers; a genteel young Negress with purple lips; a somewhat cranky young man from the Philippines who had an attachment for islands. Very few were going as far as Georgetown.

Those who were were not encouraging. They were mildly excited at first when they learned that anyone who wrote books was coming to their country, and with that pathetic belief in the might of the pen which one continually meets in out of the way places, hoped that I should persuade the Imperial Government to 'do something' about local trade conditions. The country was stiff with gold and diamonds, they said, which only needed 'development'. When I told them that I wanted to go up country, they lost interest. Of course there was always Kaieteur, they said, quite a lot of tourists went there; three or four a year; they believed it was very pretty when you got there but it cost a great deal and you might be drowned or get fever; or there was the Rupununi savannah; several white people lived there and even a white woman, but it cost a great deal to get there and you might be drowned on the way or get fever; besides it was only at certain seasons you could get there at all. I had far better winter in Trinidad, they said, where there was an excellent new country club, horse races and a lot of money about, or at Barbados where the bathing was unrivalled.

And to be honest I did gaze rather wistfully as each of the islands in turn disappeared behind us. The first was Antigua and, coming on it as we did after twelve days of unbroken horizons, it remains the most vivid – steep little hills covered in bush, a fringe of palm along the beach, brilliant blue water revealing, fathoms down, the silver sand of its bed; an old fort covering the bay; a shabby little town of wooden, balconied houses, its only prominent building a large plain Cathedral rebuilt after an earthquake, with shining towers and a good pitch-pine interior;

inquisitive black urchins in the street; women in absurd sun hats, the brims drooping and flapping over their black faces, waddling along on flat feet; ragged Negroes lounging aimlessly at corners; baskets of highly coloured fish for sale – purple and scarlet like markings of a mandril; ramshackle motor cars; and in the church-yard the memorials of a lost culture – the rococo marble tombs of forgotten sugar planters, carved in England and imported by sailing ship in the golden days of West Indian prosperity.

It is significant that marble, that most grand and delicate of all building material, the substance of almost all sculpture, has today become the symbol of the vulgar and garish – the profiteers of *Punch circa* 1920, Lyons' Corner House and the Victor Emmanuel Memorial; it is part of the flight from magnificence to which both the 'ye-olde'-pewter-and-sampler aesthetic and its more recent counterpart, the 'modern'-concrete-and-steel-tube, have given impetus. A broken column in the Syrian desert, an incised slab overwhelmed in the gross vegetation of the South American bush remain as spoors of something gracious that passed that way centuries before.

We stopped only a day at Antigua to put down passengers and cargo; one of the things we brought to the islands was holly for their Christmas decorations. It looked odd being tossed down into the lighters under a blazing sky, so completely dissociated from its traditional concomitants of Yule logs and whisky punch and Santa Claus stamping off the snow. But it was not my first Christmas in the tropics; I knew it all – the cablegram forms specially decorated with berries and robins, the puzzled native children before the crib in the Church, 'Auld Lang Syne' on the gramophone, the beggars trotting hopefully behind one in the street saying 'Happy Clistmas – me velly Clistian boy'; the prospect of hot plum pudding on a windless, steaming evening.

Blue water ends at Trinidad; there and from there onwards the sea is murky; opaque, dingy stuff the colour of shabby stucco, thick with mud sweeping down from the great continental rivers – the Orinoco, the Essequibo, the Demerara, the Berbice, the Courantyne; all along the coast their huge mouths gape amidst dune and mangrove, pouring out into the blue Caribbean the waters of the remote highlands. Later I was to tramp across part of the great continental divide, where the tributaries of the Amazon and Essequibo dovetail into one another, tiny cascading brooks, confusing in an unmapped country because they seemed always to be flowing in the direction one did not expect; I was to wade through them or scramble over them on slippery tree-trunks in the forest where they were ruby-clear, wine-coloured from the crimson timber; I was to paddle tedious days down them when they had become deep and black; leaving them months later, as I saw the water become blue and clear again I was to feel touched with regret, for they had become for a time part of my life. But now as we approached the mainland I only felt mildly depressed that bathing had ceased to be attractive.

Depression deepened as rain set in; a monotonous tropical downpour, always dreary, most monotonous and most depressing when one is on the water. We were already a day late and now we missed the tide by an hour and had to lie at anchor in the rain and a slight fog, waiting to cross the bar into Demerara. There was a lightship faintly visible a mile or so away. They told me without pride that it was a new one.

Next day, before noon, we arrived. The town lies at the mouth of the Demerara on the right bank; opposite are low, green man-grove swamps. Half a dozen small ships lay alongside the quay. We steamed up and then drifted down to our berth with the cur-rent. Low wooden sheds and low roofs beyond them; everything quite flat; rain streamed down ceaselessly; only the heavy reek of sugar occupied the senses.

Landing was simple. There was none of the jaunty cross-examination which usually greets a British subject when he arrives on British territory; an elderly Negro in a straw hat glanced at our passports; the Customs officers opened nothing; we passed through the sheds, which were full of bees attracted to the sugar bags, and out into the water-logged street; a taxi splashed and skidded to the hotel; the windows were obscured by rain.

A bare bedroom with white wooden walls, a large bed with mosquito netting, a rocking chair, a faint smell of 'Flit'. There I was.

Two coloured reporters arrived from local newspapers to inter-

190

view me. They had followed me on bicycles from the other hotel. (This, let me hasten to say, is no indication of fame. All first-class passengers are given column interviews on arrival at Georgetown.) They looked rather damp and had none of the breezy technique of their trade. They took down all I said laboriously as though I were a witness at an Archbishop's Court.

Was it true that I was a writer? Yes.

A writer who had published books or just a writer?

Was I going to write about Guiana? One of them had a cutting from a London paper in which I had facetiously said that I understood the beetles in Guiana were as big as pigeons and that one killed them with shot-guns. Had I really come to shoot beetles, they asked. They were afraid I should be disappointed. The beetles were certainly remarkably large, but not as large as that.

Had I any views about the mineral resources of the country? When I confessed that I had not, they were clearly nonplussed; this was their stock, foolproof question, because most visitors to Georgetown came there with some idea of prospecting for dia-monds or gold. They gazed at me with reproach. I volunteered the information that I was going up country.

'Ah, to Kaieteur?'

I then inwardly took the vow which I very nearly kept, that I would in no circumstances visit that very famous waterfall.

It was December 22nd when I landed, and January 3rd when I left for the interior. Most of this time was spent in trying to make some sort of plans for the future. Christmas was both a good and a bad time for this purpose; good because most of the people from up country had come down to town for the celebrations; bad because they took the holidays seriously in Georgetown. Most of my information came casually from conversation in the hotel bar.

Few of the people I talked to had even the most cursory ac-quaintance with the bush, though most of them could name someone who at one time or another had been up to Kaieteur; they were mostly discouraging, half regarding the expedition as a mild and rather tedious picnic and half as a precipitate and painful suicide. In order to dispel the suspicion that I was after diamonds, I gave it out, as was indeed the truth, that I wanted to take photographs of the primitive Indians. Here again they were discouraging. 'You'll find them all playing gramophones and working sewing-machines. They're all civilized now. We know what you want,' they said with winks, 'you want to take the girls naked. Well, your best plan is to go up to Bartika and get a few of the tarts there to pose for you. You can get the proper feather ornaments from the Self Help shop. That's what the American scientific expeditions do.' Across the Brazilian border I might find something to interest me, but not in Guiana, they said.

I had a note of introduction to a Jesuit missionary on the Takutu River. There were three Takutu Rivers marked on my map, but two were merely guesses, sketched in tentatively with dotted lines, while one was marked firmly as a place of known importance, so I assumed, correctly as it turned out, that this was the one I wanted. It ran through the furthest extremity of the Rupununi savannah forming the boundary between British Guiana and Brazil. Accordingly I made this my objective.

I was advised to go and see Bain, the Commissioner for the district, who by good chance was in Georgetown for Christmas. So with the Governor's introduction I sought him out in the boarding-house where he was staying. He was a middle-aged, emaciated man, creole with some Indian blood. Like everyone else in the colony he had at one time worked gold and diamonds; like most other people he had also been a surveyor, a soldier, a policeman and a magistrate; he had lately returned to the last avocation which included most of the other functions. He received me with great kindness and vivacity, telling me that the Rupununi was the most beautiful place in the world and that anyone with a gift for expression should be able to make a book about it. He was himself returning in a day or two by the cattle trail as far as Kurupukari which was well on my way. He had a boat of stores leaving almost at once from Bartika which he expected to find awaiting him. He offered me a place in that.

'It ought to get there before me,' he said. 'I do not know about the rains. Perhaps it will take four days, perhaps eight. But it must get there because it is full of barbed wire I need. Unless of course it's wrecked,' he added. 'Mr Winter's boat was totally destroyed in the rapids the day before yesterday.'

I had no idea where Kurupukari was, but it sounded as good as anywhere else. When I got back I looked for it on the map. Mr Bain had spoken very quickly so that when I found Yupukarri right up on the savannah I was highly delighted. It was not for two days that I found Kurupukari about a hundred miles away from it. Then I realized that I was in for a longer journey than I had anticipated, and trebled my order for stores.

I had no idea what I should need. Opinion was contradictory, some people saying, 'Just take a gun and live by that,' and others, 'Don't count on getting *anything* up country. The ranchers live on farine.'

I had no idea what farine was but I felt I should need something else. Mr Bain simply said, 'You should be like me. I can go for days without eating – like a camel. That is the way to live in the bush.'

From that moment onwards I did not have an hour's certainty of plan. It was arranged that I should take Tuesday's steamer to Bartika and start in the boat on Wednesday; then I discovered by chance that there was no steamer on Tuesdays; wires were sent and the boat delayed until Thursday.

Then Mr Bain rang up to say he was sending a black policeman with me who was to act as my servant; that sounded all right until the agents rang up to say that now the policeman was coming there would only be room for 100 lb. of my stores. There was nothing to do except countermand three-quarters of them.

Then the agents rang up to say, did I realize that it was an open boat and that since the rains were on it was imperative to take a tarpaulin. Desperate and unsuccessful attempts to secure a tarpaulin with every shop in Georgetown closed.

Then Mr Bain rang up to say that the agents said it was an open boat and that the rains were on. I should be soaked to the skin every day and undoubtedly get fever and he could not take the responsibility of sending me in it.

Then I went to see Mr Bain and he said I had better come to

193

Takama with him and perhaps there would be a horse to get me to Kurupukari.

Then I rang up the agents and said that since the boat was relieved of my weight they were to put all my stores on board.

Then Mr Bain rang up to say that he had come to the conclusion that I could have the horse which he had meant to pack with his personal stores; instead he would send them by boat.

Then I rang up the agents and said they were to take from my stores the weight equivalent to the personal stores Mr Bain was sending by boat.

All these, and other less remarkable alarms, occurred at intervals of two or three hours. Taken all in all it was a disturbed departure.

There was plenty going on in Georgetown that week.

An unknown Dutchman shot himself on Christmas morning in his room at the rival hotel, on account of feeling lonely.

A Negro known to his friends as 'the Blood of Corruption' was arrested on numerous charges. He was the leader of a criminal organization called 'the Beasts of Berlin'. They had taken the name from a cinema film; none of them had the remotest idea what Berlin was; they just liked the name. But they were perfectly serious criminals for all that.

There was a race-meeting in heavy rain and, on New Year's Eve, a large number of dances. At my hotel there was a Caledonian Ball, characterized by a marked male predominance, pipers, and quite elderly men sitting giggling on the ballroom floor; there was also a more decorous function at the club where I ate the poisoned 'crab-back'.

Through all this the preparations for the journey up country, the buying of chlorodyne and bandages, gun caps and cartridge cases, flour and kerosene, seemed fantastic and unsubstantial, and the empty forest, a few miles away, infinitely remote, as unrelated to the crowded life of the coast as it was to London. Most journeys, I think, begin and all end with a sense of unreality. Even when eventually I found myself in the train for New Amsterdam, sitting opposite Mr Bain, with our improbable baggage piled up round us, it still required an effort to convince me that we were on our way.

It is said that the railway along the Guiana coast is the oldest in the Empire. It runs in pretty, flat country over creeks and canals and through gay, ramshackle villages. The stations still bear the names of the old sugar estates, but these are mostly split up now into small holdings growing coconut and rice. The further one goes from Georgetown towards New Amsterdam, the blacker become the inhabitants, of purer Negro type and more cheerful manners. Berbice men look on Demerarans as wasters; the Demerarans look on them as bumpkins.

It was just dark by the time Mr Bain and I reached New Amsterdam. We had the carriage to ourselves and our baggage. Most of the way Mr Bain talked.

I do not know how the legend originated that the men who administer distant territories are 'strong and silent'. Some may start strong and even retain a certain wiriness into middle life, but most of them, by the time they have attained any eminence in the King-Emperor's service, are subject to one or more severe complaints. As for their silence, it seems to vary in exact inverse ratio to their distance from civilization. For silence one must go to the young diners-out of London; men in the wide open spaces are, in my experience, wildly garrulous; they will talk on all subjects – highly personal reminiscences, their dreams, diet and digestion, science, history, morals and theology. But pre-eminently of theology. It seems to be the obsession waiting round the corner for all lonely men. You start talking bawdy with some breezy, rum-drinking tramp skipper and in ten minutes he is proving or disproving the doctrine of original sin.

Mr Bain, though indefatigable in his duty, was not strong; frequent attacks of fever had left him bloodless and fleshless, and besides this he suffered from constant, appalling bouts of asthma which kept him awake for all but an hour or two every night. Nor was he silent. During the stimulating fortnight I was to spend in his company he talked at large on every conceivable topic, eagerly, confidently, enthusiastically, not always credibly, sometimes scarcely coherently, inexhaustibly; with inspired imagination, with dizzy changes of thought and rather alarming theatrical effects, in a vocabulary oddly compounded of the jargon he was accustomed to use among his subordinates and the longer, less habitual words he had noticed in print. As I have said he talked of everything at one time or another, but mostly either in metaphysical speculation or in anecdote. He himself always figured prominently in the latter and it was in these that his gestures became most dramatic. The dialogue was all in *oratio recta*; never 'I ordered him to go at once', but 'I say to him "Go! plenty quick, quick. Go!"' and at the words Mr Bain's finger would shoot out accusingly, his body would stiffen and quiver, his eyes would blaze until I began to fear he would induce some kind of seizure.

One engaging and lamentably uncommon trait in Mr Bain's reminiscences was this, that besides, like half the world, remembering and retailing all the injustices he had encountered, he also remembered and retained every word of approbation; the affection he had received from his parents as a boy; the prize given him at school for his geometry; the high commendation he had had at the technical college for his draughtsmanship; numberless spontaneous expressions of esteem from various acquaintances throughout his life; the devotion of subordinates and the confidence of superiors; the pleasure the Governor took in his official reports; testimonies from delinquents to the impartiality, mercy, and wisdom of his judicial sentences – all these were fresh and glowing in his memory and all, or nearly all, I was privileged to hear.

Many of his stories I found to strain the normal limits of credulity – such as that he had a horse which swam under water and a guide who employed a parrot to bring him information; the bird would fly on ahead, said Mr Bain, and coming back to its perch on the Indian's shoulder whisper in his ear what he had seen, who was on the road and where they would find water.

At sundown it became cold and clammy in the carriage; clouds of mosquitoes came in from windows and corridor, biting us to frenzy. Mr Bain remarked gloomily that they were probably all infected with malaria. Everyone has different theories about quinine; Mr Bain recommended constant, large doses, observing parenthetically that they caused deafness, insomnia and impotence.

We transferred from the train to a ferry steamer and drifted rather disconsolately across to the town. There was a boarding-house kept by a white gentleman in reduced circumstances; here we dined in a swarm of mosquitoes; the house had run out of drink during the New Year celebrations. After dinner to avoid the mosquitoes we walked about the streets for an hour. They were empty and ill-lit. New Amsterdam, eighty years ago, was a prosperous, if sleepy, town with a club and its own society; now there is barely a handful of whites quartered there, the rest having been driven out by mosquitoes and the decay of the sugar trade. At a street corner we met a Jordanite haranguing a few apathetic loafers and a single suspicious policeman. He wore a long white robe and a white turban and he waved a wand of metal tubing; a drowsy little boy sat beside him holding a large Bible. The Jordanites are one of the many queer sects that flourish among Negroes. They derive their name not as might be supposed from the river, but from a recently deceased Mr Jordan from Jamaica; their object seemed partially pious, partially political; they are said to favour polygamy. The present speaker ran round in little circles as he spoke, 'What for you black men afraid ob de white man? Why you ascared ob his pale face and blue eye? Why do you fear his yellow hair? Because you are all fornicators – dat is de reason. If you were pure of heart you need not fear de white man.'

Then he saw us and seemed rather embarrassed. ''Nother text, boy.' But the boy was asleep over the Bible. He cracked him sharply on the head with his wand and the child hastily read a verse of Ezekiel and the preacher took up on another subject.

'The black man got a very inferior complex,' remarked Mr Bain as we resumed our walk.

Next day we started at dawn. There was a great rainbow over the town. On the way to the quay I noticed a charming old Lutheran Church, relic of the Dutch occupation, that had been invisible the night before.

A lazy, uneventful day in the paddle steamer up the Berbice River. Monotonous vegetable walls on either bank, occasionally broken by bovianders' cabins.* Now and then an unstable, dug-out canoe would shoot out from the green shadows and an unkempt, bearded figure would deliver or receive a parcel of mail. We slung our hammocks on deck. There was a steward who made gin-swizzles of a kind and served revolting meals at intervals of two hours. On the whole a tolerable day's journey.

Our only companions on the top deck were a Belgian rancher, his Indian wife, some of their children, and his wife's sister. They were the first Indians I had seen. Since they had taken up with a European they wore hats and stockings and high-heeled shoes, but they were very shy, guarding their eyes like nuns, and giggling foolishly when spoken to; they had squat little figures and blank, Mongol faces. They had bought a gramophone and a few records in town, which kept them happy for the twelve hours we were together. Conversation was all between Mr Bain and the rancher, and mostly about horses. Quite different standards of quality seemed to be observed here from those I used to learn from Captain Hance.

'I tell you, Mr Bain, that buckskin of mine was the finest mare bred in this district. You didn't have to use no spur or whip to her. Why before you was on her back, almost, she was off like the wind and *nothing* would stop her. And if she didn't want to go any particular way *nothing* would make her. Why I've been carried six miles out of my course many a time, pulling at her with all my strength. *And* how she could rear.'

'Yes, she *could rear*,' said Mr Bain in wistful admiration. 'It was lovely to see her.'

'And if she got you down she'd roll on you. She wouldn't get up till she'd broken every bone in your body. She killed one of my boys that way.'

'But what about my Tiger?'

'Ah, he was a good horse. You could see by the way he rolled his eyes.'

* Boviander is the name given to the people of unknown descent – mostly Dutch, Indian and Negro mixtures – who live in isolated huts all along the lower waters of the big rivers; they generally have a minute clearing where they grow manioc or maize; they fish, and spend most of their time, like the water rat in *Wind in the Willows*, 'messing about in boats'.

'Did you ever see him *buck*? Why he'd buck all over the corral. And he was wicked too. He struck out at you if he got a chance.'

'That was a *good* horse, Tiger. What became of him?'

'Broke his back. He bolted over some rocks into a creek with one of the boys riding him.'

'Still you know I think that for *bucking* my Shark ...'

And so it went on. Presently I asked in some apprehension, 'And the horse I am to ride tomorrow. Is he a *good* horse too?'

'One of the strongest in the country,' said Mr Bain. 'It will be just like the English Grand National for you.'

So the day wore on. The steward trotted about with frightful helpings of curried fish; later with greyish tea and seed cake; later with more fish and lumps of hard, dark beef. The Indian ladies played their gramophone. The rancher had a nap. Mr Bain told me more. At last, about seven, we arrived at our destination, and descended in the dark into a dug-out canoe.

'Be careful, be careful, if you're not used to them you will certainly be drowned,' Mr Bain admonished me, thus giving the first evidence of what, for the next few days, was going to prove a somewhat tiresome solicitude for my safety. The trouble was this. The Governor had requested Mr Bain to look after me and, in his kindness, had stressed the fact that the conditions of the country were new to me and that he took a personal interest in my welfare. Mr Bain, in his kindness, interpreted this to mean that something very precious and very fragile had been put into his charge; if any accident were to befall me the Governor would never forgive it; danger, for one of delicate constitution, lurked in every activity of the day. If I helped to saddle the placid pack ox he would cry out, 'Stand back, be careful, or he will kick out your brains.' If I picked up my own gun he would say, 'Be careful, it will go off and shoot you.'

Fortunately this scrupulous concern began to wear thin after three days' travel, but during those three days it came as near as anything could to straining my affection and gratitude towards him.

The dug-out paddled by an indiscernible figure in the stern, swept away from the ship across the dark water; the opposite bank was lightless. We scrambled up the slippery bank (Mr Bain urging me anxiously not to fall down) and could just make out a rise in the ground surmounted by some kind of building; the boatman brought up a lantern and we climbed further. Mr Bain in the meantime asking fretfully, 'Yetto? Where's Yetto? I told him to be here with my hammock.'

'Yetto come with de horses this morning. Now him go bottomside to a party. Him no say nothing about de hammock.'

'Yetto proper bad man,' said Mr Bain lapsing into vernacular. 'Him proper Congo.'

Thus in circumstances of discredit and terms of opprobrium I first heard the name of someone to whom I was later to become warmly attached.

We climbed the little hill and reached a thatched shelter, open at the sides, where two figures lay asleep in hammocks. They woke up, sat up and stared at us. A black man and his wife. Mr Bain asked them if they knew what Yetto had done with his hammock.

'Him gone to de party.'

'Where dis party?'

'Down to de river. Indian house. All de boys at de party.'

So we went down to look for Yetto. We paddled almost noiselessly down stream, keeping into the bank. It was an effort to balance in the narrow, shallow craft. Eventually we heard music and hauled in under the bushes.

The party was in a large Indian hut. It was cosmopolitan in character, being made up of Brazilian *vaqueiros*, bovianders, blacks and a number of clothed and semi-civilized Indians. Two Brazilians were playing guitars. The hostess came out to greet us.

'Good night,' she said, shaking hands and leading us in. It was not etiquette to ask for Yetto at once, so we sat on a bench and waited. A girl was walking from guest to guest with a bowl of dark home-brewed liquor; she handed a mug to each in turn, waiting while they drank and then refilling it for the next. Two or three Negroes were dancing. The Indians sat in stolid rows, silently, soft hats pulled down over their eyes, staring gloomily at the floor. Now and then one would get up, stroll apathetically across to a girl and invite her to dance. The couple would then shuffle round in a somewhat European manner, separate without a word or a glance and resume their seats. The Indians, I learned later, are a solitary people and it takes many hours' heavy drinking to arouse any social interests in them. In fact the more I saw of Indians the greater I was struck by their similarity to the English. They like living with their own families at great distances from their neighbours; they regard strangers with suspicion and despair; they are unprogressive and unambitious, fond of pets, hunting and fishing; they are undemonstrative in love, unwarlike, morbidly modest; their chief aim seems to be on all occasions to render themselves inconspicuous; in all points, except their love of strong drink and perhaps their improvidence, the direct opposite of the Negro. On this particular evening, however, their only outstanding characteristic was inability to make a party go.

After a time Yetto was detected drinking guiltily in a corner. He was a large middle-aged black of unusual ugliness. He was comic; huge feet and hands, huge mouth, and an absurd little Hitler moustache. Mr Bain and he talked at some length about the hammock; a conversation in which 'you proper Congo' occurred frequently. Then he left the party and came away with us to find it. At last at about ten o'clock Mr Bain and I were established in the rest-house.

Next morning Yetto and some other boys appeared with the horses and my misgivings of the previous day rapidly subsided. They were very small ponies and stood placidly in the corner of the corral cropping the tops off the arid tufts of grass; they were too lethargic even to switch away the horse flies that clustered on their quarters; mine had been attacked by a vampire bat during the night and bore a slaver of blood on his withers.

The packing of the ox took some care, and it was noon before we were ready. The black man, who had shared the rest-house the night before, was coming with us. He was manager of the ranch ten or twelve miles away, which was to be our first stop. We mounted and made to start off. My pony would not move.

'Loosen de reins,' they said.

I loosened the reins and kicked him and hit. He took a few steps backwards.

'Loosen de reins,' they said.

Then I saw how they were riding, with the reins hanging quite loose, their hands folded on the front of the saddle. That is the style all over this part of the world; the reins are never tightened except in an occasional savage jerk; the aids are given on the neck instead of on the bit. Drama in movement is the object aimed at; the *vaqueiros* like a horse that as soon as they mount will give two or three leaps in the air and then start off at a gallop; it does not matter how short a time the gallop lasts provided he takes them out of sight of the spectator; then after many hours' monotonous jogging they will spur him into life when they approach either ranch or village, arrive at the gallop, the horse's mouth lathered with foam, rein him back on to his hocks and dismount in a small dust storm. I had seen this often enough in the old days of the cinema, but had not realized that it occurred in real life.

We set off across the plain cantering a little but mostly jogging at what for many weeks was to be my normal travelling gait. The country was dead flat and featureless except for ant-hills and occasional clumps of palm; the ground was hard earth and sand tufted with dun-coloured grass; thousands of lizards scattered and darted under the horses' feet; otherwise there was no sign of life except the black crows who rose at our approach from the carcasses strewn along the track, and resettled to their feast behind us. Here and in the forest we passed a carcass every half-mile. Many were recently dead, for the last drive had lost forty per cent, and these we cantered past holding our breath; others were mere heaps of bone picked white by the ants, the mound of half-digested feed always prominent among the ribs.

During the ride Mr Bain discoursed to the black rancher about history; I listened fitfully, for my horse was continually dropping behind, but I was never out of earshot of the voice, voluble, rhapsodic, now rising to some sharp catastrophe, now running on evenly, urgently, irresistibly in the shimmering noon heat.

I caught bits: '. . . once you see there was nothing but water. It says so in the Bible. Water covered the face of the earth. Then he divided the land from the waters. How did he do that, Mr Yerwood? Why, by killing de crabs, and all de shells of de crabs became ground down by the tides and became sand . . .'

'. . . then there was Napoleon. He was only a little corporal but he divorced his wife and married the daughter of an Emperor. Mark my words, Mr Yerwood, all dose Bolshevists will be doing that soon . . .'

'. . . and why did the English take so long to subdue de little Boers? Because dey were so sporting. When dey take prisoners dey let dem go again for to give dem another chance . . .'

We reached our destination in about two hours and found three sheds and a wired corral. It was less than I had expected. Through the influence of the cinema, 'ranch' had taken on a rather glorious connotation in my mind; of solid, whitewashed buildings; a courtyard with a great tree casting its shadow in the centre and a balustraded wall, wrought iron gates, a shady interior with old Spanish furniture and a lamp burning before a baroque Madonna, and lovely girls with stock-whips and guitars. I do not say that I had expected to find this at Waranana; but I did feel that the word 'ranch' had taken a fall.

Various dependants of Mr Bain's were awaiting him here – policemen returning to duty, woodmen in charge of keeping the trail open; he also had stores and saddlery and some horses, left behind on his previous journey. All these he attended to so that by next morning everything was ready for us to start out. A moody young policeman named Price was handed over to me (or me to him), to act as my personal servant. Yetto was never far away, grinning sheepishly and constantly reprimanded. He held an uncertain position, partly government runner, partly groom, partly cook, partly porter.

Mr Yerwood killed a chicken for us and, after we had dined, joined us and drank some of our rum. He and Mr Bain talked about animals, their stories growing less probable as the evening progressed. Finally Mr Yerwood described a 'water-monkey' he had once seen; it was enormous and jet black; it had a grinning mouth full of sharp teeth; it swam at a great speed; its habit was to submerge itself and wait for bathers whom it would draw down and pound to pieces on the rocks at the bottom. Just such an occurrence had happened to a friend of Mr Yerwood's; every bone in his body was broken when it floated to the surface, Mr Yerwood said.

Not to be outdone, Mr Bain related how once, when walking in the late afternoon in the neighbourhood of Mount Roraima, he had encountered two Missing Links, a man and his wife slightly over normal size but bowed and simian in their movements; they were naked except for a light covering of soft reddish down; they had stared at Mr Bain a full half-minute, then said something he did not understand, and strolled off into the bush. After that there was little to be said on the subject of animals. It was ten o'clock – late for the district – so we took to our hammocks, leaving the lamp burning as a protection against vampire bats.

It would be tedious to record the daily details of the journey to Kurupukari. Mr Bain managed everything; I merely trotted beside him; we took six days from the ranch, averaging about fifteen miles a day. Mr Bain often explained how, in normal conditions, he did the whole journey in two stages at full gallop all the way. All the time we passed only one human being – a Portuguese-speaking Indian, padding along on foot, going down to the river on some inscrutable errand. For two days we travelled over grass land and then entered the bush; it was cool and quite sunless. The green, submarine darkness of the jungle has been described frequently enough but it can never, I think, be realized until one has been there. The trail was as broad as an English lane with vast, impenetrable walls of forest rising to a hundred and fifty feet on either side; the first twenty feet from the ground were dense undergrowth, then the trunks of the trees emerged, quite bare, like architectural columns rising vertical and featureless until they broke into the solid roof of leaves, through which appeared only rare star points of direct sunlight. There were always men working to keep the trail clear of fallen timber and there were always trees lying across it at frequent intervals. Usually some kind of line had been chopped round these through the bush and we would dismount and lead our horses. There were also creeks every few miles, low at this time of year, so that we could ride through them. In the wet season, Mr Bain said, you had to crawl across a tacuba leading a swimming horse, carry your baggage across and load and reload your pack animals four or five times a day. Sometimes the trail had been completely cleared with a 'corduroy' of logs through the marshy places; elsewhere only the undergrowth had been chopped away and the trees stood up in the middle of the path; once we came to a place where the virgin forest had been burned and a second growth of low bush had taken its place; there was loose white sand here, blinding to the eyes after the gloom of the forest, and heavy going for the horses.

Everyone who has ever been there has remarked on the apparent emptiness of the bush. The real life takes place a hundred feet up in the tree-tops; it is there that you would find all the flowers and parrots and monkeys, high overhead in the sunlight, never coming down except when there is a storm. Occasionally we would find the floor of the trail strewn with petals from flowers out of sight above us.

We met the first snake on our first day in the bush. Mr Bain and I were riding abreast a mile or so ahead of the baggage. He was telling me his views on marriage ('. . . whom God has joined together let no man put asunder. Yes. But tell me this. Who is God? God is love. So when a couple have ceased to love one another . . .') when he suddenly reined up and said in a melo-dramatic whisper· 'Stop. Look ahead. Dere is a terrible great snake.' It was in the days when he still regarded my safety as peculiarly precarious. 'Don't come near – it may attack you.'

Sure enough about twenty yards ahead was a very large snake, curled up in the middle of the trail.

'What kind is it?'

'I never saw anything like him before. Look at his terrible great head,' hissed Mr Bain.

It certainly was a very odd-looking head from where we sat, swollen and brown and quite different in appearance from the mottled coils. Mr Bain dismounted and I followed. Very stealthily, step by step he approached the creature. It did not move and so, emboldened, he began to throw pieces of dead wood at it. None of them fell within six feet of their mark. He approached closer, motioning me back apprehensively. Then the snake suddenly raised his neck, retched and for a moment it appeared as though his head had fallen off. Then it became clear what had happened. We had surprised a python in the act of slowly swallowing a large toad. It had got down the back legs and was slowly sucking in the body when it had been disturbed; the 'terrible great head' was the toad's body half in and half out of the jaws. The python averted its own delicately pointed face and slipped away into the bush; the toad showed little gratitude or surprise at his escape, but dragged himself rather laboriously under a log and sat down to consider his experience.

Always, but particularly from sunset until dawn, the bush was alive with sounds. We used to turn in early, usually between seven and eight, because there was nothing to do after dark; there were no chairs to sit in or table to sit at; the lantern light was too dim for reading. As soon as we finished supper we rolled up in our hammocks and there was nothing to do but lie and listen for ten or eleven hours. There were the immediate sounds of poor Mr Bain's asthma; of the boys squatting round their fire, sometimes singing, more often arguing, always quite unintelligible when they were among themselves; there were our own beasts grazing in the corral and limping about at hobble; often we would hear the crash of dead timber falling in the forest near us, but around and above and through all these were the sounds of the bush. I am no naturalist; Mr Bain's experienced ear was able to pick out innumerable voices that to me were merged in the general chatter, but even to me there were some sounds that were unmistakable; there were the 'howler' monkeys; I never saw one except stuffed in a museum – he was a small ginger creature – but we heard them roaring like lions most days; in the far distance it was like the noise of the dredgers that once used to attend me lying sleepless night after night at Port Said. There were the frogs, some shrill like those in the South of France, others deep and hoarse. There was a bird which mooed like a cow, named, appositely enough, the 'cow-bird', and another which struck two sharp metallic notes as though with a hammer on a copper cistern; this was called the 'bell-bird'; there was a bird that made a noise like a motor-bicycle starting up; a kind of woodpecker drilling very rapidly with his beak; there were others of various kinds who whistled like errand boys. There was one which repeated 'Qu'est-ce qu'il dit?' endlessly in a challenging tone. There was one insect which buzzed in a particular manner. 'Listen,' said Mr Bain one day, 'that is most interesting. It is what we call the "six o'clock beetle", because he always makes that noise at exactly six o'clock.'

'But it is now a quarter past four.'

'Yes, that is what is so interesting.'

At one time and another in the country I heard the 'six o'clock beetle' at every hour of the day and night.

But experienced 'bush men' say that they can tell the time as accurately by the sounds of the bush as a mariner can by the sun.

Kurupukari, which we reached on the seventh day, was marked large on the map and had figured constantly in our conversation for the past week. There was a flagstaff, certainly, lying flat in the grass, still under construction; it was completed and erected during my stay; later Mr Bain hopes to obtain a flag for it. But there was no landing, no habitations, only a single wooden house standing in a clearing on a slight hill.

The Essequibo bends there, so that the place had the look of a peninsula; the river even at this season was immense, and the wooded islands round which it divided and converged made it seem larger still; a broad creek flowed into it immediately opposite the station; there were sand dunes and rocks, submerged at full flood, but now high and dry, confusing one's sense of direction; there were cascades and patches of still lake so that one seemed to be surrounded by a system of ornamental waters, and across its vast and varied expanse one could see the green precipices of forest and appreciate, as one could not when directly beneath them, the freakish height of the trees and the gay dapple of blossom at their summit.

The house, like most in the country, was of one storey, raised on piles ten or twelve feet from the ground. The verandah was the living-room with a table and two armchairs, it was also the government office; some tattered, printed regulations, a calendar and an obsolete map hung on the walls; there was a desk with pigeon-holes for licences, forms, stamps; here were transacted the multifarious functions of local government; a tax was levied on passing cattle, grants of land were registered, pilots' certificates were endorsed, letters were accepted for the irregular river service to the coast. A resident black sergeant of police took charge of them. Under us, between the supporting piles, there lived, under the minimum of restraint, a dozen or so convicts.

Mr Bain's cubicle had a cupboard, without lock, in which he kept, or attempted to keep, a few personal possessions. This busy place was the nearest thing Mr Bain had to a home, a curious contrast to the trim little official residences of British Africa. In all his huge district there was not one place which Mr Bain could lock up; his life was spent eternally jogging up and down the cattle trail and across the plain to the ultimate frontier station at Bon Success, hanging his hammock in the *vaqueiros'* shelters or putting up for the night at the scattered little ranch houses of the savannah, living from year's end to year's end in camp conditions except for rare official visits to a Georgetown boarding-house. It was not everybody's job.

Unsatisfactory news awaited us at Kurupukari; our boat from Bartika had not arrived and Mr Bain, who had hitherto been unreasonably confident about it, suddenly became correspondingly depressing. That was the way in the bush, he said, one had to be used to things like that; there was not much water in the river, no doubt they were having a difficult time at the rapids; it might be weeks before they arrived; they might never arrive at all; that was probably it – the boat had been wrecked and the men all drowned; the barbed wire and the stores anyway would be lost beyond hope. How right he had been to bring me up the trail . . . and so on.

Meanwhile we were reduced to the milder discomforts of a state of siege. We had a box and a half of biscuits and a tin of milk; and there were great sacks of farine for the convicts' rations and some *tasso*.

Farine is a vegetable product made from cassava root. It is like coarse sawdust in appearance; a granulated, tapioca-coloured substance of intense hardness and a faint taste of brown paper. It is eaten quite alone, or with hot water to soften it or more luxuriously with milk or the water in which the *tasso* has been boiled.

Tasso is prepared in this way. The killing of a beast is an event of some importance in the immediate neighbourhood. Indians get news of it and appear mysteriously like gulls round a trawler when the catch is cleaned. A few choice morsels are cut away and cooked and eaten fresh. The Indians carry off the head and the entrails. The rest is sliced into thin slabs, rolled in salt and hung up to dry. A few days of sun and hot savannah wind reduce it to a black, leathery condition in which it will remain uncorrupt indefinitely. Even the normally omnivorous ants will not touch it. It is carried under the saddle above the blanket to keep it tender and protect the horse from galling. When the time comes to eat it, it is scrubbed fairly clean of dust and salt and boiled in water. It emerges softened but fibrous and tasteless. I can conceive it might be possible for a newcomer to stomach a little farine with a rich and aromatic stew; or a little *tasso* with plenty of fresh vegetables and bread. The food of the savannah is farine and *tasso* and nothing else.

For four days there was no sign of the boat. Then, late in the afternoon, one of the convicts reported the sound of a motor. Mr Bain and I hurried down to the river bank. He too could hear it plainly, though it was half an hour before a sound reached my duller ears. Pessimistic to the last, Mr Bain said it was probably some other boat, but in the end, just at sundown, it came into sight, a grey blob very slowly approaching. Their sharper eyes – Mr Bain's and the little cluster of convicts and police – instantly recognized it as ours. In another half-hour it was there. An open boat low in the water, with an outboard engine. There was a crew of four or five, each with a story to tell. They camped near the boat and long into the night we could hear them arguing and boasting over their fire. We went to bed suffused as though by wine with renewed geniality.

The unloading took all the morning and as I saw my stores packed bit by bit against the wall of my cubicle I began to despair of ever moving them. But Yetto was confident that he and the horse and the policeman could manage them with ease. We swam the horses across the river that afternoon and hobbled them in the corral on the opposite bank so that they would be ready to start the next day. The pack horse took unkindly to the water and swallowed a good deal on the way across.

Everything seemed set for my departure. I had even some kind

of plan evolved for my ultimate route. It was possible, said Mr
Bain, to take a canoe from Bon Success down the Takutu to
Boa Vista. That meant nothing to me but Mr Bain explained that
it was an important Brazilian town – next to Manaos the most
important town in Amazonas. He had never been there himself
but he knew those who had and in his description he made it a
place of peculiar glamour – dissipated and violent; a place where
revolutions were plotted and political assassinations committed;
from there regular paddle steamers plied to Manaos – a city of
inexpressible grandeur, of palaces and opera houses, boulevards
and fountains, swaggering military in spurs and white gloves,
cardinals and millionaires; and from there great liners went direct
to Lisbon. Mr Bain made a very splendid picture of it all – so
graphic and full of passages so personal and penetrating that it
was difficult to accept his assurance that he knew it only by repute.
His eyes flashed as he told me of it and his arms swept in circles.
I felt that it was a singularly fortunate man who went to Boa
Vista and Manaos.

On the eve of my departure Mr Bain and I had an intimate and
convivial dinner. Next morning I sent the stores across with
Yetto and the policeman; they were to arrange the pack horse's
load and their own and start ahead of me. Soon after midday I
went across myself. Mr Bain came to see me off. We found and
saddled the horse; I mounted and, after many expressions of
mutual goodwill, I rode off alone up the trail.

As soon as I set out on my own, things began to go slightly
against me.

I was jogging happily up the trail, feeling for the first time a
little like an explorer, when I met the neighbouring boviander
squatting moodily on a tree stump beside a pile of tins that were
obviously part of my stores. The man grinned amiably and took
off his hat. 'Yetto and Price say to take these back,' he explained.
'Horse no can carry. Him lie down all de time.'

'Lies down?'

'All de time. Dey beat him with a stick and him goes little
little way and den him lie down again. Him no get top side. De
boys make pack lighter.'

I looked at the pile and saw that, with a minimum of discrimination, they had abandoned my entire meat ration. There seemed nothing to be done. I picked out half a dozen tins, rolled them up in the hammock at the back of my saddle and told the man to present the rest to Mr Bain with my compliments. Then I rode on less contentedly.

About six miles farther on I came upon the pack horse un-saddled and hobbled, his pack lying on the ground near him. I shouted for Yetto who eventually appeared from the bush where he and Price had been having a nap.

'Him weary,' said Yetto. 'Him no carry pack top-side.' We undid the loads and rearranged them, sifting out everything unessential from the heap. An Indian boy had appeared mys-teriously and I entrusted to him the stores we could not take, to carry back to Kurupukari. Then I rode on ahead to the shelter where we should spend the night. I waited two hours and there was no trace of the baggage. Then I resaddled my horse and rode back. About a mile from where I had left them, Yetto and Price were sitting on a fallen tree eating farine. The horse was grazing near them, the packs were on the ground.

'Dat horse am sick. Him no go at all.'

It was now late afternoon. There was nothing for it but to return to Kurupukari, so I left Price to guard the stores, told Yetto to follow with the pack horse and rode back to the river.

That ride remains one of the most vivid memories of the cattle trail. Checked and annoyed as I was, the splendour of the evening compensated for everything. Out on the savannah there is no twilight; the sun goes down blazing on the horizon, affording five or ten minutes of gold and crimson glory; then darkness. In the forest night opens slowly like a yawn. The colours gradually deepened, the greens pure and intense to the point of saturation, the tree trunks and the bare earth glowing brown; the half shades, the broken and refracted fragments of light all disappeared and left only fathomless depths of pure colour. Then dusk spread; distances became incalculable and obstacles detached themselves unexpectedly and came suddenly near; and while it was almost night in the trail the tops of the trees were still ablaze with sunlight, till eventually they too darkened and their flowers were lost. And all the pattering and whistling and chattering of the bush at night broke out loudly on all sides, and the tired little horse – who was doing a double journey and, being always on the move, had no instinct for home – suddenly pricked his ears and raised his head and stepped out fresh as though his day were only just beginning.

It was black night when I reached the corral. I hobbled him, took off his bridle and saddle and carried them down to the water's edge. The other bank showed no light. After prolonged shouting I heard an answering call and twenty minutes later a canoe appeared suddenly at my feet. Mr Bain received me without surprise. He never thought I would get far alone.

Next day there was more reorganization. The sergeant hired me a donkey named Maria and a vain young Negro named Sinclair, who had been hanging about without apparent purpose in and out of the house for some days.

Next day we set out again and reassembled at the place where I had left the stores, Yetto, Price, Sinclair, the horse, Maria, and myself, and began dividing up the loads and the duties. For his half-dollar a day a boy is assumed to be able to carry about fifty pounds for about twenty miles. It was Yetto's boast, of which the others were quick to take advantage, that he could carry a hundred pounds for fifty miles. I used to see them piling things on to Yetto's back and him taking them with pride and good humour. Sinclair was an odious youth but he knew a little about cooking. The other two hated him and on the last days went without food altogether rather than take it from him. He asked if he might drive the ass and I said yes. He then made the point that it was impossible both to carry a pack and drive the ass who strayed all over the path and needed constant goading along. In point of fact Maria did nothing of the sort. She quickly got wise to the fact that if she stayed behind with the boys, they unslung their loads as soon as I was out of sight, and put them on her back. Accordingly she used to break away and trot along happily beside the horse. This was maddening for me, because every few miles her pack would work loose and she would start scattering bits of luggage along the trail and I would have to stop and rearrange things.

Every evening Yetto had complaints against Sinclair. 'Chief, dat boy no good at all. Him too young; him not know discipline.'

Every day I used to decide to pay him off and send him back; then I used to think of Yetto's detestable cooking and hesitate. And on these occasions Sinclair always succeeded in putting me in a good temper. He would appear with my towel just when I wanted it; he would find a lime tree and unasked prepare me rum and lime when I returned from my bath in the creek; he knew exactly the things I should want, map, journal, fountain pen, glasses, and laid them out just where I needed them beside the hammock. So in spite of the fact that I knew him to be lazy, untruthful, disloyal, sulky and conceited, he remained in my service to the end as far as the frontier.

To this rather absurd little band there attached himself a spectral figure named Jagger. I had seen him, too, moping on the steps at Kurupukari and heard Mr Bain upbraiding him on more than one occasion on some obscure subject connected with the post office. He was a coloured youth in the technical Georgetown sense of the word and in that sense only; for I never saw a face so devoid of a nameable hue. It was a ghastly *grisaille* except for his eyes which were of a yellowish tinge, the colour of trodden snow, and circled with pink. He loped along with us carrying his own food and belongings; never asking for anything except company, always eager to help with advice. He spoke accurate and elaborate English, in a toneless, lisping voice that would have sounded supercilious had it not been accompanied by his expression of inflexible misery and self-disgust.

I never fully mastered the history of his downfall which was connected in some way with litigation, wills and money-lenders. Yetto explained it quite simply, 'Him was robbed by his brudders.'

He had fever badly, and on the second day arrived at the midday halt well behind the others, dragging himself along unsteadily. He hung up his hammock, rolled into it and lay with averted face, unwilling to eat or talk. As I rode on that afternoon I began to worry about Jagger. It really looked as though he might be going to die on our hands; in his present state he would never reach the savannah on foot. Here I felt was the time for a Christian gentleman to show his principles; to emulate Sir Philip Sidney.

213

'Yetto,' I said that evening, 'I think that tomorrow Jagger had better ride my horse. I can easily walk the next few stages.'

'Dat's all right, Chief,' said Yetto. 'Him not come on.'

'Not come on?'

'Him plenty sick. Him stay in his hammock, back where us had breakfast.'

'But will he be all right?'

'Oh yes, Chief, him'll be all right. Him sick, dat's all.'

Later that evening half a dozen *vaqueiros* arrived with a drove of fifty cattle. I gave them quinine for Jagger and instructions to look after him, but I never heard whether or no he reached the savannah.

During the first week's ride, when I had been with Mr Bain, continually entertained by the fresh spate of his reminiscences, I had had practically no conversation with the boys. Now in the evenings, and particularly after wet days when I issued a ration of rum, I found them very sound company, particularly Yetto.

Like most people in the colony Yetto had done a variety of jobs in his time. He had formed one of the police guard of honour when the Prince of Wales visited Georgetown and the Prince had shaken hands with him. He had once set out on an ill-fated expedition to Cuba – a story which was introduced by: 'Chief, did you ever know a black man from Grenada named Adams?'

'No, I'm afraid not.'

'Him stole twenty dollars off of me.'

Adams had taken charge of the joint funds and absconded in Trinidad.

Yetto had been married but had not liked it. He had seen the Georgetown riots. But the high summit of his experience had been a lucky strike as a 'pork knocker'. He had come back to Georgetown with $800 and had spent it in six weeks.

'Why, Chief, me took an automobile and drove round and round de town with three girls and me give them gold bangles and went to all de best rum shops and hotels. But me didn't drink no rum, no Chief, nor beer either. It was gin and whisky all de time. Me didn't get no sleep for days, driving round all night with the girls.'

'But tell me, Yetto, did you get any better girls for all this money you were spending?'

'No, Chief, just de same girls but me like to see dem happy. Dey was fine girls but you could get dem for a dollar a night. But me give dem gold bangles and gin and whisky and a drive round and round in an automobile. All de girls plenty fond of Yetto when he had de money. ... But me was young den. Now me learned wisdom.'

'What would you do if you had the money now?'

There was a pause and I expected Yetto to tell me that he would buy a farm or a shop and settle down from the arduous and unsettled life he was now living. 'Well, Chief, me tell you dis. Me would spend all de money on myself. Me would buy fine clothes and rings. Den de girls would go wid me for de hope of what me was going to give dem. And in de end me would give dem nothing.' And he opened his vast mouth and roared with laughter, his gold teeth flashing in the firelight.

But his pleasures had not been wholly philistine. During that rapturous six weeks an Italian opera singer had given a concert in Georgetown (... shadow and spangle of cheap tragedy ... the ageing prima donna, Grand Dukes and English Milords behind her, pitifully touring, in the company of her seedy and devoted manager, yearly to more remote and less lucrative audiences to the final, tartarean abyss of a Georgetown concert hall ...).

'De cheapest ticket was two dollars but me went with my girl. Dere was all white people dere and de way her sung was wonderful, wid a different coloured dress for each song and dey was in all de languages, French and English and Italian and German and Spanish. Dat lady knew everything. Her made us cry.'

The last time that Yetto had come up the trail had been in the company of a government vet. and his wife and the presence of the lady gave the occasion a peculiar lustre in Yetto's eyes. It had been altogether a very magnificent expedition with collapsible camp tables, picnic baskets and a cocktail shaker. They had travelled ten miles a day on foot with a troop of porters. Every place where they had halted was sanctified in Yetto's eyes. 'Dis is where Mrs McDougal shot an accouri' ... 'Dis is where Mrs McDougal was so weary dat Mr McDougal had to take off her

boots' ... 'Dis is where Mrs McDougal had a bath' ... Yetto
had not missed a detail of her habits or idiosyncrasies. 'Mrs
McDougal had a great fancy for me. Her took my snapshot. Her
said, "Now I must take Yetto," and her did. Doctor McDougal
promised to send me a print. Tomorrow me show you de very
tree where Mrs McDougal took my snapshot. When we get to
Takama her say, "I don't know what we should have done
without Yetto." Dere's nothing me wouldn't do for Mrs
McDougal.'

On the third day from Kurupukari we crossed a dry creek and
came into a little savannah named after the creek, Surana, where
there was an Indian village. These were sophisticated Macushis
who were in constant contact with the ranches and the traffic of
the trail.

About a dozen or fifteen huts could be seen at Surana. A
polite English-speaking young man came out to meet me and
showed me an empty mud and thatched hut where I could spend
the night, and the water hole, half a mile distant, where I could
wash. Later some of the women brought me a present of bananas.
It was a hospitable place. Many of them assembled to stare and
talk to the boys.

'Dey all love Yetto,' said Yetto.

Next day we reached Anai on the edge of the savannah. It
was exhilarating to see open country again after the cramped
weeks in the forest.

'Dat house is so healthy,' said Yetto, 'dat yo shiver all night.'

There were other occupants on the evening of my arrival; a
surly Syrian, with a flabby white face, grotesque in riding clothes.

'Dat a very cruel man. Him tie up de Indians all night and
beat dem until Mr Bain stop him.'

Yetto's predictions about the healthiness of the place proved
quite accurate. It was deadly cold after the soft, close nights of the
forest.

Next day a painful ride, the first of many that were to follow.
The heat was intense, glaring up off the earth so that my face was
skinned under the shade of a broad-brimmed hat. Exhaustion was
infectious; I felt it seeping up from the stumbling horse, seeping

down into him from me. Constant urging was necessary to keep him at a trot. When he fell into a walk the dead hardness of the saddle was intolerable. Above all there was thirst. Later I had many longer and hotter days without water, but this was the first of them and I was fresh from the deep shade and purling creeks of the forest. The trail, clear enough in places, would sometimes dwindle and peter out among patches of dried sedge; then it was necessary to cast round in widening circles until I picked it up again after a loss of time and strength. Often it would split and divide into two equally prominent branches. In this way I must have covered nearly double the real distance, when, at about five in the afternoon, I arrived at my destination.

This was the ranch of a man named Christie. I knew nothing about him except what I had been told the previous evening; that he was very old and 'very religious'. His religion, I was warned, took the form that he did not participate in the open hospitality of the savannah. He allowed – he could scarcely have prevented it – passers-by to hobble their horses in his corral and sleep under his shelter, but that was the full extent of his goodwill.

Visibility is poor on the savannah by reason of the 'sand-paper' trees. These low shrubs, six or ten feet in height, are scattered loosely all over the country at intervals of twenty yards or so; sometimes they are thicker and from a distance give the impression of a copse, but when approached always resolve into isolated units; they throw almost no shade; their leaves are very rough on one side and it is from this peculiarity that they get their name; their wood is brittle and useless for any practical purpose. Their only good quality, that I was able to discover, was the element of surprise that they gave to travelling. In some countries one sees the day's objective from the start; it is there in front of one, hour after hour, mile after mile, just as remote, apparently, at noon as it had been at dawn; one's eyes dazzle with constant staring. The 'sand-paper' trees often hid a house from view – particularly the low, dun houses of the district – until one was practically inside it. Then there would be a sudden, exultant, a scarcely credulous, inward leap of delight as one realized, at the worst and almost desperate hour of the day, that one's distress was over. Horse and I were both unsteady with fatigue when an Indian home came into view quite near us. Then another, with some women squatting in front. They ran in and hid at my approach but I rode up to the door and shouted into the darkness, making the motions of drinking. After some giggling and nudging one of them brought me out a calabash of cold water. Then I said 'Christie' and they repeated 'Christie' and giggled more. Finally one of them came out and pointed. Another twenty minutes brought me to the ranch. It was a handful of huts, thrown out haphazard on the ground like the waste stuff of a picnic party. There was no one about. I dismounted and walked round. The central and largest house was only half built but there was another near it with dilapidated thatch, open at all sides, which was distinguishable from the others by a plank floor, raised a couple of feet from the earth. Here, reclining in a hammock and sipping cold water from the spout of a white enamelled teapot, was Mr Christie.

He had a long white moustache and a white woolly head; his face was of the same sun-baked, fever-blanched colour as were most faces in the colony but of unmistakable Negro structure. It is illegal for blacks – or for that matter, whites, unless they get permission – to settle in Indian country and I learned that for the first ten years or so of his residence there had been repeated attempts by the government to evict him; after that they had let him be. I greeted him and asked where I could water my horse. He smiled in a dreamy, absent-minded manner and said, 'I was expecting you. I was warned in a vision of your approach.'

He climbed out of the hammock, looked about for shoes, found only one, and hobbled across to shake hands with me.

'I always know the character of any visitors by the visions I have of them. Sometimes I see a pig or a jackal; often a ravaging tiger.'

I could not resist asking, 'And how did you see me?'

'As a sweetly toned harmonium,' said Mr Christie politely.

He pointed out the tenuous straggle of footpath that led to the water hole. I took off saddle and bridle and led the horse down by his rope halter. He whinnied at the smell of water and we both drank immoderately; he was trembling in the legs and lathered in sweat but, I was glad to find, not galled. I sluiced him down, turned him into the corral, and left him happily rolling in the dust. Then I slung my hammock under a shelter near Mr Christie's house and fell asleep until, two hours later, the rest of my party arrived. They had my change of clothes with them. As soon as they arrived I got out of boots and breeches, had a bath and a mug of rum. I drank a lot of rum that evening; how much I did not realize until next morning when I discovered the empty bottle. Sinclair, knowing that there was a row in the air, had picked a handful of limes on his way. He filled up the mug assiduously with rum and limes and brown sugar and cold, rather muddy water. I did not investigate the boys' quarrel and Sinclair did not get the sack. The sweet and splendid spirit, the exhaustion of the day, its heat, thirst, hunger and the effects of the fall, the fantastic conversations of Mr Christie, translated that evening and raised it a finger's breadth above reality.

The lamp stood on the floor in the middle of the shelter so that all the faces were illumined as faces are not meant to be seen; from below with cheek bones casting shadows across their eyes and strong light under the brows and chin and nostrils. Everyone in the vicinity came round to watch me eat supper. Mr Christie stalked round and round the lamp telling me about God.

He asked me whether I were a 'believer' and I said yes, a Catholic.

'There are *some* good Catholics,' conceded Mr Christie, 'they are far from the truth but they are in the right direction. Only the other evening I was looking at the choir of the blessed singing before the throne of God and to my great surprise, I recognized the late Bishop of Guiana ... but they take too much on themselves. Their ministers like to be called "father". There is only one "Father" – the one above.'

'Have you the same objection to children addressing their male parent in that way?'

'It is a terrible thing to be a male parent' – Mr Christie had a large family by an Indian mistress – 'Verily it is written' – and he quoted some text I cannot remember to the effect that children are a curse. 'Why only the other day my eldest son begat a child by a woman of no cultivation. He even speaks of marrying her.'

'But living as you do out here in the savannah, is lack of cultivation a very serious matter?'

'It is very serious when she will not sing,' said Mr Christie severely.

We spoke of the uncle of some friends of mine who had worked in this district as a missionary and retired to England as the result of a complete breakdown.

'That man had the devil in him,' said Mr Christie. 'Do you know what he did? He boiled a chicken in the place where I used to say my prayers. I have never been there since. It was defiled.'

I told him that the priest had since recovered his health and was working on the South Coast.

'No, no, I assure you that the contrary is the case. He appeared to me the other night and all the time he spoke to me his head rolled about the floor in a most horrible manner. So I knew he was still mad.'

Every Sunday he preached for four or five hours to the neighbouring Indians. I asked him whether his work among them was successful. 'No, not successful, you could not call it successful. I have been here for thirty years and so far have made no converts at all. Even my own family have the devil in them.'

He told me that he was at work on a translation of the scriptures into Macushi, 'but I have to change and omit a great deal. There is so much I do not agree with ... but I am not worried. I expect the end of the world shortly.' Some years back he had seen a number flashed in the sky and that was the number of days remaining. I asked him how he knew that that was the meaning of the number.

'What else could it be?' he asked.

As I sat soaking rum he told of numerous visions. How when his mistress died he had heard a voice from heaven say, 'The old horse is dead.'

'It did not mean that she was like a horse. In some ways she was very pretty. It meant no more riding for me.'

Lately he had been privileged to see the total assembly of the elect in heaven.

'Were there many of them?'

'It was hard to count because you see they had no bodies but my impression is that there were very few.'

I asked if he believed in the Trinity. 'Believe in it? I could not live without it But the mistake the Catholics make is to call it a mystery. It is all quite simple to me.' He told me how the Pope had had a French admiral murdered and his heart sent to Rome in a gold box; also that Freemasons stole bodies out of the cemetery and kept them in a cellar below every Lodge. You could always tell a Freemason, he said, because they had VOL branded on their buttocks. 'It means volunteer, I suppose,' he said. 'I can't think why.'

Presently some of the onlookers in the outer circle came into the hut and squatted down round the lamp. I had some cocoa made and handed round. One of Mr Christie's daughters had married an East Indian. The man put a naked child on my knee and attempted to interest me in a row he was having with the policeman at Anai about illicit tobacco selling. It was all a trumped-up charge, he said, the result of spite. But I was not in the mood to follow his difficulties.

After a little I fell asleep and woke up to find the party still going on and Mr Christie still talking of visions and mystic numbers. When I next awoke they had all gone away, but I could hear Mr Christie prowling round in the darkness outside and muttering to himself.

Next day was easy going.

The ranch I was making for was the property of a Georgetown Chinaman named Mr Wong, who was one of Yetto's heroes on account of his reputation for high play at cards. The manager was a swarthy, genial man, with a well-trained Indian mistress. He was clever with his fingers and the eaves of the huts were hung with bridles and whips of plaited hide and ornamented saddles of his own making. There was a certain swagger in his clothes; he had a big-brimmed, leather-bound Brazilian hat, large silver buckles down the sides of his leggings and a silver-hilted knife stuck into one of them; large spurs were strapped on to his bare, horny heels.

I asked the way to wash and was shown a path through the vegetable garden into a belt of bush. I went down and, pushing through, suddenly found a sharp precipice at my feet and a dark, swift river of some breadth. It was unexpected and dramatic after the great stretch of arid savannah all round. On the opposite side there was the same clay cliff and a fringe of bush; that was Brazil. I had not taken in – for the ranch was not marked on the map – that I was already at the frontier and that this was the Ireng. I was to see plenty of this river later on and grow to hate it.

The river bank was infested by cabouri fly, odious insects so small that they easily penetrate any ordinary mosquito curtain; they breed in running water and attack in great numbers. You cannot feel their bite until they have finished sucking; then they leave a little black spot behind them and a circle of burning flesh.

Insects played a prominent part in my experience throughout all this period. For the preceding week I had been discomforted by *bêtes rouges*, a minute red creature which brushes off the leaves of the bush on to one's clothes and finds its way below one's skin where it causes unendurable itching. My arms and legs were covered with these in spite of crab oil and antiseptic soap and I scratched until I was raw. It is quite accurate to say that in the weeks from leaving Kurupukari until some time after my final return to Georgetown, there was not a two-inch square on my body that was not itching at some time of the day or night.

A Portuguese family came to call that afternoon with a guitar. They all came in and solemnly shook hands with me – about eight of them – on arrival and on departure.

Two wild-eyed, shaggy Patamona Indians also arrived in a canoe from upstream, trying to trade a monkey for some gunpowder, for Wong's ranch is at one extreme angle of the savannah, the nearest civilized spot to the Pakaraima district.

Two days later we reached St Ignatius, where I was to spend ten days as the guest of Father Mather, the kindest and most generous of all the hosts of the colony.

He was at work in his carpenter's shop when we arrived and came out to greet us, dusting the shavings off his khaki shirt and trousers, and presenting a complete antithesis of the 'wily Jesuit' of popular tradition. Most of the simple furniture of the living-room was his work – firm, finely jointed and fitted, delicately finished, a marked contrast to the botched, makeshift stuff that prevailed even in Georgetown. He loves and studies all natural things, in particular woods and birds about which he has huge

222

stores of first-hand knowledge. It is very rarely that he goes down to the coast; when he does the river-side scenery – to me unendurably monotonous – provides a luxurious orgy of observation; occasionally some call will take him into the hills, but for the most part his work keeps him in the desolate surroundings of St Ignatius, and his researches are confined to the insects that collect round his reading-lamp in the evenings.

I paid off Yetto, Sinclair and Price, for blacks are not encouraged to stay long among the Indians. Before they left they each asked to be photographed and in turn wore Yetto's old cloth cap and Price's spotted handkerchief for their portraits.

St Ignatius was very unlike the missions of Africa – the crowded compounds, big school houses with their rows of woolly black heads patiently absorbing 'education'; the solid presbyteries and packed, devout congregations; the native priests and nuns, methodical in white linen and topees; the troops of black children veiled for their first Communion; the plain chant and the examination papers. It was as lonely an outpost of religion as you could find anywhere. If it had not been for the Calvary on the river-bank, it might have been one of the smaller ranches.

Near the house was a small church built of tin and thatch and furnished with a few benches six inches high from the mud floor; it was open at the west end for light and ventilation, and, in spite of every discouragement and a barrier of wire netting, a hen used regularly to lay her eggs behind the altar.

Here Father Mather lived quite alone for the greater part of the year. Another priest, Father Keary, used the home as his headquarters but except in the wet weather he was continually on circuit among the villages. Father Mather kept the home going and managed the ranch and stores.

I have often observed that the servants of the religious are, as a class, of abnormally low mentality. I do not know why this should be – whether it is that good people in their charity give jobs to those whom no one else will employ, or whether, being poor, they get them cheap, or whether they welcome inefficient service as a mortification, or whether unremitting association with people of superior virtue eventually drives sane servants off their heads. Whatever the explanation, that is usually the state of affairs. Father Mather's establishment, however, was an exception. It is true that there was an idiot Macushi boy who constantly obtruded a moon face round the door at meal-times, asking for tobacco, but he was employed only on casual labour outside the house. The two Indian widows who cooked, wove hammocks, drove the guinea fowl out of the bedrooms and generally 'did for us' were exemplary people. So was David Max y Hung, the head *vaqueiro*. This pious and efficient young man spoke two Indian languages, English, and Portuguese, perfectly. He was half Chinese, half Arawak Indian and his wife was Brazilian. He was away at a round-up at the time of my arrival (every ranch sends a representative at every round-up to identify his own cattle and see that there is no tampering with the brands) and it was his absence that prolonged my stay so pleasantly, for on the first evening Father Mather explained to me that it was quite hopeless to think of reaching Boa Vista by canoe at that season. It was easy, however, to ride there, and on David's return I could have horses and David himself for a guide. So I stayed on, glad of the rest and learning hourly from Father Mather more about the country.

The life of the Brazilian frontier must, I should think, be unique in the British Empire. In its whole length from Mount Roraima to the Courantyne – a distance of about five hundred miles – Bon Success is the only British government station, and that is under the admirable management of Mr Melville, who is half Indian by birth and married to a Brazilian. On the other side there is no representative of law nearer than Boa Vista. There are no flags, no military, no customs, no passport examinations, no immigration forms. The Indians have probably very little idea of whether they are on British or Brazilian territory; they wander to and fro across the border exactly as they did before the days of Raleigh.

Throughout the whole district, too, there is only one shop and that is in two parts, half in Brazil and half in British Guiana. The proprietor is a Portuguese named Mr Figuiredo. On his own side of the river he sells things of Brazilian origin, hardware, ammunition, alcohol in various unpalatable forms, sugar and *farine*, a few decayed-looking tins of fruit and sweets, tobacco, horses, saddlery and second-hand odds and ends extorted from bankrupt ranchers; on the British side he sells things brought up from Georgetown, mostly male and female clothing, soaps and hair oils, for which the more sophisticated Indians have a quite un-sophisticated relish, and brands of patent medicines with en-graved, pictorial labels and unfamiliar names – 'Radways Rapid Relief', 'Canadian Healing Oil', 'Lydia Pynkham's Vegetable Product'. If a Brazilian wants anything from the British side he and Mr Figuiredo paddle across the river and he buys it there; and vice versa. Any guilt of smuggling attaches to the customer.

Father Mather and I went to breakfast with Mr Figuiredo one day. He gave us course after course of food – stewed *tasso* with rice, minced *tasso* with *farine*, fresh beef with sweet potatoes, fresh pork, fried eggs, bananas, tinned peaches and crème de cacao of local distillation. His women folk were made to stand outside while we ate, with the exception of one handsome daughter who waited. After breakfast we went into the shop and Mr Figuiredo made an effortless and unembarrassing transition from host to shopkeeper, climbing behind the counter and arguing genially about the price of coffee. He has no competition within two hun-dred miles and his prices are enormous; but he lives in a very simple fashion, dressing always in an old suit of pyjamas and employing his family to do the work of the house.

After a week David returned from the round-up – suave, spectacled, faultlessly efficient – and took over the arrangements for my journey to Boa Vista.

David's Brazilian brother-in-law Francisco joined us; the luggage was divided – unequally, for I took only hammock, blanket and change of clothes – between our three horses. Then after breakfast on 1st February, we set off for the border. The sun was obscured and a light drizzle of rain was falling.

The ford was about three miles upstream from St Ignatius. Our horses waded through the shallow water, stretching forward to drink; half way over we were in Brazil. A lurch and scramble up the opposite bank; we forced our way through the fringe of bush, leaning low in the saddle to guard our faces from the thorn branches; then we were out into open country again, flat and desolate as the savannah we had left; more desolate, for here there was no vestige of life; no cattle track, no stray animals; simply the empty plain; sparse, colourless grass; ant-hills; sand-paper trees; an occasional clump of ragged palm; grey sky, gusts of wind, and a dull sweep of rain.

On the fourth day we reached the bank of the Rio Branco at an empty hut immediately opposite Boa Vista.

Since the evening at Kurupukari when Mr Bain had first mentioned its name, Boa Vista had come to assume greater and greater importance to me. Father Mather had been there only once, and then in the worst stage of malignant malaria, so that he had been able to tell me little about it except that some German nuns had proved deft and devoted nurses. Everybody else, however, and particularly David, had spoken of it as a town of dazzling attraction. Whatever I had looked for in vain at Figuiredo's store was, he told me, procurable at 'Boa Vist''; Mr Daguar had extolled its modernity and luxury – electric light, cafés, fine buildings, women, politics, murders. Mr Bain had told of the fast motor launches, plying constantly between there and Manaos. In the discomfort of the journey there, I had looked forward to the soft living of Boa Vista, feeling that these asperities were, in fact, a suitable contrast, preparing my sense for a fuller appreciation of the good things in store. So confident was I that when we first came in sight of the ramshackle huddle of buildings on the further bank, I was quite uncritical and conscious of no emotion except delight and expectation.

The river was enormously broad and very low; so low that as we gazed at the town across sand dunes and channels and a fair-sized island it seemed to be perched on a citadel, instead of being, as was actually the case, at the same dead level as the rest of the plain. Two *vaqueiros* were lying in hammocks by the bank, and from these David elicited the information that a boat was expected some time in the next few hours to ferry them across. The *vaqueiros* studied us with an air that I came to recognize as characteristic of Boa Vista; it was utterly unlike the open geniality

226

of the ranches; conveying, as it did, in equal degrees, contempt, suspicion and the suggestion that only listlessness kept them from active insult.

With David's assistance, I began some enquiries about accommodation. There was none, they said.

'But I understood there were two excellent hotels.'

'Ah, that was in the days of the Company. There was all kinds of foolishness in the days of the Company. There is nowhere now. There has not been an hotel for two years.'

'Then where do strangers stay?'

'Strangers do not come to Boa Vist'. If they come on business, the people they have business with put them up.'

I explained that I was on the way to Manaos and had to wait for a boat. They showed complete indifference, only remarking that they did not know of any boat to Manaos. Then one of them added that possibly the foreign priests would do something for me – unless they had left; last time he was in Boa Vist' the foreign priests were all sick; most people were sick in Boa Vist'. Then the two men started talking to each other.

My enthusiasm had already cooled considerably by the time we saw a boat put out from the opposite shore and make slowly towards us. We all got in, David, Francisco, I, the two surly *vaqueiros*, the saddles and the baggage, so that the gunwales were only an inch clear of the water. Then partly paddling, partly wading and pushing, we made our way across. There were women squatting on the further shore, pounding dirty linen on the rocks at the water's edge. We hauled our possessions up the steep bank and found ourselves in the main street of the town. It was very broad, composed of hard, uneven mud, cracked into wide fissures in all directions and scored by several dry gulleys. On either side was a row of single-storeyed, whitewashed mud houses with tiled roofs; at each doorstep sat one or more of the citizens staring at us with eyes that were insolent, hostile and apathetic; a few naked children rolled about at their feet. The remains of an overhead electric cable hung loose from a row of crazy posts, or lay in coils and loops about the gutter.

The street rose to a slight hill and half-way up we came to the Benedictine Mission. This at any rate presented a more imposing aspect than anything I had seen since leaving Georgetown. It was built of concrete with a modestly ornamented façade, a row of unbroken glass windows, a carved front door with an electric bell, a balustraded verandah with concrete urns at either end; in front of it lay a strip of garden marked out into symmetrical beds with brick borders.

We approached rather diffidently, for we were shabby and stained with travelling and lately unaccustomed to carved front doors and electric bells. But the bell need have caused us no misgiving, for it was out of order. We pressed and waited and pressed again. Then a head appeared from a window and told us, in Portuguese, to knock. We knocked several times until the head reappeared; it was Teutonic in character, blond and slightly bald, wrinkled, with a prominent jaw and innocent eyes.

'The gentleman is a stranger too. He speaks Portuguese in a way I do not understand,' said David. 'He says there is a priest but that he is probably out.'

I was used to waiting by now, so we sat on the doorstep among our luggage until presently an emaciated young monk in white habit appeared up the garden path. He seemed to accept our arrival with resignation, opened the door and led us into one of those rooms found only in religious houses, shuttered, stuffy and geometrically regular in arrangement; four stiff chairs ranged round four walls; devotional oleographs symmetrically balanced; a table in the exact centre with an embroidered cloth and a pot of artificial flowers; everything showing by its high polish of cleanliness that nuns had been at work there.

The monk was a German-Swiss. We spoke in halting French and I explained my situation. He nodded gloomily and said that it was impossible to predict when another boat would leave for Manaos; on the other hand a new Prior was expected some time soon and that boat must presumably return one day. Meanwhile I was at liberty to stay in the house if I chose.

'Will it be a question of days or weeks?'

'A question of weeks or months.'

David thought the Boundary Commission had a boat going down in a few days; he would go into the town and enquire. With rather lugubrious courtesy the monk, who was named Father

Alcuin, showed me a room and a shower bath; explained that he and the other guest had already breakfasted; sent across to the convent for food for me. I ate the first palatable meal since I had left St Ignatius, changed and slept. Presently David returned with reassuring information. The Commission boat was passing through in four or five days; a week after that there would be a trade launch. He smiled proudly both at bringing good news and because he had bought a startling new belt out of his wages. Then he and Francisco bade me good-bye and went to rest with the horses on the other bank of the river.

Already, in the few hours of my sojourn there, the Boa Vista of my imagination had come to grief. Gone; engulfed in an earthquake, uprooted by a tornado and tossed sky-high like chaff in the wind, scorched up with brimstone like Gomorrah, toppled over with trumpets like Jericho, ploughed like Carthage, bought, demolished and transported brick by brick to another continent as though it had taken the fancy of Mr Hearst; tall Troy was down. When I set out on a stroll of exploration, I no longer expected the city I had had in mind during the thirsty days of approach; the shady boulevards; kiosks for flowers and cigars and illustrated papers; the hotel terrace and the cafés; the baroque church built by seventeenth-century missionaries; the bastions of the old fort; the bandstand in the square, standing amidst fountains and flowering shrubs; the soft, slightly swaggering citizens, some uniformed and spurred, others with Southern elegance twirling little canes, bowing from the waist and raising boater hats, flicking with white gloves indiscernible particles of dust from their white linen spats; dark beauties languorous on balconies, or glancing over fans at the café tables. All that extravagant and highly improbable expectation had been obliterated like a sand castle beneath the encroaching tide.

Closer investigation did nothing to restore it. There was the broad main street up which we had come; two parallel, less important streets and four or five more laid at right angles to them. At a quarter of a mile in every direction they petered out into straggling footpaths. They were all called Avenidas and labelled with names of politicians of local significance. The town had been planned on an ambitious scale, spacious, rectangular, but most of the building lots were still unoccupied. There was one fair-sized store, a little larger and a little better stocked than Figuiredo's, half a dozen seedy little shops; an open booth advertising the services of a barber-surgeon who claimed to wave women's hair, extract teeth and cure venereal disease; a tumble-down house inhabited by the nuns, an open schoolhouse where a fever-stricken teacher could be observed monotonously haranguing a huge class of listless little boys; a wireless office, and a cottage where they accepted letters for the post; there were two cafés; one on the main street was a little shed, selling *farine*, bananas and fish, there were three tables in front of it, under a tree, where a few people collected in the evening to drink coffee in the light of a single lantern; the second, in a side street, was more attractive. It had a concrete floor and a counter where one could buy cigarettes and nuts, there were dominoes for the use of habitués and, besides coffee, one could drink warm and expensive beer.

The only place, besides the Benedictine Priory, which had any pretensions to magnificence was the church, a modern building painted in yellow and orange horizontal stripes, with ornate concrete mouldings; there were old bells outside, and inside three sumptuous altars, with embroidered frontals and veils, carved reredoses, large, highly coloured statues, artificial flowers and polished candlesticks, decorated wooden pews, a marble font bearing in enormous letters the name of the chief merchant of the town, a harmonium; everything very new, and clean as a hospital – not a hen or a pig in the building. I was curious to know by what benefaction this expensive church had come into being and was told that, like most things, it had started 'in the days of the Company'.

I discovered one English-speaking person in the town; a singularly charmless youth, the illegitimate son of a prominent Georgetown citizen whom I had met there at Christmas time. This served as a fragile link between us, for the young man told me that he hated his father and had thought of shooting him on more than one occasion. 'Now I have been married and have written five times for money and had no answer.'

230

He was completely fleshless like all the inhabitants of Boa Vista, with dank, black hair hanging over his eyes, which were of slightly lighter yellow than the rest of his face. He spoke in a melancholy drawl. He was almost the only person I saw doing any work in the whole town. He owned a small blacksmith's shop where he made branding irons and mended guns. Most of the other inhabitants seemed to have no occupation of any kind, being caught up in the vicious circle of semi-starvation. Perhaps they picked up a few casual wages during the flood season when boats ran from Manaos fairly frequently and the ranchers came in for stores and needed labour for shipping their cattle. All the time that I was there I scarcely saw anyone except the school teacher earn anything – or spend anything. Even in the café the majority of customers came to gossip and play dominoes and went away without ordering a cup of coffee. At some miles distance was a settlement of soldiers who brought a few shillings into the town; they were reservists bedded out with wives on small allotments. An aged town clerk presumably received some sort of wages; so no doubt did the itinerant government vet. who appeared from time to time; so did the wireless operator and an official of villainous aspect called the 'Collector'. But the other thousand odd inhabitants spent the day lying indoors in their hammocks and the evenings squatting on their doorsteps gossiping. Land was free, and, as the nuns proved, could produce excellent vegetables, but the diet of the town was *farine, tasso* and a little fish, all of which were of negligible cost. But it was far from being a care-free, idyllic improvidence. Everyone looked ill and discontented. There was not a fat man or woman anywhere. The women, in fact, led an even drearier life than the men. They had no household possessions to care for, no cooking to do, they left their children to sprawl about the streets naked or in rags. They were pretty – very small and thin, small-boned and with delicate features; a few of them took trouble with their appearance and put in an appearance at Mass on Sundays in light dresses, stockings and shoes, and cheap, gay combs in their hair.

From fragmentary and not altogether reliable sources I picked up a little history of Boa Vista. It was a melancholy record. The most patriotic Brazilian can find little to say in favour of the inhabitants of Amazonas; they are mostly descended from convicts, loosed there after their term of imprisonment as the French loose their criminals in Cayenne, to make whatever sort of living they can in an inhospitable country. Practically all of them are of mixed Indian and Portuguese blood. There is no accurate census, but a recent medical survey in the *Geographical Magazine* reports that they are dying out, families usually becoming sterile in three generations; alien immigrants, mostly German and Japanese, are gradually pushing what is left of them up country; Boa Vista is their final halting place before extinction. The best of them go out into the ranches; the worst remain in the town.

They are naturally homicidal by inclination, and every man, however poor, carries arms; only the universal apathy keeps them from frequent bloodshed. There were no shootings while I was there; in fact there had not been one for several months, but I lived all the time in an atmosphere that was novel to me, where murder was always in the air. The German at the Priory constantly slept with a loaded gun at his bedside and expressed surprise at seeing me going shopping without a revolver; the blacksmith, partly no doubt owing to his avocation, spoke of little else; one of his main preoccupations was altering trigger springs so that they could be fired quick on the draw.

There was rarely a conviction for murder. The two most sensational trials of late years had both resulted in acquittals. One was the case of a young Britisher who had come across from Guiana, panning gold. He had no right there and one evening in the café tipsily expressed his willingness to shoot anyone who interfered with him. The boast was accepted as constituting provocation when, a few nights later, he was shot in the back and robbed, while entering his house.

The other case was more remarkable. Two respected citizens, a Dr Zany and a Mr Homero Cruz, were sitting on a verandah talking, when a political opponent rode up and shot Dr Zany. His plea of innocence, when brought to trial, was that the whole thing had been a mistake; he had meant to kill Mr Cruz. The judges accepted the defence and brought in a verdict of death from misadventure.

232

From time to time attempts have been made to raise the condition of the town. A little before the War a German appeared with ample capital and began buying cattle. He offered and paid a bigger price than the ranchers had ever before received; he fitted out a fleet of large motor launches to take the beasts down to market at Manaos. The project was perfectly sound financially and would have brought considerable advantage to the district, but it was destined to failure. Before the first convoy had reached the market, he had been shot and killed by an official whom he had neglected to bribe. The defence was that he had been shot while evading arrest on a charge of collecting turtles' eggs out of season. The murderer was exonerated and the boats never reappeared at Boa Vista.

A more recent enterprise had been that of 'the Company', so frequently referred to. I never learned the full story of this fiasco, for the Benedictines were deeply involved in it and I did not like to press the question at the Priory. The blacksmith gravely assured me that the scandal had been so great that the Archbishop had been taken to Rome and imprisoned by the Pope. There certainly seemed to have been more than ordinary mismanagement of the affair. Father Alcuin never mentioned it except to say that things had not gone as well as they had hoped. So far as I could gather the facts are these:

A year or two ago, inflamed by charitable zeal, the wealthy Benedictines at Rio conceived the old plan of bringing prosperity and self-respect to Boa Vista. Geographically and politically the town held the key position to the whole, immense territory of the Northern Amazon tributaries. The monks saw that instead of its present position as a squalid camp of ramshackle cut-throats, it might be a thriving city, a beacon of culture illuminating the dark lands about it, a centre from which they could educate and evangelize the Indians. They imagined it, even, as a miniature ecclesiastical state where industry, commerce, and government should be in the benevolent hands of the Church; a happy dream, glowing with possibilities of success to those imperfectly acquainted with the real character of Boa Vista.

Accordingly 'the Company' was launched, under the highest ecclesiastical patronage, financed by Benedictine money and

233

managed by the brother of one of the hierarchy. The method by which the town was to be raised to prosperity was, again, sensible enough to anyone who expected normal working conditions. Instead of the cattle being transported to the slaughter-houses at Manaos, they were to be butchered on the spot and tinned. Cheap corned beef, it was assumed, would rapidly take the place of the unnourishing *tasso* and would provide a more valuable and more manageable export than live cattle. The factory would provide regular and remunerative employment to all in the district and, following the best tradition of big business, 'the Company' would also provide the necessaries and amusements on which their wages should be spent; the profits, rapidly circulating, would be used in public services. No one had any ulterior motive; the whole scheme was for the glory of God and the comfort of the people of the place. In Rio, on paper, it all seemed faultless. Operations were begun on a large scale.

The canning factory was built and installed with the best modern machinery, an electric plant was set up, providing the streets and the houses with light; a fine Church, a hospital and a small school were built; there was soon to be a larger school, a Priory and a convent; liberal wages were paid out, two hotels and a cinema opened; a refrigerator provided Boa Vista with the first ice it had ever seen. Everything seemed to be going admirably.

But the monks at Rio had reckoned without the deep-rooted, local antagonism to anything godly or decent; a prejudice which at the moment was particularly inflamed by the unforeseen arrival of an irresponsible American with a rival scheme for improvement. His more ambitious proposal was to run a motor road and railway through the impassable bush that separated the town from Manaos, a project more or less equivalent in magnitude to the making of the Panama Canal. Finding that concessions had already been granted to the Benedictines which made his already impracticable railway legally impossible, he fell back on explaining to the inhabitants the great advantages of which they had been deprived, the higher wages he would have paid, the greater prosperity which he would have initiated. The citizens, naturally disposed to see a sinister purpose in any activity, however small, had already become suspicious of the great changes that were taking place. The American emphasized the foreign birth of most of the Order and the relationship between the manager of the company and the high ecclesiastic in Rio, with the result that by the time the monks and nuns reached their new home, they found everyone fairly convinced that a swindle was being perpetrated at their expense. It was only with difficulty and some danger that they succeeded in landing, being attacked with hostile demonstrations and showers of stones.

From then onwards everything went against the Benedictines, who were insulted and boycotted. The canning factory proved a failure; no one would use the ice – an unnatural, impermanent substance, typical of everything foreign; dishonest stuff that had lost half its weight even before you got it home – they didn't want the hospital, much preferring to sicken and die in their hammocks in the decent manner traditional to the place; no one paid his electric light bill and the plant had to be stopped. The priests went down with fever and, one by one, had to be sent back to Manaos. 'The Company' became bankrupt and all further work was stopped. No Priory was built, no big school, no convent. At the time of my arrival things were at their lowest ebb. Father Alcuin was the last priest left and he was so ill that only supernatural heroism kept him at his work. Often he was only able to totter to the Church to say his Mass and then retire to bed in high fever for the remainder of the day. The palatial house in which he was living was the building originally intended for the hospital. Its two big wards were now occupied by a carpenter engaged in making benches for the Church, and a government vet. who fitted up a laboratory there, which he used from time to time between his rounds of the ranches; he was investigating a pre-valent form of paralysis in horses which he attributed to worms. Whatever minute flicker of good still survived in the town was preserved by the nuns, silent, devoted, indefatigable, who lived in appalling quarters near the river-bank, kept a school for the handful of bourgeois daughters, and nursed a Negro and an aged diamond prospector who had arrived separately in a dying condition from up country and were in no mood to respect the prejudices of the town. It was, as I have said, the lowest point;

a new Prior was expected daily to reorganize things and set them to rights.

The Priory – as the hospital was now called – was no exception to the rule formulated a few pages above, that the religious are served by idiots. A single Indian boy of impenetrable stupidity looked after us. He had a round, brown face and a constant, mirthless grin which revealed rows of sharply filed teeth. He giggled when observed and would, in occasional bursts of confidence, produce for inspection a grubby sheet of lined paper on which he had tried to copy an alphabet written for him by Father Alcuin. He was absolutely honest, and dazed with delight when, on leaving, I gave him a small tip. His chief duty was to fetch the meals from the convent kitchen, a quarter of a mile away. They arrived cold and dusty, but with surprising regularity. He also rang the Angelus and could always be found by the bell rope half an hour before the time, waiting for the clock hands to reach the appointed place. The rest of his day was spent in talking to a captive monkey that was tethered to a tree in the garden, or in gaping, hour after hour, at the jars of worms which filled the vet.'s laboratory.

The only other occupant of the house was the German who had first greeted our arrival; a man typical, except in his eccentricities, of the men of his race which one encounters in remote places all over the globe; part of the great exodus of disillusioned soldiers and students that followed the defeat of 1918, from Germany and the German colonies.

Mr Steingler was not a particularly attractive man. I never discovered what he was doing in Boa Vista. He had a minute and unprofitable plantation up the River Uraricuera where he lived in complete solitude and, I gathered from his conversation, great privation. He spoke vaguely of business he had to do in the town and would often go shuffling off to gossip at the stores; he spoke of some mail he was expecting, but when eventually the boat arrived from Manaos, there was nothing for him; he would sometimes announce his imminent departure, but always stayed on. He said he did not like to leave while Father Alcuin was so ill. The truth was, I think, that he could not bear to leave a place where there were people to talk to him in German; and he liked the food. He was a demonstratively greedy man and used to give great boyish whoops and guffaws of delight as he helped himself to the dishes, for at his farm, as he often explained, he had only *farine* and *tasso*.

It is possible that he was staying on at the Priory because absolute destitution awaited him at his farm.

He was a firm atheist and did not disguise his contempt for the activities of his hosts. I tried to point out to him once that it was particularly fortunate for him that some people still had such curious notions – the nuns had nursed him through a grave illness the year before – but he said, 'No, it is nonsense. It is only for children,' and of the new Prior who was coming, 'No doubt it is a step in his career.'

His appearance was extremely odd, for he carried himself with the stiff back of an infantryman while his loose sandals made him drag his feet in an incongruous manner, when he walked. He wore a shiny and threadbare suit of blue serge, a 'boater' straw hat, a crumpled white collar and a narrow black tie. His ankles were bare and his sandals of his own manufacture. He invariably carried an absurd little ebony cane with a dented silver crook. We went to the café together most nights, but he would seldom accept a drink, saying at first that he could not drink beer when it was not iced; later I realized it was because he could not afford it himself and in this one form would not take hospitality he could not return, so to cover his pride I used to invent reasons – that a boat was expected, that Father Alcuin was better, that it was my birthday – and then he would drink the warm beer with relish and laugh loudly at whatever was said.

We talked in a laborious mixture of French and English, over neither of which languages Mr Steingler had much command; indeed he seemed to be barely intelligible in any language; his fluent Portuguese seemed to cause endless misunderstandings at the café and even his German seemed to puzzle Father Alcuin. The difficulty lay chiefly in discovering which of his many languages Mr Steingler was trying to speak. Conversation at meals was always uneasy, for Father Alcuin knew no English and only the most formal French; most of the time he and Mr Steingler would stumble along in German, occasionally explaining some obscure point in Portuguese; then, feeling that I was being left out of things, they would attempt to draw me in. Mr Steingler would suddenly bow towards me, beam, and make curious animal sounds in the roof of his mouth.

As a rule Father Alcuin was too ill to eat; when he was in fever he kept to his room but in the days of intermission he usually sat at table with us, drinking a little soup. I do not think he ever liked me much or understood what I was doing in his house, but he accepted my presence without complaint as he accepted all the other hardships of Boa Vista. Only on the subject of Freemasons did he show any violent emotion. It is possible that they had taken some sinister hand in the fiasco of 'the Company'.

Was it really true that the King of England was a Mason?

I replied that I thought he was.

'Is that how he became King? Did the Masons put him on the throne?'.

'No, he is king by legal hereditary right.'

'Then how did the poor man fall into their power?'

It was useless to explain that English Masons were for the most part Headmasters and Generals with, as far as I knew, no criminal activities.

'That is what they say until they have you in their power. And the Prince of Wales, is he a Mason too? Is that why he does not marry? Do the Masons forbid it?'

I think he began to suspect me of secret Masonry after a time, in spite of my conscientious assistance at Sunday Mass.

The Church was, considering the villainy of the place, surprisingly well attended; largely, I suppose, because the nasal singing of the girls' school provided the only kind of entertainment of the week. These children, shepherded to their places by the nuns, were dressed up in clean muslin veils and, the wealthier of them, long white cotton gloves; they wore innumerable medals and coloured ribbons and sashes, proclaiming their different degrees of piety. They sang sugary little vernacular hymns in tremulous, whining voices. They occupied the greater part of the Church. Beside them were the elderly women in best dresses and clean stockings. What with this weekly blossoming of femininity, and the concrete architectural ornaments of the building, the candles and the artificial flowers, Sunday Mass was the nearest thing to a pretty spectacle that Boa Vista provided, and the men assembled in fair numbers to enjoy it. They did not come into the Church, for that is contrary to Brazilian etiquette, but they clustered in the porch, sauntering out occasionally to smoke a cigarette. The normal male costume of the town was a suit of artificial silk pyjamas, which many of the more elegant had washed weekly, so that on Sundays they carried themselves with an air of great refinement and caution. Some minutes before the Elevation they might be seen unfolding their handkerchiefs and spreading them on the bare boards of the floor; then, when the bell rang, they would delicately kneel on one knee, rise, shake out the handkerchief, refold it and tuck it away in the breast pocket. This, however, was the practice only of the most pious; the majority remained throughout propped against the walls, staring at the napes of the girls' necks. A priest told me that when he was new to the country he had remonstrated with the men, telling them that this was no fashion in which to hear Mass.

'We haven't come to hear Mass,' they had replied, fingering the revolver butts in their holsters. 'We're here to see you don't interfere with our women.'

I found very little to occupy my time. There was an edition of Bossuet's sermons and a few lives of the Saints in French for me to read; I could walk to the wireless office and learn that no news had been heard of the Boundary Commissioner's boat; I could visit the English-speaking blacksmith and watch him tinkering with antiquated automatic pistols. This young man would not come with me to the café on account of his having recently beaten the proprietor – an act of which he was inordinately proud, though it can have required no great courage since he was a very old man and slightly crippled. I could give bananas to the captive monkey and I could study the bottled worms in the laboratory; I could watch the carpenter in his rare moments of industry, sawing up lengths of plank. There was really quite a number of things for me to do, but, in spite of them all, the days seemed to pass slowly.

The blacksmith, who knew all that was going on in the town,

promised to tell me as soon as the Commissioner's boat was sighted, but it so happened that he forgot to do so, and I only learned from Mr Steingler, one morning after I had been six days in the Priory, that it had arrived the previous evening and was due to leave in an hour; the Commissioner was at that moment at the wireless station. I hurried off to interview him. Things might have been less difficult if Father Alcuin had been able to accompany me, but it was one of the days when he was down with fever. Alone I was able to make no impression. The Commissioner was an amicable little man, in high good humour at the prospect of a few days' leave in Manaos, but he flatly refused to have me in his boat. I cannot hold it against him. Everyone in that district is a potential fugitive from justice and he knew nothing of me except my dishevelled appearance and my suspicious anxiety to get away from Boa Vista. I showed my passport and letters of credit, but he was not impressed. I besought him to cable to Georgetown for my credentials, but he pointed out that it might take a week to get an answer. I offered him large wads of greasy notes. But he was not having any. He knew too much about foreigners who appeared alone and unexplained in the middle of Amazonas; the fact of my having money made me the more sinister. He smiled, patted my shoulder, gave me a cigarette, and sharp on time left without me.

I cannot hold it against him. I do not think that the British Commissioners would have done any more for a stray Brazilian. But it was in a despondent and rather desperate mood that I heard his boat chugging away out of sight down the Rio Branco.

From then onwards my only concern was to find some other means of getting away from Boa Vista. The trade boat of which David had spoken became increasingly elusive as I tried to pin its proprietor down to any definite statement of its departure. He was the manager of the chief store, a low-spirited young man named Martinez. I went to see him every day to talk about it; he seemed glad of a chat but could hold out only the vaguest hopes for me. The boat had to arrive first. It should be on its way with the new Prior; when it came, there would be time enough to discuss its departure. All sorts of things had to be considered –

cargo, mail, other passengers. Day after day went by until all faith I had ever cherished in the trade boat slowly seeped away. Ordinary vexation at the delay began to give place to anxiety, for everyone in the town seemed to spend at least three days a week in fever. It seemed to me a poor gamble to risk becoming semi-invalid for life for the dubious interest of a voyage down the Rio Branco. So I abandoned the idea of Manaos and decided to return to Guiana.

This journey, so simple from British territory, where one was supported by the good will of the mission and the ranchers, presented endless difficulties from the other side. Mr Martinez said he could arrange it, but days passed and no horses appeared. He found me a guide, however, in the person of a good-natured boy named Marco; he was fifteen or sixteen, in from the country, and had been hanging round the store for some weeks in search of employment; this youth, after a house to house enquiry lasting several days, eventually secured the hire of a horse for himself, belonging, as it turned out, to Mr Martinez and quartered at the ranch on the other side of the river. I still needed another horse – if possible two – and provisions. Mr Martinez had some tins of sweet biscuits and sardines, another shop had two tins of sausage; the nuns made bread and cheese. These would comfortably take us the three days' ride to Dadanawa. Horses were still an unsolved difficulty when help came from an unexpected quarter.

Mr Steingler had hitherto listened apathetically to my complaints, merely remarking from time to time, 'Les peuples ici sont tous bêtes, tous sauvages; il faut toujours de patience,' until one day the thought came to him that there might be something in it for him. He opened the subject cautiously, saying one evening that even if I secured a horse, it would be impossible to get a saddle; both were equally important. I agreed. He then went on to say that it so happened that he had a very good saddle himself, one that he would not readily part with to anyone, a particularly fine, new saddle of European workmanship, a rare and invaluable possession in a country like this. However, seeing my difficulty, and feeling the kinship that one European feels for another in a savage country, he was willing to part with it to me.

He took me to his room and dragged it out from under his bed. It was made on the English pattern but clearly of the most slip-shod local workmanship; moreover, it was of great age and in deplorable condition, half unsewn, with padding as hard as metal, every leather frayed and half worn through, several buckles missing. I asked him what he wanted for it.

Between European gentlemen, he said, it was impossible to bargain over money. He would call in a friend to make an assessment. The friend was the carpenter from the next room who was transparently in the racket up to his eyes. He turned over the saddle, praised it (embarrassing himself and Mr Steingler by inadvertently detaching another buckle while he spoke) and said that, all things considered, 20,000 *Reis* (£5) would be a moderate price. I accepted the assessment and then began, in my turn, to point out that, necessary as a saddle was, and much as I admired this particular one of Mr Steingler's, it was of very little use to me without a horse. I would buy it at his price, if he would find me a mount to put under it.

From that moment onwards Mr Steingler worked for me indefatigably. He set out there and then in his boater hat, twirling his ridiculous cane, and by evening was able to report that the Collector had the very horse for me; a beast of some age, he admitted, but immensely strong, big boned, well-conditioned; just what was needed for savannah travelling. We went to see him. He was of much the same quality as the saddle and, curiously enough, commanded exactly the same price. Presumably 20,000 *Reis* was a unit in their minds, the highest figure to which avarice could aspire. I bought him on the spot. I do not know what rake-off Mr Steingler got on the transaction, or whether he merely wished to keep in with the Collector. I preferred to be thought a mug and get away, rather than to achieve a reputation for astuteness and risk spending an unnecessary hour in Boa Vista.

That evening Mr Steingler did a further bit of business, by producing the town clerk, a venerable old man with a long white beard, who was willing to hire me a pack horse he owned in the corral on the further bank – 4,000 *Reis* for the journey to Dadanawa. I paid him and went to bed well contented with the prospect of immediate escape.

Next morning I bade farewell to Father Alcuin. The plans for my departure had been freely discussed at table for over a week, but had not penetrated the feverish trance in which the poor monk lived. He was greatly surprised, and when I handed him a donation to the house to cover my board and lodging, he woke suddenly to the fact that he had exerted himself very little on my behalf; it was then that he revealed, what before he had kept carefully hidden, that he had a wooden pack saddle which he could put at my disposal. Thus equipped and blessed I felt that I was at last on my way.

But it was not to be as easy as that; the forces of chaos were still able to harass my retreat and inflict some damaging attacks. The next two days, in fact, were slapstick farce, raised at moments to the heights of fantasy by the long-awaited appearance of the Prior.

News of his approach and imminent arrival came on the morning of the day that I had fixed for my departure. Instantly the Priory was overrun by nuns. They worked in the way nuns have, which is at the same time sub-human and superhuman; poultry and angels curiously compounded in a fluttering, clucking, purposeful scurry of devoted industry; they beat up the Prior's mattresses and dusted every crevice of his quarters, they trotted to and fro with wicker rocking-chairs and clean sheets, they lined the corridor to his room with potted shrubs, put palm leaves behind all the pictures, arranged embroidered tablecloths on every available shelf and ledge, decorated the bookcase with artificial flowers, built a triumphal arch over the front door and engrossed programmes for a hastily organized concert. I regretted very much that I should not be there to see his reception.

My plans were that I should cross the river in the afternoon with the grey cob I had bought from the Collector; see to the rounding in of the other two horses, sleep by the corral on the further side and start for Dadanawa first thing the next morning.

Mr Martinez had organized the crossing, for which he had hired me a canoe and another boy, whom I was to meet with Marco at three o'clock. At half past four they arrived; the other boy turned out to be a child of eight or nine. Mr Martinez explained that he was taking the place of his elder brother who had fever that day.

We carried the saddles and baggage down the bank, found the canoe, which when loaded was dangerously low in the water. The descent at the usual landing place was too steep for a horse, so it was arranged that the small boy and I should paddle to a point up stream where the bank shelved down more gently, where Marco would meet us with the horse. It was half past five when we reached the place and found no sign of Marco. The sun sets at six. For half an hour the small boy and I sat hunched in the canoe – I cramped and fretful, he idly playful with my belongings – then we paddled back in the darkness to the landing place. Sundry whistlings and catcalls ensued until presently Marco loomed up through the shadows riding the grey. We neither spoke a word of the other's language but by repetitions and gestures, and that telepathy which seems to function between two people who have something of urgency to communicate, we got to understand that the horse had taken some catching, that Marco was quite ready to try swimming him across in the dark, that I thought this lunacy, that the baggage was to be left where it was, that Marco was to sling his hammock by the bank and guard it all night, that I would come at dawn and we would cross over then. I cannot explain how we discussed all this, but in the end the situation was well understood. Then I hurried back to the Priory which I had left a few hours before with so many formal thanks and good wishes.

In my vexation I had entirely forgotten about the Prior. I now came to the refectory, ten minutes late for dinner, out of breath and wet to the knees, to find him sitting at table. He was, as it happens, in the middle of the story of his own sufferings on the way up. It was a problem of good manners of the kind that are solved so astutely on the women's pages of the Sunday papers. What should I do? It was clearly impossible to escape unobserved, for the Prior had already fixed me with a look of marked aversion. I could not slip into a chair with a murmured apology for my lateness, because some explanation of my reappearance was due to Father Alcuin, and of my existence to my new host, the Prior. There was nothing for it but to interrupt the

Prior's story with one of my own. He did not take it too kindly. Father Alcuin attempted to help me out, explaining rather lamely that I was an Englishman who had waited here on the way to Manaos.

Then what was I doing attempting to cross the Rio Branco in the dark? the Prior demanded sternly.

I said I was on my way to Dadanawa.

'But Dadanawa is nowhere near Manaos.'

Clearly the whole thing seemed to him highly unsatisfactory and suspicious. However, with the charity of his Order he bade me sit down. The idiot boy removed the soup plates and the Prior resumed his story. In honour of his arrival a fish course had been added to the dinner; nothing could have been less fortunate, for he had lived on fish for the last ten days and on that particular sort of coarse and tasteless fish that was now offered him. He glared at it resentfully over his spectacles and ordered it to be removed. Mr Steingler watched it go with evident distress.

The Prior was no doubt a very good man, but he did not add to the ease of the refectory. He was thoroughly exhausted by his journey and in no mood to bustle off to the nuns' concert. He had already formed a low opinion of Mr Steingler and my arrival confirmed him in his general disapproval. He was there on a mission of reorganization and Mr Steingler and myself were obviously the kind of thing that had to be investigated and cleaned up. He finished his narration of delays and discomforts, took a dislike to the pudding, and before Mr Steingler had nearly finished his first helping, rose to recite an immensely long grace. Then, with hostile adieux, stumped away grumbling to the celebrations at the school.

Next day at dawn I saw him on his way to Mass and he was more amicable. I bade him good-bye with renewed thanks and went down to the river. The small boy and Marco were there; the baggage was intact; after an hour's perilous and exhausting work we got the canoe and the horse across to the other side; the child paddled back and I settled down to wait until Marco had collected the other horses. The pack horse was easily identified by some *vaqueiros* who were waiting there. He was a wretched creature, down in the pasterns, but our baggage was very light and it seemed probable that he would get it to Dadanawa. Mr Martinez's horse could not be found. After two hours Marco returned, smiling and shrugging and shaking his head.

Back to Boa Vista once more. We had to wait until noon for a canoe. I arrived at the Priory once more, a good quarter of an hour late for luncheon. The Prior's doubts of my honesty became doubts of my sanity. Once more I made my adieux, repeating the same thanks with increased apologies. Mr Martinez, at last roused to activity, decided to accompany me himself to the other side and find the horse. He issued a number of peremptory orders which were lethargically obeyed. His motor launch was brought up, four or five men were recruited, and a formidable expedition set out. After some hours, the horse was discovered straying some miles distant, lassoed and led in. Then a further disaster occurred. A large sow which had been nosing round the baggage for some time discovered a way into the kit bag and ate the whole of the bread and cheese on which I had been counting as my main sustenance in the next few days.

Back to Boa Vista; back to the Priory, just as they were finishing dinner. The Prior now regarded me with undisguised despair. I was able, however, to buy another loaf and more cheese from the convent. Next morning, without further contact with my hosts, I slipped out of the Priory and left Boa Vista for the last time.

CHAPTER FIVE

A War in 1935

(From *Waugh in Abyssinia*)

Addis Ababa

IN the summer of 1935 the *Evening Standard* published a cartoon representing the Throne of Justice occupied by three apes who squatted in the traditional attitude, each with his hands covering his eyes, ears or mouth; beneath was the legend, '*See no Abyssinia; hear no Abyssinia; speak no Abyssinia*'.

This may have expressed the atmosphere of Geneva; it was wildly unlike London. There the editorial and managerial chairs of newspaper and publishing offices seemed to be peopled exclusively by a race of anthropoids who saw, heard and spoke no other subject.

Abyssinia was News. Everyone with any claims to African experience was cashing in. Travel books whose first editions had long since been remaindered were being reissued in startling wrappers. Literary agents were busy peddling the second serial rights of long-forgotten articles. Files were being searched for photographs of any inhospitable-looking people – Patagonian Indians, Borneo head-hunters, Australian aborigines – which could be reproduced to illustrate Abyssinian culture. In the circumstances anyone who had actually spent a few weeks in Abyssinia itself, and had read the dozen or so books which constituted the entire English bibliography of the subject, might claim to be an expert, and in this unfamiliar but not uncongenial disguise I secured employment with the only London newspaper which seemed to be taking a sane view of the situation, as a 'war correspondent'.

There followed ten inebriating days of preparation, lived in an attitude of subdued heroism before friends, of knowledgeable discrimination at the tropical outfitters. There was a heat wave at the time. I trod miasmic pavements between cartographers and consulates. In the hall of my club a growing pile of packing cases, branded for Djibouti, began to constitute a serious inconvenience to the other members. There are few pleasures more complete, or to me more rare, than that of shopping extravagantly at someone else's expense. I thought I had treated myself with reasonable generosity until I saw the luggage of my professional competitors – their rifles and telescopes and ant-proof trunks, medicine chests, gas-masks, pack saddles, and vast wardrobes of costume suitable for every conceivable social or climatic emergency. Then I had an inkling of what later became abundantly clear to all, that I did not know the first thing about being a war correspondent.

After the bustle, ten tranquil days on the familiar route. On 19th August, Djibouti; the familiar stifling boulevards; spindly, raffish Somalis, the low-spirited young man at the Vice-Consulate; the tireless, hopeless street pedlars; the familiar rotund Frenchmen, their great arcs of waistline accentuated with cummerbunds; the seedy café clientèle, swollen at this moment by refugees – Dodecanesan mostly – from up the line and by despondent middle-aged adventurers negotiating for Ethiopian visas; the familiar after-dinner drive to the café in the palm grove; the fuss about train and luggage. A torrid, almost sleepless night. On the 20th, shortly before midday, we crossed the Ethiopian frontier.

The occupants of the railway carriage were typical of the rising tide of foreigners which was then flowing from all parts of the world to the threatened capital.

There were six of us, sipping iced Vichy water from our thermos flasks and gazing out bleakly upon a landscape of unrelieved desolation.

One of them had been my companion from London, a reporter from a Radical newspaper. I saw him constantly throughout the succeeding months and found his zeal and industry a standing reproach. I did not know it was possible for a human being to identify himself so precisely with the interests of his employers. The situation, obscure to most of us, was crystal clear to him – the Emperor was an oppressed anti-fascist.

My other colleague was a vastly different character. From time to time he gave us visiting cards, but we never remembered his name, and for the next few weeks he became a prominent and richly comic figure in Addis life, known to everyone as 'the Spaniard'. He was vivacious and swarthy and stout, immensely talkative and far from intelligible in English, French, and German. His equipment, as he proudly admitted, was largely acquired at a sixpenny store. He changed his clothes in the train, putting on breeches, a pair of chocolate-coloured riding boots, and a Boy Scout's belt and revolver holster. He then placed a tin aneroid on the seat beside him and proclaimed the changes of altitude with boyish excitement, peeling and devouring one by one throughout the journey an enormous basket of slightly rotten bananas.

It was clear to us that Spanish journalism was run on quite different lines from English. From the moment we left Marseilles he had been composing articles for his paper – one about Haifa, two about de Lesseps, one about Disraeli. 'I have a very good history of Africa in German,' he explained. 'When I have nothing to report I translate passages from that. Mine is the most important paper in Spain, but it is a great thing for them to send a correspondent as far as this. They must have news all the time.' While the rest of us were leading a life agreeably unembarrassed by the financial cares that occupy so much attention in normal travel, the Spaniard was in a chronic high fever of anxiety about his expenditure; for many days after his arrival at Addis Ababa he was to be found with a stub of pencil and sheet of paper working out how many thalers he should have got for his francs at Djibouti and brooding sceptically over the results; he was apparently an easy prey for the dishonest; his cabin, he complained, was rifled on board ship and a wad of money stolen; at Djibouti he had a still odder misfortune; he gave me his pocket-book to guard while he went for a swim and on his return maintained that a thousand francs had disappeared from it. He bewailed the loss at length and in piteous terms, saying that he was saving it for a present to his little daughter. But I made no offer to reimburse him and he soon recovered his jollity. It was a great surprise to him to discover that three of the English journalists beside myself were new and probably temporary members of our staffs and that all except one were entirely new to the work of foreign

249

correspondent. 'I am the most important and expensive man on my paper,' he said.

'English editors would not send anyone whose life they valued on a job of this kind,' we told him.

'I have my revolver. And the boots are snake-proof. How much do you think they cost?'

Someone suggested ten shillings.

'*Very* much less,' he said proudly.

He was one of the few people who, I really believe, thought that the coloured races were dark-skinned because they did not wash. He did not intend to stay long in Ethiopia, because, he explained, he was his paper's Paris correspondent and it was impossible to do both jobs satisfactorily at the same time. 'I shall merely make a rapid tour of the front on a motor bicycle,' he said.

In the absence of any more probable alternative, it was later put about in Addis Ababa, where everyone was credited with some sinister activity, that the Spaniard was a papal spy.

The fourth member of the party was a sturdy American doctor who had come to offer his services to the Ethiopian Red Cross. With him was Mr Prospero, whom he had rescued from an indefinite sojourn in the Djibouti hotel. Mr Prospero was photographer for an American newsreel. A few weeks before he had been a contented resident in Japan, where he owned a house, a dog, had lately paid the last instalment on a saloon car, and employed his time making pictures of cherry blossom and court ceremonial. At a few hours' notice he had been whisked away from this life of lotus eating and deposited, penniless – his funds having been cabled in advance to Addis – at Djibouti, than which there can be no town in the world less sympathetic to strangers desirous of borrowing a railway fare. His life thereafter was a protracted martyrdom gallantly but gloomily endured, which seemed to typify the discouragement which in less degrees we all suffered. At Addis he was accommodated at the Imperial Hotel in a ground-floor room immediately next to the only entrance; as more camera men arrived, they joined him there with camp beds and mountains of technical apparatus until the little room, heaped with cameras and crumpled underclothes, packing-cases of film and half-empty tins of baked beans, presented a scene hideously compounded of workshop, warehouse, and slum dormitory. I saw Mr Prospero constantly, and always in distress; now soaked to the skin pathetically grinding the handle of his camera in an impenetrable pall of rain; now prostrate under the bare feet of a stampeding mob, like a football in a rugger scrum; now lamed; now groaning with indigestion; now shuddering in high fever. He became a figure from classic tragedy, inexorably hunted by hostile fates. After we had been in Addis Ababa some time a copy of a poster arrived from America advertising his newsreel. It represented a young man of military appearance and more than military intrepidity, standing calmly behind his camera while bombs burst overhead and naked warriors rolled interlocked about his knees. In vast letters across this scene of carnage was printed:

'O.K., BOYS, YOU CAN START THE WAR NOW.
PROSPERO IS THERE.'

The sixth and by far the gayest of us was an Englishman who was soon, suddenly, to become world-famous: Mr F. W. Rickett. He had joined our ship at Port Said and throughout the succeeding week had proved a light-hearted companion. From the first he was invested with a certain mystery. Anyone travelling to Addis Ababa at that moment attracted some speculation. Mr Rickett spoke openly of a 'mission', and when tackled by the Radical on the subject hinted vaguely that he was bringing Coptic funds to the Abuna. He spoke more freely about a pack of hounds which he had in the Midlands, and when, as often happened, he received lengthy cables in code, he would pocket them nonchalantly, remarking, 'From my huntsman. He says the prospects for cubbin' are excellent.' The Radical and I put him down as an arms salesman of whom large numbers were said to be frequenting Addis Ababa. In the gaudy reports of his concession which flooded the papers of the world a fortnight later great emphasis was laid upon Mr Rickett's 'unobtrusive entrance' into the country and his residence at 'an obscure boarding-house'. Nothing could have been further from his intentions or expectations. He had ordered the one luxury carriage of the Ethiopian railway and treasured the most extravagant hopes about its character – even to the belief that it contained a kitchen and cook. He had, in fact, very kindly offered me a place in it. But when we got to the station we found that we had to take our places in the ordinary coach. In the same way he had ordered a suite at the Imperial Hotel. It was only when we found there was no other accommodation, that we went to Mrs Heft's excellent *pension*.

The day wore on, more oppressive after luncheon at a wayside buffet; the little train jerked and twisted through an unendurable country of stone and anthills. There were no signs of rain here, the sand was bare, the few tufts of scrub colourless as the surrounding stone; the watercourses were dry. At sunset we stopped for the night at Dirre-Dowa. I remembered how gratefully I had left it five years before. Now in the cool of the evening, with the lights of the hotel terrace revealing sombre masses of flowering bougainvillea, it seemed agreeable enough. The head of the railway police came up from the station with us for a drink. He was one of the new school of Ethiopian official – clean-shaven, khaki-clad, French-speaking. He told us the latest news from Europe. Mr Eden had walked out of the Paris discussions. That meant that England was going to fight against Italy, he said. 'That depends on the League of Nations,' we said.

'No, no. It is because you do not want Italy to be strong. It is good. You know that Ethiopia cannot threaten you. We are friends. Together we will defeat the Italians.'

We did not disabuse him; instead we accepted our temporary popularity as easily as we could, clinked glasses and drank to peace.

Next morning at dawn we resumed our places in the train and reached Addis that evening.

I little suspected what a large part in our lives that stretch of line was going to play in the coming months. I covered it six times before Christmas and learned every feature – the transition from desert to downland, the view of the lakes, the cinder fields, the Hawash gorge, the candle-lit hotel at Hawash where on every journey but this the train deposited us for the night, the station where there was an ostrich, a beggar who recited prayers, a little girl who mimed; the painted arch of the lake hotel at Bishoftou which told that the climb was nearly over and that we were in measurable distance of Addis, the silly coon-face of the ticket collector outside the window as he climbed along the running-boards to enquire who wanted to lunch at the buffet. But at this time we all assumed that, when war was declared, we should at once be isolated. On the first day Hawash bridge would be bombed and the line cut in a hundred places. We had all planned routes of escape to Kenya or the Sudan. Of the various fates which from time to time we predicted for Haile Selassie – rescue by British aeroplanes, death in battle, murder, suicide – no one, I think, ever seriously suggested what was actually to happen; that in the final catastrophe, desperate and disillusioned, betrayed by the League, deserted by his army, hunted by insurgent tribesmen, with his enemies a day's march from the Palace and their aircraft regularly reconnoitring over his head, he would quietly proceed to the station, board the train and trip down to Djibouti by rail. The least romantic of us never suggested that.

Addis Ababa on the eve of war seemed little changed in character and appearance from the city I had known five years before. The triumphal arches that had been erected for the coronation had grown shabbier but they were still standing. The ambitious buildings in the European style with which Haile Selassie had intended to embellish his capital were still in the same rudimentary stage of construction; tufted now with vegetation like ruins in a drawing by Piranesi, they stood at every corner, reminders of an abortive modernism, a happy subject for the Press photographers who hoped later to present them as the ravages of Italian bombardment.

There were several hotels in Addis Ababa, all, at the time of our arrival, outrageously prosperous. 'Kakophilos's', at which we all assumed we should stay, was completely full with journalists and photographers living in hideous proximity, two or three to a room even in the outbuildings. It was a massive, shabby building of sepulchral gloom, presided over by the eponymous, sturdy, middle-aged, misanthropic Greek, who had taken it over as a failing concern just before the troubles. There was something

admirable about the undisguised and unaffected distaste with
which he regarded his guests and his ruthless disregard of their
comfort and dignity. Some attempted to be patronizing to him,
some dictatorial, some ingratiating; all were treated with uniform
contempt. He was well aware that for a very few months nothing
that he did or left undone could affect his roaring prosperity;
after that anything might happen. The less his guests ate the
greater his profits, and from his untidy little desk in the corner he
watched with sardonic amusement the crowds of dyspeptic
journalists – many of them elderly men, of note in their own
countries – furtively carrying into his dining-room paper bags of
fresh bread, tins of tuck and pocketfuls of oranges and bananas,
like little boys trooping into tea at their private schools. Mr
Kakophilos never apologized and very rarely complained. Nothing of the smallest value was endangered in the scenes of violence
which became increasingly frequent as the journalists made
themselves at home. When his guests threw their bedroom furniture out of the window, he noted it in the weekly bill. If they fired
their revolvers at the night watchman he merely advised the
man to take careful cover. Menageries of unclean pets were
introduced into the bedrooms; Mr Kakophilos waited uncon-
cerned until even their owners could bear their presence no
longer. His was the chief hotel of the town and nothing could
shake its status. Here, intermittently, the government posted its
communiqués; here the Foreign Press Association held its
acrimonious meetings; here every evening, when the wireless
station was shut, we all assembled, in seedy wicker chairs in the
large, bare, flea-ridden hall, to drink and grumble.

The Deutsches Haus, where Mr Rickett and I were taken, was
humbler and very much more hospitable. It stood near the
Splendide in a side street, but its immediate surroundings were
not imposing. Opposite was a tannery run by a Russian Prince,
from which, when the wind was in the wrong quarter, there came
smells so appalling that we were obliged to shut our windows and
scatter in different parts of the town; sometimes a lorry of
reeking pelts would be left all day at our gates; once, for some
purpose connected with his hideous trade, His Highness acquired
a load of decomposing cows' feet. He was a debonair figure,

given to exotic tastes in dress. When he first arrived at Addis he was asked to luncheon at the British Legation and the guard turned out for him. A few days later he opened a house of ill fame. Now he was mainly, but not exclusively, interested in the fur trade. He often spoke wistfully of a convoy of girls who had been on order from Cairo since the battle of Walwal but were held up somewhere, mysteriously and unjustly, in the customs.

But though the surroundings were forbidding, the hospitality inside the gates (which were kept by a grizzled warrior armed with a seven-foot spear) was delightful. Mrs Heft was one of the Germans who had drifted to Abyssinia from Tanganyika when it was confiscated by the British government after the war. There were a large number of her compatriots in the town, mostly in very poor circumstances, employed as mechanics or in petty trade. The Deutsches Haus was their rendezvous where they played cards and occasionally dined. The Hefts could never quite get used to the disregard of small economies or the modest appetites of her new boarders. Many of our demands seemed to her painfully complex. 'The journalists pay well,' she confided. 'But they are very difficult. Some want coffee in the morning and some want tea, and they expect it always to be hot.' But she worked untiringly in our service.

She was a housewife of formidable efficiency. Daily from dawn until noon a miniature market was held on the steps of the dining-room. Half a dozen native hawkers squatted patiently, displaying meat, eggs, and vegetables. Every half-hour she or Mr Heft would emerge, disparage the goods, ask the price, and, in simulated rage, tell the salesmen to be off. Eventually, when it was time to start cooking luncheon, she made her purchases.

Mr Heft had a deafening little car, which at any moment of the day or night he would take out for our use. There was also a hotel taxi, which the bearded chauffeur used as a crèche for his baby. When his services were required he would whisk the infant out of the back seat and nurse it as he drove.

There were two geese loose in the yard who attacked all comers. Mr Heft was always promising to kill them, but they were still alive when I left the country. There was also a pig, which he did kill, from which Mrs Heft made a magnificent abundance of

255

sausages and *pâtés*. The food, for Addis, was excellent. Mr Heft hovered over the tables at meal times watching all we ate. 'No like?' he would say, in genuine distress, if anyone refused a course. 'Make you eggies, yes?'

The Hefts' bedroom opened from the dining-room, and it was there that everything of value in the house was kept. If one wanted change for a hundred thaler note, an aspirin, a clean towel, a slice of sausage, a bottle of Chianti, the wireless bulletin, a spare part for a car, a pack of cards, one's washing or one's weekly bill, Mrs Heft dived under her bed and produced it.

The Deutsches Haus soon became the headquarters of most of the English journalists and photographers. We employed our own servants, decorated our rooms with monkey-skin rugs from the Russian Prince and native paintings from the itinerant artists, and were, on the whole, tolerably comfortable. The Americans, more Baedeker-minded, stayed resolutely with Mr Kakophilos.

There were two places of entertainment in the town, *Le Select* and the *Perroquet*, usually known by the names of their proprietors, Moriatis and Idot. Both had a bar and a talking cinema. Mme Idot had also a kitchen and put it about that her cooking was good. From time to time she would placard the town with news of some special delicacy – *Grand Souper. Tripes à la mode de Caen* – and nostalgic journalists would assemble in large numbers, to be bitterly disillusioned. She came from Marseilles, Mme Moriatis from Bordeaux. They were bitter rivals, but while Mme Moriatis affected ignorance of the other's existence, Mme Idot indulged in free criticism. 'Poor woman!' she would say. 'What does she think she is doing here? She should go back to Bordeaux. She has a face like Lent.' M. Moriatis was a very handsome cad-Greek; M. Idot a hideous cad-Frenchman. Both, by repute, whipped their wives, but Mme Idot professed to enjoy it. Mme Idot shed an atmosphere of false gaiety, Mme Moriatis of very genuine gloom. One talked gravely to Mme Moriatis about the beauties of France and the wickedness of Abyssinian character; she was always apologizing for the inadequacy of her entertainment and one tried to encourage her. 'It is not *chic*,' she would say very truly. 'It is not as I should like it. If the Italians were here we should have dancing at the aperitif time and upstairs an

hotel with bathrooms – completely European.' Everyone pinched
Mme Idot and slapped her behind, told her that her films were
unendurable and her wines poisonous. *Le Select* had pretensions
to respectability and occasionally held charity matinées attended
by members of the diplomatic corps. There was no nonsense of
that kind about the *Perroquet*. Both prospered on the contrast,
because, after an hour in either place, one longed for the
other.

Most visitors to Addis Ababa arrive feeling ill. I had mild
dysentery and a heavy cold, and lay in my room for two days,
dizzy, torpid and acutely miserable, until a series of peremptory
cables from Fleet Street roused me to a sense of my responsi-
bilities: *Require comprehensive cable good colourful stuff also all
news*, shortly followed by *Please indicate when can expect
comprehensive cable*, followed by *Presume you are making
arrangements getting stuff away* and *What alternative means communication in event breakdown?*

The method by which telegrams were distributed gave limitless
opportunity for loss and delay. They were handed out to the
messengers in bundles of about a dozen. The men were unable to
read and their system of delivery was to walk round the town to
the various hotels and places where foreigners might be expected
to congregate and present their pile of envelopes to the first white
man they saw, who would look through them, open any that might
seem of interest, and hand back those that were not for him. Often
it took more than a day for a message to reach us and, as the
commands of Fleet Street became more and more fantastically
inappropriate to the situation and the enquiries more and more
frivolous, we most of us became grateful for a respite, which
sometimes obviated the need of reply.

However, on the third day one of these messengers found his
way to my room with the first, very reasonable request, so I left
my bed and set out rather shakily into the pouring rain to look for
'colour'.

First steps as a war correspondent were humdrum – a round of
the Legations with calling cards, a sitting at the photographers' to

obtain the pictures needed for a journalist's pass, registration at the Press Bureau.

This last was a little tin shed at the further extremity of the main road. It might well have been classed among the places of entertainment in the town. Here morning and afternoon for the first six weeks, until everyone, even its organizers, despaired of it ever performing any helpful function, might be found a dozen or so exasperated journalists of both sexes and almost all nationalities, waiting for interviews. It was an office especially constituted for the occasion. At the head of it was a suave, beady-eyed little Tigrean named Dr Lorenzo Taesas. He was a man of great tact and many accomplishments, but since he was also Judge of Special Court, head of secret police, and personal adviser to the Emperor, it was very rarely that he attended in person. His place was taken by another Tigrean, named David, equally charming, a better linguist, an ardent patriot, who was unable on his own authority to make the most trivial decision or give the simplest information. 'I must ask Dr Lorenzo,' was his invariable answer to every demand. In this way a perfect system of postponement and prevarication was established. If one approached any government department direct, one was referred to the Press Bureau. At the Press Bureau one was asked to put one's enquiry in writing, when it would be conveyed to the invisible Dr Lorenzo. At this early stage the Abyssinians had no reason to be hostile to the Press. Most of them in fact – and particularly the Emperor – were eager to placate it. But this was the manner in which Europeans had always been treated in the country. Just as many white men see a Negro as someone to whom orders must be shouted, so the Abyssinians saw us as a people to be suspected, delayed, frustrated in our most innocent intentions, lied to, whenever truth was avoidable, and set against one another by hints of preferential treatment. There was no ill-will. The attitude was instinctive to them; they could not alter it, and closer acquaintance with us gave them good reason to stiffen rather than relax.

Almost all those impatient figures on Dr Lorenzo's doorstep were after one thing. We wanted to get up country. Travelling in Ethiopia, even in its rare periods of tranquillity, was a matter of the utmost difficulty. Many writers have left accounts of the intricate system of tolls and hospitality by which the traveller was passed on from one chief to another and of the indifference with which the Emperor's *laissez-passer* was treated within a few miles of the capital. Now, with torrential rains all over the highlands flooding the streams and washing away the mule tracks, with troops secretly assembling and migrating towards the frontiers, with the subject peoples, relieved of their garrisons, turning rebel and highwayman, the possibilities of movement in any direction were extremely slight. But, at any rate for the first weeks after our arrival, we most of us cherished a hope, and the Press Bureau constantly fostered it, that we should get to the fighting. No one ever got there. My last sight of Lorenzo, more than three months later at Dessye, was of a little figure, clad in khaki then in place of his dapper morning coat, surrounded by a group of importunate journalists in the Adventist Mission compound, promising that very soon, in a few days perhaps, permission would be granted to go north. Actually it was only when the front came to them, and the retreat of the government headquarters could not keep pace with the Italian advance, that any of them saw a shot fired.

But meanwhile there still lingered in our minds the picture we had presented of ourselves to our womenfolk at home, of stricken fields and ourselves crouching in shell holes, typing gallantly amid bursting shrapnel; of runners charging through clouds of gas, bearing our despatches on cleft sticks. We applied, formally, for permission to travel, absolving the government of all responsibility for our safety, and awaited an immediate reply.

The Radical, who knew his job, had no illusions of the kind. The court, the government offices and the Legations were the 'news centres'. His place was near the wireless office. Not so my immediate neighbour in the Deutsches Haus, an American who proclaimed his imminent departure for the Tigre. A squad of carpenters was noisily at work under our windows boxing his provisions, his caravan of the sturdiest mules was stabled nearby. He had already discarded the dress of a capital city and strode the waterlogged streets as though he were, even at that moment, pushing his way through unmapped jungle. Poor chap, he was one of the group surrounding Lorenzo at Dessye.

In Addis everything seemed to be at a standstill.

Mr Rickett, it is true, held out hopes of a story. On the second day of our visit he had promised me an important piece of news on Saturday evening. Saturday came and he admitted, rather ruefully, that he had not been able to arrange anything; it would probably be next Wednesday, he said. It seemed clear that he was involved in the endless postponements of Abyssinian official life, and that in ten days' time I should find him at the Deutsches Haus, still negotiating. Accordingly, with Patrick Balfour, an old friend who had preceded me as correspondent for the *Evening Standard*, I decided to leave for the South by the Monday train.

It was full of refugees. The Greeks from Rhodes and the Dodecanese formed a more sombre body. Many of these had been born in Abyssinia; almost all had come to the country as Greek or Turkish nationals. It was the only home they had known; they were artisans earning a better living than they could have got among their own people. Then, by changes in the map that were incomprehensible to them, they found that they had suddenly become Italians, and now they were being hustled down to the coast with the prospect of being recruited into labour gangs or soldiers to fight against the country of their adoption. There were several of them in our train, wistfully sucking oranges in the second-class coach.

Until three years before, the journey from Dirre-Dowa to Harar took two days. Now there was a motor road.

We left Dirre-Dowa shortly before midday. Patrick and I and his servant had now been joined by another Englishman, an old acquaintance named Charles G., who had come out primarily in search of amusement. There was also a youthful and very timid Abyssinian nobleman, who wanted a lift and raised entirely vain hopes of his being useful to us.

We left in two cars and, twisting and groaning up the countless hairpin bends and narrow embankments of the new road, were very soon at the top of the pass, which formerly had taken four hours of arduous riding. Here was a military post, a barricade and new corrugated-iron gates, which were later described by many poetic correspondents as 'the ancient "Gates of Paradise"'.

They certainly emphasized the contrast between the Harar

province and the surrounding wilderness. Behind lay the colourless, empty country which one saw from the train; mile after mile
of rock and dust, anthill and scrub, and, on the far horizon, the
torrid plain of the Danakil desert, where the Hawash river
petered out in a haze of heat. In front, beyond the surly Abyssinian guard, the uplands were patterned with standing crops,
terraces of coffee, neat little farms in flowering stockades of
euphorbia, the pinnacles of their thatched roofs decorated with
bright glass bottles and enamelled chamber-pots. In less than four
hours after our departure from Dirre-Dowa we were in sight of
the walls and minarets of Harar.

Perhaps I had been unduly eloquent in describing to my companions the beauties that awaited us.

After all I had remembered, and all I had said, the reality was a
little disappointing. There had been changes. The first sight to
greet us, as we came into view, was a vast, hideous palace, still
under construction; a white, bow-fronted, castellated European
thing like a south-coast hotel. It stood outside the walls, dominating the low, dun-coloured masonry behind it. The walls had been
breached and, instead of the circuitous approach of medieval
defence, the narrow, windowless lane which had led from the
main gates, under the walls, bending and doubling until it reached
the centre of the town, a new, straight track had been driven
through. There was an hotel, too, built in two storeys, with a
balcony, a shower-bath and a chamber of ineffable horror,
marked on the door, *W.C.* It was kept by a vivacious and
avaricious Greek named Carassellos, who, everyone said, for no
reason at all, was really an Italian. This building, where we took
rooms, had been erected immediately in front of the Law Courts,
and the space between was a babel of outraged litigants denounc-
ing to passers-by the venality of the judges, the barefaced perjury
of the witnesses, and the perversions of the legal system, by
which they had failed in their suits. About twice every hour they
would come to blows and be dragged inside again by the soldiers
to summary punishment.

But the main change seemed to be in the proportions of
Abyssinians to Hararis. It was at the moment, by all appearance,
an Abyssinian town. Great numbers of troops were being drafted

there. A Belgian training school was established. Abyssinian officials had been multiplied for the crisis, and with their women and children filled the town. The Hararis were rapidly melting away; those that could afford it, fled across the frontiers into French and British territory, the majority to the hills. They were a pacific people who did not want to get involved on either side in the coming struggle; particularly, they did not want their women to get into the hands of the Abyssinian soldiers. In place of the lovely girls I had described, we found the bare, buttered, sponge-like heads, the dingy white robes, the stolid, sulky faces and silver crosses of the Abyssinian camp followers.

Later the chief of the police dropped in for some whisky. He was an officer of the old school, greatly given to the bottle. He was suffering at the time from a severe cold and had stuffed his nostrils with leaves. It gave him a somewhat menacing aspect, but his intentions were genial. Very few journalists had, as yet, visited Harar, and the little yellow cards of identity from the Press Bureau, which were an object of scorn in Addis, were here accepted as being evidence, possibly, of importance. Patrick's servant, whose French was fluent but rarely intelligible, acted as interpreter. That is to say, he carried on a lively and endless conversation, into which we would occasionally intrude.

'What is he saying, Gabri?'

'He says he has a cold. He hopes you are well.'

Then they would carry on their exchanges of confidences. The end of this interview, however, was a promise that we should have a pass to take us as far as Jijiga.

During our day of waiting for permission to go to Jijiga, Patrick and I each engaged a spy. They were both British 'protected persons', who had for a long time made themselves a nuisance at the Consulate. That was their only point in common.

Mine, Wazir Ali Beg, was an Afghan, an imposing old rascal with the figure of a metropolitan policeman and the manner of a butler. He wrote and spoke nearly perfect English. At some stage of his life he had been in British government service, though in what precise capacity was never clear. Lately he had set up in Harar as a professional petition writer. He put it about among the

British Indians, Arabs, and Somalis who thronged the bazaar that he was a man of personal influence in the Consular Court, and thus induced them to part with their savings and brief him to conduct their cases for them. To me he represented himself as the head of a vast organization covering the Ogaden and Aussa countries. He never asked for money for himself but to 'reimburse' his 'agents'. On the occasion of our first meeting he gave me an important piece of news: that a party of Danakil tribesmen had arrived at Dirre-Dowa to complain to the Governor of Italian movements in their territory; a force of native and white troops had penetrated the desert south-west of Assab and were making a base near Mount Moussa Ali. It was the verification of this report, a month later, which provoked the order for general mobilization and precipitated the war. Wazir Ali Beg had a natural flair for sensational journalism and was so encouraged by my reception of this report that he continued to recount to me by every mail more and more improbable happenings, until, noticing letters in his scholarly hand addressed to nearly every journalist in Addis Ababa, I took him off my pay roll. He then used my letter of dismissal to put up his prices with his other clients, as evidence of the sacrifices he was making to give them exclusive service.

Patrick's spy was named Halifa, but he was soon known to the European community as Mata Hari. He was an Aden Arab whose dissolute appearance suggested only a small part of the truth. He approached us that evening without introduction on the balcony of the hotel, squatted down on his haunches very close to us, glanced furtively about him, and with extraordinary winks and gestures of his hands expressed the intention of coming with us to Jijiga as interpreter.

His frequent appearances at the Consular Court were invariably in the capacity of prisoner, charged with drunkenness, violence, and debts of quite enormous amounts. He made no disguise of the fact that most of his recent life had been spent in gaol. When he found that this amused us, he giggled about it in a most forbidding way. He wore a huge, loose turban which was constantly coming uncoiled like the hair of a drunken old woman, a blue blazer, a white skirt, and a number of daggers. Gabri,

Patrick's Abyssinian servant, took an instant dislike to him. 'Il est méchant, ce type arabe,' he said, but Gabri, once outside the boundaries of his own country, was proving a peevish traveller. He did not at all like being among Mohammedans and foreigners. Harar he could just bear on account of the abundance of fellow countrymen, but the prospect of going to Jijiga filled him with disgust.

The chief of police had given us two effeminate little soldiers, who trotted at our heels wherever we went, weighed down by antiquated rifles, looking as though they would burst into tears at every moment of crisis.

After protracted negotiations we had taken seats in a coffee lorry, bound for Hargeisa. There were the usual delays as the Somali driver made a last-minute tour of the town in the endeavour to collect additional passengers, and it was soon clear that we should not reach Jijiga by nightfall. Our two soldiers began nervously to complain of danger from brigands, but the journey was uneventful.

Rain came on at sunset and for four hours we made slow progress. The headlights pierced only a few feet of darkness; we skidded and splashed through pools of mud. Our driver wanted to stop and wait for dawn, saying that, even if we reached Jijiga, we should find ourselves locked out. We induced him to go on and at last came to the military post at the outskirts of the town. Here we found another lorry, full of refugees, which had passed us on the road earlier in the day. They had been refused admission and were now huddled together in complete darkness under sodden rugs, twenty or thirty of them, comatose and dejected. Our soldiers climbed down and parleyed; the driver exhibited the consular mailbag which he was carrying; Patrick and I produced our cards of identity. To everyone's surprise the barrier was pulled back and we drove on to the town. It was to all appearances dead asleep. We could just discern through the blackness that we were in a large square, converted at the moment to a single lake, ankle-deep. We hooted, and presently some Abyssinian soldiers collected round us, some of them drunk, one carrying a storm lantern. They directed us into a kind of pound; the gates were shut behind us and the soldiers prepared to return to bed.

There was no inn of any kind in Jijiga, but the firm of Mohamed Ali kept an upper room of their warehouse for the accommoda‑ tion of the Harar consul on his periodic visits. We had permission to use this and had wired the local manager to expect us. His representative now appeared in pyjamas, carrying an umbrella in one hand and a lantern in the other.

Fresh trouble started, which Mata Hari tried to inflame into a fight, because the soldiers in command refused to let us remove our bags. They had to be seen by the customs officer, who would not come on duty until next morning. As they contained our food, and we had had nothing to eat since midday, the prospect seemed discouraging. The Indian from Mohamed Ali's told us it was hopeless and that we had better come to our room. Mata Hari, Charles, and I set out with one of our own soldiers to find the customs officer. We knocked up his house, where they refused to open the door but shouted through the keyhole that the customs office was at the French House. A handful of Abyssinians had now collected in the darkness. Mata Hari did all he could to pro‑ voke them to violence, but our Harari guard was more concilia‑ tory and eventually we were led through what appeared to be miles of mud to another house which showed a light and a posse of sentries. The nature of the 'French House' was not at the moment clear. Sounds of many loud voices came from the interior. After Mata Hari had nearly got himself shot by one of the sentries, the door opened and a small Abyssinian emerged, clean-shaven, dressed in European clothes, horn-spectacled; one of the younger generation. We later learned that he was new to his position, having spent the previous year in prison on a charge of peculation. He came with us to the lorry, apologizing in fluent French for the inconvenience we had suffered. Our bags were sur‑ rendered and the Indian led us to our room, where, after supper, we slept on the floor until daybreak.

One of the wonders of travel is where native servants sleep. They arrive at any hour in a strange place and seem immediately to be surrounded by hospitable cousins-in-law, who embrace them, lead them home and for the rest of the stay batten upon one's stores. Our party broke up and disappeared cheerfully into the night; all except Gabri, who did not like Jijiga. He was intensely xenophobic where Somalis were concerned; he would not eat anything himself, saying that the food was not suitable for an Abyssinian; he nearly starved us by refusing to buy provisions on the grounds that the prices were excessive.

Mata Hari seemed to have slept in the mud, to judge by his appearance next morning, but perhaps he had merely found his fight. He came to our room in a kind of ecstasy, almost speechless with secrecy. He had news of the highest importance. He could not say it aloud, but must whisper it to each of us in turn. Count Drogafoi, the French Consul, had been thrown into prison. We asked him to repeat the name. He shook his head, winked and produced a stub of pencil and a piece of paper. Then, glancing over his shoulder to make sure he was not observed, he wrote the word, laboriously, in block capitals, DROGAFOI. It was to Drogafoi's house, he said, that we had been the night before. They were going to shoot Drogafoi that day. They had also arrested twelve Roman Catholics; these would be sewn up in skins and burned alive. There were four Maltese popes in the town. They would probably be shot too. He would return shortly, he said, with further information, and with that and another meaning wink he tip-toed downstairs.

In a somewhat puzzled state of mind we sat down to a breakfast of tinned partridge and Chianti. While we were still discussing what, if any, truth could be concealed in this story, the customs officer, our friend of the night before, came to introduce himself by name – Kebreth Astatkie – and to enquire about our welfare. Dedjasmach Nasebu, the Governor of Harar, was in Jijiga that day, he told us, on his way south, and would be pleased to see us. Accordingly we set out on foot for the Gebbi.

Rain had stopped and the town presented a more cheerful appearance. It consisted of a single main square and two side streets. The single European in the town, besides the mysterious Drogafoi and the Maltese popes, was a Greek, whom Mata Hari pointed out to us, riding a bicycle.

'That is the Alcohol,' he explained; a title which, we found later, meant that he owned the local liquor monopoly.

The Gebbi, like most Abyssinian official buildings, was a

nondescript assembly of tin-roofed sheds, the largest of which had some upper rooms, reached by an outside staircase. Two half-grown lions were tethered outside the main door; the slave in charge wrestled with one of them for our benefit, and was rewarded with a thaler and a deep scratch on the thigh. There was the inevitable small army of ragged retainers, squatting on their heels, nursing their old rifles.

We were first shown into the presence of the governor of Jijiga, Fitaurari Shafarah, an officer of the old school, who sat, surrounded by local notables, in a very small room, hung with carpets; the shutters were closed and the atmosphere was stupefying. He was a grizzled, gloomy little man who had been present at the battle of Walwal and had gained some discredit there, through being discovered, at the height of the action, squatting in his tent selling cartridges to his own troops. His own interpreter introduced us, and after the exchange of a few civilities we sat in unbroken silence for rather more than half an hour. Eventually we were led into the open and upstairs to Nasebu's quarters. The Dedjasmach wore European uniform and spoke French. Like everyone else in Abyssinia who spoke French – with the single exception of the Emperor – he was clean shaven. He was well up in European affairs. We drank coffee together and discussed the constitution of the Committee of Five, the Committee of Thirteen, the Council of the League, and such topics as, in those days, seemed important.

Patrick then asked him what truth there was in the story that a Frenchman had been arrested in Jijiga.

'A Frenchmen arrested?' he enquired with innocent incredulity. 'I will ask about it.'

He clapped his hands and sent a servant for Kebreth. They talked together for a few seconds in Amharic; then he said, 'Yes, it appears that something of the sort has occurred,' and proceeded to tell us the whole story, while Kebreth produced from various pockets about his person a collection of all the relevant documents.

Drogafoi was a Count Maurice de Roquefeuil du Bousquet, who had come to Ethiopia nine years before in search of a livelihood. For some time the police had been keeping a watch on his house. He was said to live in guilty splendour, but when Patrick and I visited his home later we found two simple and clearly impoverished little rooms. On the day before our arrival, an elderly Somali woman had been arrested leaving his house and, when she was searched, a film tube was found in her armpit, which, she confessed, she was taking to the Italian Consulate at Harar. Kebreth showed us the contents: a snapshot of some motor lorries and five pages of inaccurate information (of the kind which Wazir Ali Beg used regularly to write to me) describing the defences of Jijiga.

The Count and Countess had been arrested and their house searched. Kebreth said it was full of correspondence with Italian officers across the frontier, and of the names of native agents who were now being rounded up. He showed us the Count's passport and finally the Count himself, who, with his wife, was now under guard in an outbuilding of the Gebbi. As a large proportion of the Count's agents were boys who had been educated at the mission school, unfounded suspicion had also fallen upon the Franciscan friars. We took photographs of the Gebbi and the Count's house, of the lion cubs and the place of his imprisonment, of the slave in charge of the lions and the captain of the guard. A dramatic moment came when we expressed a wish to photograph the detective responsible for the arrest.

'You wish to photograph the detective?' said Kebreth. 'He stands before you. It was I.'

So we photographed Kebreth too, beaming through his horn-rimmed spectacles, and returned to Mohamed Ali's with the feeling that we were on to a good thing. It seemed to have all the ingredients of a newspaper story – even an imprisoned 'bride'. Moreover, there was no possibility of any other journalist having got it. We happily imagined cables arriving for our colleagues in Addis. '*Badly left Roquefeuil story*' and '*Investigate imprisoned countess Jijiga.*' It was now Friday morning. If we were to reach the Saturday papers it must be cabled by seven o'clock. Patrick and I feverishly typed out our reports while Charles engaged a car to take them to the nearest wireless station at Hargeisa, in British Somaliland, and Kebreth obligingly made out a pass for his journey.

When our cables were safely on their way, Patrick and I walked out into the town and there had another stroke of good luck. It was midday and the people were trooping into the little mosque to their prayers. A car drove up and there emerged a stocky figure in a black cossack hat. It was Wehib Pasha, a Turkish veteran of the Gallipoli campaign, one of the major mystery men of the country. He had left Addis in the greatest secrecy. There had been rumours that he was bound for the Ogaden. Some said he was on a religious mission, to preach a Moslem crusade against the Italians; others that he was to be the new Moslem Ras, whose appointment was hinted at. Patrick had interviewed him in Addis and found him profoundly uncommunicative.

His disgust at seeing us was highly gratifying. He shot into the mosque and sent his secretary-companion – an elegant Greek youth with a poetic black beard and immense, sorrowful eyes – to inform us that we were not to follow him about, and that if we took any photographs he would have our cameras destroyed. We sent Mata Hari into the mosque after him and told him to make enquiries in the market about what the Pasha was doing. The reply, which we got some hours later, disentangled from Mata Hari's more obvious intentions, was that the Pasha had recruited a large labour gang and was leaving next day for the south in a train of lorries, to dig lion pits for the Italian tanks.

Feeling that our trip to Jijiga had been a triumphant success, Patrick and I made our arrangements with a half-caste lorry driver to return next day to Harar. There remained the delicate question of whether or no we should tip Kebreth. Gabri and Mata Hari, when consulted, said of course all officials must be tipped on all occasions; Gabri alone showed some anxiety that we would give too much. Accordingly when Kebreth came in that evening for a drink with us, Patrick produced a note and with great tact suggested that we should be glad if he would distribute a small sum to the poor of the town in acknowledgement of our enjoyable visit.

Kebreth had no respect for these euphemisms; he thanked us, but said with great composure that times had changed and Ethiopian officials now received their wages regularly.

Five hours' delay next morning in getting on the road. Our half-caste driver made one excuse and then another – he had to take some mail for the government, he was awaiting another passenger, the municipal officer had not yet signed his pass. At last Mata Hari explained the difficulty; there was shooting on the road; a handful of soldiers in the manner of the country had taken to the bush and were at war with the garrison. 'This driver is a very fearful man,' said Mata Hari.

Presently, when the half-caste had at last been taunted into activity by our staff, the danger passed. Less than a mile outside the town we met soldiers coming back, dragging some very battered prisoners. 'Perhaps they will be whipped to death. Perhaps they will only be hanged,' said Mata Hari.

We were still in a mood of self-approval. We wondered whether any of our messages had yet arrived in London and whether Patrick had got in first with the Saturday evening edition, or I on Monday morning. We expected cables of congratulation. There was a cable for me. It said, '*What do you know Anglo American oil concession?*' Evidently our messages had been delayed; but as there was no possible competitor, we were not alarmed. I replied '*Apply local agent for commercial intelligence Addis*', and, still in good humour, went up to dine at the Consulate.

Next morning there was another cable, a day old: '*Must have fullest details oil concession.*' I replied: '*Absolutely impossible obtain Addis news Harar.*' Before luncheon there was a third: '*Badly left oil concession suggest your return Addis immediately.*'

It was now clear that something important had happened in our absence, which eclipsed our stories of Roquefeuil and Wehib Pasha. A two-day train left Dirre-Dowa for Addis on Tuesday morning. In low spirits Patrick and I arranged for our departure.

Harar had suddenly lost its charm. News of the events at Jijiga had filtered through in wildly exaggerated forms; the town was inflamed with spy-mania. Mata Hari was promptly gaoled on the evening of his return. We bought him out, but he seemed to expect hourly re-arrest. The chief of police may have had some reprimand for allowing us to go to Jijiga or perhaps it was only that his cold was worse; whatever the reason, his manner had entirely changed towards us and he was now haughty and suspicious. Mr Carassellos was in a condition of infectious agitation. Half his friends had just been arrested and cross-examined under suspicion of complicity with Roquefeuil. He was expecting the soldiers to come for him any minute.

Roquefeuil and the native prisoners arrived on Sunday night. Throughout the day on Monday, Mata Hari popped in on us with fragments of unlikely news about his trial; that he was in the common prison, that the Emperor was coming in person to supervise his execution; that he had boasted, 'In seven days' time this town will be in the hands of Italy and I shall be avenged.' But the story had lost its interest for us.

No one in Harar knew anything about an oil concession. The first information we received was at Dirre-Dowa, where a young official explained that the Emperor had leased most of the country to America. At Awash we learned that Mr Rickett was associated with the business. At Addis, on Wednesday night, we found that the story was already stale. It was a sensational story which, for a few days, threatened to influence international politics.

Mr Rickett, as the agent of a group of American financiers, had secured from the Emperor a concession for mineral rights of unprecedented dimensions. The territory affected was that bordering on the Italian possessions over which the Italian troops would presumably seek to advance, and which, presumably, they hoped to annex.

Had the concession been made in 1934, it is difficult to see how the United States government could have permitted Italian occupation. As it was, in Septemper 1935, with war already inevitable, the States Department at Washington intervened against the Emperor and forbade the ratification of the concession. By doing so they virtually recognized Italy's right to conquer, for, while he was still a sovereign ruler, they refused to recognize the Emperor's right to grant concessions within his own dominions. The Emperor had reverted to the traditional policy of balancing the self-aggrandizement of the white peoples one against another, and it failed. After that he was left with no cards to play except international justice, collective security and the overweening confidence of his fighting forces. He played the first two astutely enough; the third turned out to be valueless.

On our return to Addis Ababa we found the temporary white population still further increased. Before the outbreak of war the number of accredited journalists and photographers was rather more than a hundred. They showed almost every diversity which the human species produces. There was a simian Sudanese, who travelled under a Brazilian passport and worked for an Egyptian paper; there was a monocled Latvian colonel, who was said at an earlier stage of his life to have worked as ring-master in a German circus; there was a German who travelled under the name of Haroun al Raschid, a title, he said, which had been conferred on him during the Dardanelles campaign by the late Sultan of Turkey; his head was completely hairless; his wife shaved it for him, emphasizing the frequent slips of her razor with tufts of cotton wool. There was a venerable American, clothed always in dingy black, who seemed to have strayed from the pulpit of a religious conventicle; he wrote imaginative despatches of great length and flamboyancy. There was an Austrian, in Alpine costume, with crimped flaxen hair, the group leader, one would have thought, of some Central-European Youth Movement; a pair of rubicund young colonials, who came out on chance and were doing brisk business with numberless competing organizations; two indistinguishable Japanese, who beamed at the world through horn-rimmed spectacles and played interminable, highly dexterous games of ping-pong in Mme Idot's bar. These formed an exotic background that was very welcome, for the majority of the regular pressmen were an anxious, restless, mutually suspicious crowd, all weighed down with the consciousness that they were not getting the news.

It was a disheartening quest. The situation throughout the whole of September was perfectly clear. Everyone was waiting for Italy at her own convenience to begin the war.

There were reports from all over the country of extensive troop movements. The order for general mobilization had not been made. The news of its promulgation was cabled back almost daily by one or other of the special correspondents: '*War drums beating*

in the North – the Emperor raises the Standard of Solomon.'
Almost daily enquiries came from Fleet Street, ' *What truth general mobilization ?*' Like almost every important event in the war it was so often anticipated and so often denied that, when it actually happened, it had lost all its interest.

No answer was given to our applications for leave to travel. We were obliged to rely for information about what was happening in the interior upon the army of Greek and Levantine spies who frequented Mme Moriatis's bar. Most of these men were pluralists, being in the pay not only of several competing journalists at once but also of the Italian Legation, the Abyssinian secret police, or both.

The railway station was a centre of minor information. Half the white population and practically all the Press were on the platform for each departure. There was seldom any very sensational occurrence; sometimes an Indian would be arrested smuggling dollars; there were always tears; once or twice an Abyssinian dignitary left on an official mission, attended by a great entourage, bowing, embracing his knees, and kissing him firmly on his bearded cheeks. At any time there was a fair amount of rough and tumble at the Addis terminus between Arab porters and station police. This served to give colour to the descriptions of panic and extravagant lamentation which were dutifully cabled to Fleet Street.

The arrivals in the evening were more interesting, for anyone visiting Addis at this season was a potential public character, perhaps another Rickett. Two humane English colonels excited feverish speculation for a few days until it was discovered that they were merely emissaries of a World League for the Abolition of Fascism. There was a Negro from South Africa who claimed to be a Tigrean, and represented another World League for the abolition, I think, of the white races, and a Greek who claimed to be a Bourbon prince and represented some unspecified and unrealized ambitions of his own. There was an American who claimed to be a French viscount and represented a league, founded in Monte Carlo, for the provision of an Ethiopian *Disperata* squadron, for the bombardment of Assab. There was a completely unambiguous British adventurer, who claimed to have been one of Al Capone's bodyguards and wanted a job; and an ex-officer of the R.A.F. who started to live in some style with a pair of horses, a bull terrier and a cavalry moustache – he wanted a job too. All these unusual characters were good for a paragraph.

There was also a mysterious and, I am now inclined to believe, non-existent force of Yemen Arabs which made a fitful appearance in our despatches. By some accounts they were still in the Yemen and were waiting orders for the attack from the Imam of Sana. They were to cross the Red Sea in a fleet of dhows, fall upon Assab and massacre the garrison. Another version had it that they were already in Addis, organized as a fighting corps. They were constantly reported as parading at the palace and offering their arms and fortune in the Emperor's service. There was in fact a number of venerable old traders from the Yemen, dotted about the bazaar quarter. If two of them sat down together for a cup of coffee it was described as a military consultation.

By every post, until I told him to stop, Wazir Ali Beg sent me a budget of news.

He had no difficulty in finding other correspondents and, as the situation became darker and reporting more speculative, Wazir Ali Beg's news service formed an ever-increasing part of the morning reading of the French, English, and American newspaper publics.

Whenever Mata Hari was out of prison, he too wrote:

'THE ETHUPIAN NEWS OF THE 11TH SEPTEMBER
'*Troubles at 3 p.m.*
'Soldiers. *Fieghts near Bazara doors some of the Soldiers entered Bazara house as some brack heads bloods come out* ...
'Dagash Mazh *said the Ethupian troops will assault the Italian troops before the time of the rain* ...
'Dagash Mazh *regarding to the lecture of the 8th advise the soldiers, regret to say, at 3 p.m. the soldiers to their misfortune and endignity on the peoples, robing the vegetables, etc.*
'Truck *passed on to leg of one Somalee.*
'News *from the Arabic news papers, the warfare will be between six Governments shortly.*
'Somali Merchant Mahmood Warofaih *made trench in his*

garden and put his money, few days repeat to see his money and not found, at once come mad.'

This last trouble was by no means peculiar to Mahmood Warofaih. During the crisis it seemed to be happening all over the country. The gardener at the Deutsches Haus suffered in exactly that way and showed every sign of losing his reason until, to the disappointment of the other servants, who were enjoying the spectacle immoderately, Haroun al Raschid charitably reimbursed him.

The Foreign Press Association held occasional meetings, which were highly enjoyable, having a character of combined mock-trial and drinking bout. The Americans and French did most of the talking; the English endeavoured to collect the subscriptions and maintain some semblance of constitutional order. The Spaniard was elected a member of committee, with acclamation. The Radical made a conscientious and rather puzzled treasurer. The Americans were facetious or ponderously solemn, according as their drink affected them. There was one of them who was constantly on his feet crying: 'Mr Chairman, I protest that the whole question is being treated with undesirable levity.' Every now and then the French walked out in a body and formed an independent organization.

Our chief function was to protest. We 'protested unanimously and in the most emphatic manner' or we 'respectfully represented to the Imperial Government' that the cabling rates were too high, that the Press Bureau was inconveniently situated and inadequately staffed, that a Negro aviator had insulted a French reporter, that preferential treatment was given to certain individuals in the despatch of late messages, that the official bulletins were too meagre and too irregular; we petitioned to be allowed to go to the fronts, to be told definitely whether we should ever be allowed to go there. No one paid the smallest attention to us. After a time the protesting habit became automatic. The Association split up into small groups and pairs protesting to one another, cabling their protests to London and Geneva, scampering round to the palace and protesting to the private secretaries of the Emperor at every turn of events. But that was later; in these early days the Foreign Press Association showed some of the lightheartedness of a school debating society.

Week succeeded week, full of whispered rumours; more journalists and cinema men arrived. I bought a petulant and humourless baboon which lived in my room at the Deutsches Haus, and added very little to the interest of these dull days. There were rowdy evenings at *Le Select* and the *Perroquet*. The Spaniard went back to resume his duties in Paris. Patrick and I gave a dinner-party in his honour, which was overclouded for him by the loss of his sixpenny fountain-pen. 'Who of you has taken my feather?' he kept asking with great earnestness. 'I cannot work without my feather.'

At last, on October 2nd, came the announcement which had been so often predicted, that general mobilization would be proclaimed on the morrow. It was preceded by the formal complaint that Ethiopian territory had been violated at Mount Moussa Ali. Notices were posted inviting the Press to attend 'a ceremony of great importance' which was to be held next day at the old Gebbi. Everybody knew what that meant.

It was particularly gay that evening in the bars. Next morning we all assembled at the Palace at half past ten. We were shown straight into an airless gallery and kept there.

No one knew quite what to expect, and even the most daring of the journalists had decided to wait and see what happened before composing their reports. Various almost liturgical ceremonies were expected; we were told in some quarters that the Emperor would set up his standard in person; that his crimson tent would be pitched as a rallying point for the armies; that the great drum of Menelik would be beaten, which had not sounded since 1895.

The drum was there; we could hear it clearly from our place of confinement, beating a series of single thuds, slow as a tolling bell. When eventually the doors were thrown open and we emerged on to the terrace, we saw the drum, a large ox-hide stretched over a wooden bowl. It may or may not have belonged to Menelik; all the whites said that it had and Mr David politely agreed.

A flight of stone steps led from the terrace to the parade ground, where a large, but not very large, crowd had assembled.

They were all men. Over his shoulder I watched a journalist typing out a description of the women under their mushroom-like umbrellas. There were no women and no umbrellas; merely a lot of black fuzzy heads and white cotton clothes. The Palace police were trying to keep the crowd back, but they pushed forward until only a small clearing remained, immediately below the steps. Here Mr Prospero and a half a dozen of his colleagues were grinding away behind tripods.

The drum stopped and the people were completely silent as the Grand Chamberlain read the decree. It took some time. He read it very loudly and clearly. At the end there were three concerted bursts of clapping. Then the men made a rush for the Palace; it was unexpected and spontaneous. They wanted to see the Emperor. Most of them had swords or rifles. They flourished these wildly and bore down upon the little group of photographers, who, half fearing a massacre, scuttled for safety, dragging along their cumbrous apparatus as best they could. The crowd caught poor Mr Prospero, knocked him down and kicked him about, not in any vindictive spirit, but simply because he was in the way. One of them eventually put him on his feet, laughing, but not before he had sustained some sharp injuries.

Upstairs the decree was being read to the journalists in French by Dr Lorenzo. He could not make himself heard above the shouting. He stood on a chair, a diminutive, neat, black figure, crying for attention. A great deal of noise came from the journalists themselves. I had seldom seen them to worse advantage. Dr Lorenzo had in his hand a sheaf of copies of the decree. The journalists did not want to hear him read it. They wanted to secure their copies and race with them for the wireless bureau. Lorenzo kept crying in French, 'Gentlemen, gentlemen, I have something of great importance to communicate to you.'

He held the papers above his head and the journalists jumped for them, trying to snatch, like badly brought up children at a Christmas party.

The soldiers had now worked themselves into high excitement and were streaming past, roaring at the top of their voices.

Lorenzo led a dozen of us into the Palace, where in comparatively good order he was able to make his second announcement. He was clearly in a state of deep emotion himself; the little black hands below the starched white cuffs trembled. 'His Majesty has this morning received a telegram from Ras Seyoum in the Tigre,' he said. 'At dawn this morning four Italian war planes flew over Adowa and Adigrat. They dropped seventy-eight bombs, causing great loss of life among the civilian population. The first bomb destroyed the hospital at Adowa, where many women and children had taken refuge. At the same time Italian troops invaded the Province of Agame, where a battle is now raging.'

The excitement barely survived the transmission of our cables. By afternoon the cheering crowd had melted away and was dozing silently in their *tukals*. Shutters were put up on the Greek–Italian grocery store and a guard posted before it, while at the back door journalists competed with the French Legation to buy the last tins of caviare.

That afternoon and evening we drove round the town in search of 'incidents', but everything was profoundly quiet. News of the bombardment of Adowa was now all over the bazaars, but it seemed to cause little stir. Adowa was a very long way off. Practically no one in Addis had ever been there. It was known to them by name, as the place where the white men had been so gloriously cut to pieces forty years before. It was inhabited by Tigreans, a people for whom they had little liking.

The Europeans, Levantines and Americans, on the other hand, fell into a cold sweat of terror. The Emperor's white adviser had at this time organized a daily tea party of specially sympathetic correspondents. This group became a centre from which Ethiopian propaganda radiated. On the afternoon of October 3rd, 'the Leaker', as he was familiarly known, gave it out that an air raid was expected on Addis that evening. The effect was galvanic. One group of journalists hastily concluded a deal for the lease of a mansion immediately next door to the Italian Legation. They packed up their stores and luggage and their accumulations of trashy souvenirs and set off in secrecy to their new home. Unfortunately they were contravening a municipal bye-law which forbade a change of address without previous permission. I

cannot help suspecting that Mr Kakophilos must have tipped off
the police; there was a touch of saturnine triumph in the air with
which he welcomed their return, an hour later, under guard, to his
hotel. A similar fate befell a neurotic young Canadian who set
out to hide on the top of Mount Entoto. Other journalists took
refuge in outlying missions and hospitals, or shared their bedrooms with their chauffeurs for fear that, when the alarm came,
they might find their cars usurped by black women and children.
Others are said to have sat up all night playing stud poker in gas
masks. Timidity was infectious. A passing motor bicycle would
have us all at the window staring skywards. A few hardened
topers remained sober that evening for fear of sleeping too heavily.
But the night passed undisturbed by any except the normal
sounds – the contending loudspeakers of the two cinemas, the
hyaenas howling in the cemetery. Few of us slept well. The first
two hours after dawn were the most likely time for a raid, but the
sun – at last it was full summer – brought reassurance. After a
slightly strained week-end we settled down to our former routine.
On Monday night there was a bacchanalian scene at Mme Idot's,
where, among other songs of international popularity, 'Giovan-
ezza' was sung in a litter of upturned tables and broken crockery.

The communiqué, read in dramatic circumstances by Dr
Lorenzo, asserted that the first bomb of the attack had fallen on
'the hospital', destroying it and killing many women and
children. When we began to look for details, our doubts were
aroused whether there had ever been a hospital there at all. No
such thing existed as a native hospital; no Red Cross units had
yet appeared in the field; the medical work of the country was
entirely in mission hands. The headquarters of these organizations
knew nothing about a hospital at Adowa, nor did the Consulates
know of any of their nationals engaged there. The publication of
the news was already having the desired effect in Europe; a letter,
which caused great amusement when it reached us, appeared in
The Times expressing the hope that 'the noble nurses had not died
in vain', but at Addis Ababa suspicions were aroused that our
legs were being pulled. Mr David and Dr Lorenzo, when pressed,
had to admit that they knew no more than was disclosed in the

first bulletin; there *had been* a hospital – it was now destroyed, they maintained stoutly, and added that it was clearly marked with the red cross; apart from that they had no information.

But suddenly, from other sources, a flood of detail began to reach us. There was an Abyssinian servant who had been treated there two years ago for a pain in his leg by a great number of American doctors and nurses; the hospital was a fine building in the centre of the town.

There was a Greek who knew the place well. It was managed by Swedes and lay at a short distance along the Adigrat road.

There was a Swiss architect and government contractor – a jolly fellow, married to a half-caste; he was responsible for most of the ugliest of the recent public buildings – who was able to give Patrick confidential but absolutely authentic information about the nurse who had been killed; she was of Swedish birth but American nationality; she had been blown to bits. He had heard all about it on the telephone from a friend on the spot.

The most circumstantial story came from an American Negro who was employed as aviator by the Ethiopian government. I met him at his tailor's on the Saturday morning, ordering a fine new uniform. He had been at Adowa, he claimed, at the time of the bombardment. More than this, he had been in the hospital. More than this, he had been drinking cocoa with the nurse five minutes before her death. She was a handsome lady, thirty-two years old, five foot five in height. They had been sitting in the hospital – clearly marked by the red cross – when the first bomb had fallen. The airman's first thought, he said, was for the safety of his machine, which was lying a mile outside the town. Except for himself and the doctor there were no other men in the town. It was populated solely by women and children. He had lain near his aeroplane for some hours while the bombs fell. The Italians had flown very badly, he said, and bombed most erratically ('Mr Waugh, do you realize, *I* might have been killed *myself*?'). Eventually he had returned to see the place demolished and the nurse dead. He had then flown back to Addis, where the Emperor had been deeply moved by his story.

Cables were soon arriving from London and New York: '*Require earliest name life story photograph American nurse up-*

blown Adowa.' We replied '*Nurse unupblown*', and after a few days she disappeared from the news.

We still believed that the railway was doomed. On Tuesday the 8th 'positively the last' train left for Djibouti. There was something very like a riot at the station as frantic refugees attempted to board it, and the station police locked out legitimate passengers who had reserved their places. For the first time the scene approximated to the descriptions which, as early as August, had been filling the world's Press. It was now too late to be of interest – another example of the inverted time lag between the event and its publication which marked all our professional efforts in the country.

The camera men were even more unhappily placed than the correspondents. Their apparatus rendered them conspicuous and most of the native soldiers had an exaggerated idea of the value which their portraits might be to the enemy. The cinema companies in particular had invested huge sums in their expeditions and were getting very little in return for it.

One group of cinema men purchased the good will of a chief who was encamped with his men in the hills behind Addis and were able to stage some fairly effective charades of active service. Later at Dessye the 'Ethiopian Red Cross' lent itself to a vivid imposture, staging a scene of their own heroic services under fire, with iodine to counterfeit blood and fireworks and flares for a bombardment. One prominent photographer had brought out with him a set of small bombs which he was able to discharge from his position at the camera by means of an electric cable. He had some difficulty explaining them at the French customs and I do not know if they were ever used. Those who had worked during the Chinese wars – where, it seemed, whole army corps could be hired cheaply by the day and even, at a special price, decimated with real gunfire – complained bitterly of the standard of Abyssinian venality.

The white population of the town pursued their normal routine. Mme Moriatis showed signs of despair, spoke daily of a massacre, and tried to persuade her husband to pack up. One evening, when she was showing a French version of *Peg o' My Heart*, her cinema was visited by the picturesque retinue of one of the provincial magnates, who came with women, bodyguard and two half-grown lions who were left on the steps in charge of his slaves. The brief run on the bank came to an end. The thaler went up in value; the engine drivers of the railway did a brisk trade in smuggling silver. Various statesmen and warriors returned from exile and were reconciled to the Emperor. The French population organized itself in a defence corps. Issa tribesmen shot down an Italian aeroplane and hid for days, not knowing if they had done well or ill. An Egyptian prince arrived to establish a Red Crescent hospital. The Yemen Arabs were reported to be active. We eked out our despatches with such small items of news. Already some correspondents began to talk of leaving, and the most distinguished veteran actually left. The rest of us centred all our hopes on the long-deferred trip to Dessye. Various dates – the anniversary of his accession, St George's Day – were suggested as the time of the Emperor's departure.

At the beginning of November the long-awaited permission to go to Dessye was at last granted. Enthusiasm for the trip simultaneously began to wane. It was said that the Emperor would not in fact go there; that it was a ruse to get the pressmen under close observation and out of harm's way; that there would be no wireless facilities; that the big southern campaign would begin in our absence. In the end only a small number of those who had been clamouring for permission decided to avail themselves of it. The Radical was among them, and he and I agreed to travel together.

As soon as this was known we became a centre of interest. All the boys at the Deutsches Haus, and the girl of no fixed occupation who pottered about the outbuildings, giggling, and occasionally appeared in the bedrooms with a broom, applied to accompany us. A saturnine Syrian, named Mr Karam, who had lately formed the habit of waylaying me on Sunday mornings after Mass and asking me to drink coffee with him, offered to sell us a motor lorry. The trouble about this lorry was that it did not in fact belong to Mr Karam. He had secured an option on it from a fellow Syrian and hoped to resell it at a profit. This was not clear until later, when he suffered great embarrassment about the spare parts. We said we would not take the lorry until it was fully equipped; he promised to equip it as soon as the agreement was signed. It was only when we went with him to the store that we discovered that he could not get the spare parts on credit, and could not pay for them until we had paid him an instalment of the price. There was a further embarrassment. We demanded a trial run up Entoto to test the engine. He could not get the petrol for the trip. In the end we filled up the tanks. James, my interpreter, who was not getting the rake-off he expected and had consequently taken up a suspicious attitude to Mr Karam, reported in triumph next morning that Mr Karam had hired out the lorry to a building contractor and was consuming our petrol. Poor Mr Karam was merely trying to raise the money for a new tyre. In the end we hired the machine for a month, at what I suspect was very near its full purchase price. From that moment Mr Karam was obsessed by anxiety that we would make off with his lorry. He hung about the garage, where a gang was at work enhancing its value with a covered top and built-in boxes for petrol cans, pathetically canvassing our signatures to bits of paper on which we guaranteed not to drive beyond Dessye. It happened that the various agreements were made out in my name. When, a month later, the Radical and I separated and I returned to Addis Ababa in another car, poor Mr Karam's suspicions became feverish. He was convinced that there had been a plot against him and that the Radical had deserted with his lorry to the Italians.

With James's help we got together a suitable staff for the journey. He and my own boy, an Abyssinian, had long been at enmity. In the hiring of the servants they frequently came to tears. The most important man was the cook. We secured one who looked, and as it turned out was, all that a cook should be. A fat, flabby Abyssinian with reproachful eyes. His chief claim to interest was that his former master, a German, had been murdered and dismembered in the Issa country. I asked him why he had done nothing to protect him. '*Moi, je ne suis pas soldat, suis cuisinier, vous savez.*' That seemed a praiseworthy attitude, so I engaged him. He suffered a great deal from the privations of the journey and cried with cold most evenings, the tears splashing and sizzling among the embers of his fire, but he cooked excellently, with an aptitude for producing four or five courses from a single blackened pan over a handful of smoking twigs.

The chauffeur seemed to be suitable until we gave him a fortnight's wages in advance to buy a blanket. Instead he bought cartridges and *tedj*, shot up the bazaar quarter and was put in chains. So we engaged a Harari instead who formed a Moslem alliance with James against the other servants. The Radical and I found ourselves in almost continuous session as a court of arbitration. A cook's boy and chauffeur's boy completed the party. We had brought camping equipment and a fair quantity of stores from England; we supplemented these with flour, potatoes, sugar and rice from the local market; our Press cards were officially endorsed for the journey; our servants had been photographed and provided with special passes; and by November 13th, the day announced by the Press Bureau for our departure, everything was ready.

Rumours came back that there were disturbances on the Dessye road. Part of it ran through the fringe of the Danakil country and these unamiable people had been resorting to their traditional sport of murdering runners and stragglers from the Abyssinian forces; there had also been sharp fighting between the Imperial Guard and the irregular troops, causing a number of casualties which reached us in a highly exaggerated form. A Canadian journalist who had arranged to start a week earlier with a caravan of mules had his permission cancelled abruptly and without explanation. David and Lorenzo refused to commit themselves; both were unapproachable for the two days preceding the 13th, but on the night of the 12th no official announcement had been made of postponement, our passes were in order, and the Radical and I decided to see how far we could get. At the best we might arrive before the road had been cleared of traces of the recent troubles; at the worst it would be an interesting experiment with Ethiopian government methods. The correspondent of the *Morning Post* decided to join us.

Most of the loading was done on the day before. That night we kept the lorry in the road outside the Deutsches Haus and put two boys to sleep in it. We meant to start at dawn, but, just as we were ready, James accused the cook of peculation, the Abyssinians refused to be driven by a Harari, and my personal boy burst into tears. I think they had spent the evening saying good-bye to their friends and were suffering from hangovers. The only two who kept their composure were those who had guarded the lorry. It was nearly nine before everyone's honour was satisfied. The streets were then crowded and our lorry, painted with the names of our papers and flying the Union Jack, made a conspicuous object. We drove past the Press Bureau, glancing to see that there was no notice on the door. We let down the side curtains, and the three whites lay low among the cases of stores hoping that we should pass as a government transport.

For nearly an hour we sprawled under cover in extreme discomfort as the heavily laden lorry jolted and lurched along the rough track. Then James told us that all was clear. We sat up, tied back the curtains, and found we were in open country. Addis was out of sight; a few eucalyptus trees on the horizon behind us marked the extreme of urban expansion, before us lay a smooth grassy plain and the road, sometimes worn bare, scarred by ruts and hoof marks, sometimes discernible only by the boulders that had been distributed along it at intervals to trace its course. There was brilliant sunshine and a cool breeze. The boys at the back began to unwrap their bundles of luggage and consume large quantities of an aromatic spiced paste. An air of general good humour had succeeded the irritation of early morning.

We drove on for five or six hours without a stop. The way was easy. Galla girls came out to wave to us, tossing their bundles of plaited hair. The men bowed low, three times; no one had travelled by car on that road for many months except Abyssinian officials or officers, and they had learned to associate motor traffic with authority.

After the first twenty miles we found soldiers everywhere. Some at noon, still encamped; others wandering along in companies of a dozen; some with mules to carry their loads, some with women. These were stragglers from Ras Getatchu's army which had gone through Addis a week before.

The road turned and wandered, following the lie of the ground;

every now and then we ran across the line of the telephone, a double overhead wire running straight across country. This, we knew, constituted our danger.

The first telephone station was named Koromach. We reached it at three o'clock. A uniformed Abyssinian stood across the road signalling us to stop. James and the Harari were all for running him down; we restrained their enthusiasm and climbed out of our places. The office was a small, lightless *tukal* a hundred yards or so off the road. There were twenty or thirty irregular soldiers there, squatting on their heels with rifles across their knees, and a chief in a new khaki uniform. By means of James the telephone officer explained that he had received an order from Addis to stop two car loads of white men travelling without permits. This constituted the strong point of our argument, for we were clearly only one car load and we had our permits; we showed them to him. He took them away into a corner and studied them at length; yes, he admitted, we had our permits. He showed them to the chief and the two sat for some time in colloquy. 'The chief is a good man,' said James. 'The telephone man very bad man. He is saying we are not to go on. The chief says we have permission and he will not stop us.'

Since the man in charge of the guns was on our side, we took a more arrogant line. What proof had the clerk that he had received a message at all? How did he know who was speaking? How did he know the message, if message there was, referred to us? Here were we being held up in our lawful business by the hearsay statement of the telephone. It was evident that the chief really distrusted the telephone. A piece of writing on a printed card had more weight with him than a noise coming out of a hole in the wall. At this stage of the discussion James left us and disappeared into the lorry. He returned a moment later with a bottle of whisky and a mug. We gave the chief a good half-pint of neat spirit. He tossed it off, blinked a little, and apologized for the delay we had been caused; then he conducted us, with his men, to the lorry and, the telephone man still protesting, waved us a cordial farewell.

We had been held up for half an hour. It got dark soon after six, so, since we had as yet had no practice in making camp, after an hour and a half's further drive, we turned off the track and stopped for the night under the lee of a small hill.

It was deadly cold. None of us slept much that night. I could hear the boys shivering and chattering round the fire whenever I woke. An hour before dawn we rose, breakfasted and struck camp under a blaze of stars. With the first sign of the sun we were on the road. Our hope was to get through Debra Birhan before the Gebbi officials at Addis were awake to warn them of our approach. Debra Birhan was about three hours' drive away. It was the last telephone station on the road. Once past that the way lay clear to Dessye.

We were out of Galla country now and among true Abyssinians, but this part was sparsely populated and many of the farms had been left empty by their owners who were marching to the front. There were fields of maize here and there, standing high on either side of the road, many of them showing where they had been trampled down by passing soldiers; the track was tolerably level and we made good time. When we were a couple of miles from Debra Birhan, James warned us that it was time to hide. We drew the curtains, lay down as before and covered ourselves as well as we could with sacks and baggage.

It seemed a very long two miles and we had begun to believe that we were safely past the station when the lorry came to a halt and we heard a loud altercation going on all round us. We still lay low, hoping that James would bluff our way through, but after about five minutes his head appeared through the curtain. It was no good; rather shamefacedly we crept out of hiding. We found ourselves on the green of a large village. On one side stood the church of considerable size from which the place took its name. Next to it was the Governor's compound and courthouse; on all sides irregular clusters of huts; some sizeable trees; a pretty place. A less agreeable prospect was the collection of soldiers who surrounded us. They were the crocks left behind when the young men went to the war. They were ragged and dilapidated, some armed with spears but most of them with antiquated guns. 'I am sorry to disturb you,' said James politely, 'but these people wished to shoot us.'

In the centre stood the mayor – a typical Abyssinian squireen, tall, very fat, one-eyed. It was not clear at first whether he was disposed to be friendly; we tried him with whisky, but he said he was fasting – a bad sign.

He said he had received a message to stop us. We told him we had heard that story before at Koromach; we had cleared the whole matter up there. It was a mistake. We showed him our permits. Yes, he admitted, they were quite in order. He must just make a note of our names and write a letter of commendation for us to the other chiefs on the road; would we come with him to Government House.

It sounded hopeful, but James added to his interpretation, 'I think, sir, that this is a liar-man.'

A leper woman had now joined the party; together we all sauntered across the green to the mayor's compound.

The main building was a rectangular, murky hut. We went inside. The telephone operator was not well that day; he lay on his bed in the darkest corner. The chief of police sat by his side: a toothless little old man with an absurd military cap on the side of his head. These three talked at some length about us. 'They do not want to let us go, but they are a little afraid,' said James. 'You must pretend to be angry.' We pretended to be angry. 'They are *very* afraid,' said James.

The argument followed much the same course as yesterday's, but the one-eyed mayor was much less impressed by our written permits. First he affected not to be able to read them; then he complained that the signature looked fishy; then he said that although we had indeed permission to go to Dessye we had neglected to get permission to leave Addis Ababa. It was a mere formality, he said; we had better go back and do it.

Then we made a false step. We proposed that he should do this for us by telephone. He jumped at the suggestion. It was exactly what he would do. Only it would take some time. It was unsuitable that people of our eminence should stand about in the sun. Why did we not pitch a tent and rest? His men would help us.

If we had gone on being angry we might still have got through; instead we weakly assented, pitched a tent and sat down to smoke. After an hour I sent James to enquire how things were getting on. He came back to say that no attempt was being made to telephone to Addis. We must come back and be angry again.

We found the chief holding a court, his single, beady eye fixed upon a group of litigants who at a few inches' distance from him were pleading their case with all the frantic enc₁gy common in Abyssinian suits. He was not at all pleased at being disturbed. He was a great man, he said. We said we were great men too. He said that the telephone operator was far from well, that the line was engaged, that the Gebbi was empty, that it was a fast day, that it was dinner-time, that it was late, that it was early, that he was in the middle of important public business, that James was offensive and untruthful and was not translating what he said and what we said, but instead, was trying to make a quarrel of a simple matter which admitted of only one solution, that we should wait until the afternoon and then come and see him again.

I do not know what James said, but the result was an adjournment of the court and a visit to the telephone hut, where the chief of police demonstrated, by twirling the handle, that the machine was out of order. We wrote out a telegram to Lorenzo protesting in the customary terms of the Foreign Press Association that we were being unjustly held prisoner in defiance of his own explicit permission to proceed. We had little hope of moving Lorenzo; we thought it might impress the mayor. 'They are *very* frightened,' said James. But they proceeded to their luncheon with the utmost composure and our message remained in the hands of the bedridden and now, apparently, moribund telephonist. 'They are too frightened to send it,' said James, trying to put an honourable complexion on the affair.

When we returned to our tent we found that, in our absence, the entire male and female labour of the village had been recruited and a barricade built of stones and tree trunks across the front of the lorry. Walking a little way back along the road we had come, we found another barricade. Any hopes which we might have entertained of the mayor's good will were now dispelled.

The afternoon passed in a series of fruitless negotiations. The chief would not send our message to Lorenzo, nor subsequent messages which we wrote to other officials. We tried to get him to endorse them with a note that they had been presented and refused. That was no good. We made up our minds to spending the night at Debra Birhan and pitched the other tents.

Our sudden docility disconcerted the chief and for the first time he showed some sign of the fears which James had attributed to him. He clearly feared that we intended to make a sortie by night. To prevent this he tried to separate us from the lorry; he and the chief of police came waddling down at the head of their guard – now reinforced by the village idiot, a stark-naked fellow who loped and gibbered among them until they drove him away with stones, when he squatted out of range and spent the rest of the day gesticulating at them obscenely. They said that we had chosen a very cold and dangerous camping ground. We might be attacked by robbers or lions; the tents might be blown down; would we not prefer to move to a more sheltered place? We replied that if they had been solicitous of our comfort earlier, we could no doubt have found a better camping ground on the road to Dessye.

Later they tried a stupendous lie. The Emperor was on the telephone, they said; he had rung up to say that ten lorry loads of journalists were on the way to join us; would we mind waiting for them until tomorrow morning, when we could all travel together?

Finally, to make things certain, they set a guard round us; not a mere posse of sentries but the whole village, leper, idiot, police chief and the mayor himself. The latter pitched a tent a few paces from us; a ramshackle square thing which, to the loud derision of our boys, who were enjoying the situation to the full, blew down twice. The others squatted with spears and rifles in a circle all round us. It was a bitterly cold night. By dawn they looked frozen. We breakfasted, struck camp, loaded the lorry and waited. At eight the chief came to say that we must go back. The barrier behind us was removed. We climbed into the lorry. Even now the chief feared a sudden dash for Dessye; he drew up his men across the road with their rifles ready. The chief of police spoiled the gravity of the defence by trotting forward and asking us to take his photograph. Then, in a cheerful mood, we drove back to Addis Ababa, which with some rather ruthless driving we made before nightfall.

Our little trip had caused a mild scandal. As soon as it became known we had gone, officials from the Press Bureau had trotted round all the hotels with typewritten notices, dated the day before, saying that leave for Dessye was indefinitely postponed. A stout barricade and a military post were set up on the road out of Addis. The French journalists had lodged a formal protest that preferential treatment was being given us; Belattingetta Herui announced that we were enjoying a little holiday in camp five miles outside the capital; an American journalist cabled home that we were in chains. Mr Karam hung round us rather tentatively offering a bill for ten pounds; the return trip to Debra Birhan, he claimed, had not been specified in our original contract. We had missed no news of importance and had picked up through James, who had earned the esteem of one of our guards with the present of six matches, some interesting details of the Danakil raids and inter-regimental fighting near Dessye. On the whole it had been an enjoyable excursion.

Two days after our return general permission for Dessye was again issued, this time in earnest. In the end it was a scratch caravan which set out for Dessye. The Radical, the *Daily Express* correspondent, and I were the only regular English journalists; an American preacher, a free-lance communist, and an unemployed German Jew deputized for more august principals. Only the cinema companies travelled impressively.

There was no possible advantage to be gained by priority, but habitual competition had by now unbalanced many, so that some lorries made a race of it. The adolescent Canadian far outdistanced the rest of the field and arrived in Dessye a day ahead; I believe that on his return he was accorded a civic reception in his home-town for this feat. Others preferred a more leisurely journey; stopped to fish and shoot on the way and compose descriptions of the scenery, which, a few hours after Debra Birhan, became varied and magnificent.

Early in the afternoon of the second day we came suddenly and without warning – for the road was recent and not yet marked on any published map – upon an enormous escarpment, a rocky precipice open before our wheels; far below lay a broad valley, richly cultivated and studded with small hemispherical hills, each crowned with a church or a cluster of huts. Down this awful cliff the track fell in a multitude of hairpin bends; surveyed from above the gradient seemed, in places, almost perpendicular; there was barely clearance for the wheels; on the off-side the edge crumbled away into space; at the corners the road was sharply inclined in the wrong direction. Our Harari driver gave a sigh of despair. Straight down the face of the cliff transecting the road at each turn led a precipitous footpath. Ostensibly to lighten the truck, actually because we were thoroughly scared, the Radical and I decided to go down on foot. It was a stiff descent; with every step the air became warmer as though we were scrambling across the seasons. When we reached more tolerable ground we waited for the lorry, which presently arrived, the driver speechless but triumphant. All that night, James reported, he was talking in his sleep about braking and reversing.

We found a warm and sheltered camping place a few miles from the foot of the escarpment, and here, shortly before sundown, we were visited by heralds from the local governor, Dedjasmach Matafara, who was living nearby in temporary quarters, to ask us our business. I sent James to explain. He returned rather drunk to say that the Dedjasmach was 'very gentleman'. He was accompanied by slaves bearing a present of *tedj*, native bread, and a young sheep; also an invitation to breakfast the next morning.

The Dedjasmach was a very old man, a veteran of the first battle of Adowa, corpulent, ponderous in his movements, with unusually dark skin and a fine white beard.

He occupied a series of huts behind a well-made stockade. There was a circular *tukal* where he slept and where, on our arrival, he was completing his toilet; there was a larger, square building for eating and the transaction of business, a cook-house, women's and soldiers' quarters, and in the centre an open space, part farmyard and part barrack square. Soldiers, slaves, and priests thronged the place, disputing it with cattle and poultry.

The Dedjasmach greeted us with great politeness and dignity, slipped on a pair of elastic-sided boots and led us across to the dining-room. The preparations were simple. One of the sheets was taken from the Dedjasmach's bed and stretched across the centre of the hut to shield us from public view; behind it, in almost complete darkness, a low wicker table was laid with piles of native bread. The Radical and I, the Dedjasmach and two priests, sat down at little stools. James stood beside us. Two women slaves stood with horsehair whisks, fanning away the flies. Abyssinian bread is made in thin, spongy discs. It is used very conveniently as both plate and spoon. The curry – a fiery but rather delicious dish which forms the staple food of those who can afford it – is ladled out into the centre of the bread; morsels are then wrapped up in pieces torn from the edge and put into the mouth. The Dedjasmach courteously helped us to tit-bits from his own pile. Other slaves brought us horn mugs of *tedj* – a heavy drink at eight in the morning. Conversation was intermittent and rather laborious; it consisted chiefly of questions addressed to us by our host and the priests. They asked us our ages, whether we were married, how many children. One of the priests recorded this information in a little exercise book. The Dedjasmach said he loved the English because he knew that they too hated the Italians. The Italians were a poor sort of people, he said; one of his friends had killed forty of them, one after the other, with his sword. He asked us if we knew General Harrington; he had been a good man; was he still alive? Then he returned to the question of the Italians. They did not like the smell of blood, he said; when they smelled blood they were afraid; when an Abyssinian smelled blood he became doubly brave; that was why the sword was better than the gun.

Besides, he said, the Italians disliked fighting so much they had to be given food free before they would do it; he knew this for a fact; he had seen it himself forty years ago; they had great carts loaded with food and wine to persuade the men to fight; Abyssinians scorned that; each man brought his own rations and, if he had one, his own mule.

Water was brought for us to bathe our hands; then little cups of bitter coffee. Finally we made our adieux. He asked us to take two soldiers with us to Dessye. Slightly drunk, we stepped out into the brilliant morning sunshine. One of the soldiers who was accompanying us had to sell his mule before he could start. At last the transaction was complete. He bundled in at the back with the boys; we were saved the embarrassment of the second by the arrival, just as we were starting, of a French journalist. We told him that the Dedjasmach had sent the soldier for him and he accepted the man gratefully.

Then we resumed the journey.

It had been more than a pleasant interlude; it had been a glimpse of the age-old, traditional order that still survived, gracious and sturdy, out of sight beyond the brass bands and bunting, the topees and humane humbug of Tafari's régime; of an order doomed to destruction. Whatever the outcome of the war: mandate or conquest or internationally promoted native reform – whatever resulted at Geneva or Rome or Addis Ababa, Dedjasmach Matafara and all he stood for was bound to disappear. But we were pleased to have seen it and touched hands across the centuries with the court of Prester John.

On a later day we passed an army – Dedjasmach Bayana's, which had left Addis fourteen days before; they had found a sugar plantation, and every man was sucking a cane as he shambled along; Bayana himself maintained the same pomp as when he had paraded before the Emperor; he rode under a black umbrella, surrounded by his domestic slaves and led-mules adorned with their ceremonial trappings; a team of women followed him carrying jars of *tedj* under crimson cotton veils. We passed through belts of forest, full of birds and game and monkeys and brilliant flowers. On the fourth day Dessye lying high up in a cup in the mountains, surrounded on all sides by hills.

It is a place of recent creation; an Abyssinian military outpost in the Mohammedan Wollo country. In appearance it was very much like a miniature of Addis Ababa – the same eucalyptus trees, the same single shopping street, the same tin roofs, a Gebbi built on an eminence dominating the town. The inhabitants were Abyssinian squatters; the Wollo Gallas came in for the weekly market but lived in the villages.

The place was full of soldiers; a detachment of the Imperial Guard was quartered in the grounds of the Italian consulate; the irregulars slept in a ring of encampments along the surrounding hillside. They came into town at dawn and remained until sunset, drinking, quarrelling and sauntering about the streets; more were arriving daily and the congestion was becoming perilous. The chiefs were under orders to leave for the front, but they hung on, saying that they would not move until the Emperor led them in person.

We reported to the mayor, a stocky, bearded figure who had disgraced himself in London and now happily compromised in his costume between the new and old régimes by wearing beard and cloak of a traditional cut and, below them, shorts and red and white ringed football stockings. He passed us on to the chief of police, who, that afternoon, was tipsy. Eventually we found a camping ground for ourselves.

For so many weeks now Dessye had been our goal – a promised land sometimes glimpsed from afar, sometimes impenetrably obscured, sometimes seen in a mirage a stone's throw away in crystal detail, always elusive, provocative, desirable – that its pursuit had become an end in itself. Now that, at length, we found ourselves actually there, when the tents were pitched and the stores unpacked and all round us a village of tents had sprung up, we began to wonder what precisely we had gained by the journey. We were two hundred or so miles nearer the Italians, but for any contact we had with the battlefield or information about what was happening, we were worse off than at Addis Ababa. A field wireless had been established on the hill side a mile out of the town. Here we all hurried to enquire about facilities and were told, to our surprise, that messages of any length might be sent. At Addis there had been a limit of two hundred words. All messages from Dessye had to be retransmitted from Addis. It seemed odd, but we were used to unaccountable happenings. That evening all over the camp typewriters were tapping as the journalists spread themselves over five hundred, eight hundred, a thousand word messages describing the perils of the journey. Two days later we were cheerfully informed that none of the messages had been sent, that no more could be accepted until further notice, that when the station reopened there would be a limit of fifty words and a rigid censorship. So there, for the time being, our professional activities ended.

A week passed in complete idleness. The Emperor's arrival was daily predicted and daily postponed. Lij Yasu died, and James, who had been dining with Mohammedan friends in the town, and drinking in Christian fashion, returned in a high state of excitement to say that the Emperor would be murdered if he attempted to show himself among the Wollo Gallas.

The native members of the 'Ethiopian Red Cross' had a beano, stripped to the skin and danced round the tent of their American officer, who had only that evening moved his quarters to avoid contamination from his more worldly Irish colleagues.

The governing Dedjasmach made a strenuous and partly successful attempt to get some of the soldiers to the front. He organized a parade, and, himself at their head, drums beating and bugles playing, led them Pied-Piper fashion up the Makale road, returning by himself after dark to the more agreeable accommodation of his own bedroom.

Relieved of the itch to cable, the journalists displayed amiable characteristics which they had hitherto concealed. We became house proud; the Radical and I set a popular vogue by erecting the first latrine. Mr Prospero contrived an arc-light. We began to entertain and competed mildly in kitchen and service. Except for a Finnish misanthrope who maintained a front of unbroken hostility – and later on his return to Addis indulged in litigation at the American consular court against a colleague who punched him – the grimmest characters seemed to grow soft in idleness. On 28th November there was a Thanksgiving Dinner, attended by all except the Finn, and after it a drinking competition won – dishonestly we discovered later – by one of the Irishmen.

Next day it was announced officially that the Emperor was on the road, and on the 30th he arrived. The soldiers waited for him all day, squatting along the route, reeling and jostling about the streets. They had been surly and hostile for some days; now, exhilarated at the prospect of the Emperor's arrival, they became menacing, held up the cars of the cinema men, scowled and jeered through the heat of the day; then, towards evening, as it became cold, crowded shivering and morose. The royal mules in brilliant saddle cloths waited to take the Emperor on the last stage of his journey, up the hill to the Crown Prince's Gebbi, but the sun went down, the crowds began to melt away and the photographers were again deprived of a picturesque shot. At length he arrived, unobtrusively, in the darkness. From now on Dessye became his headquarters; in the new year he moved north; he was not to see Addis again until he arrived in the spring, in flight to the coast.

There was no mistaking the sincerity of the Court's optimism; three weeks before they had professed the same confidence but in a strained and anxious fashion; now, reverting to the simpler habits of their upbringing, they were openly jubilant.

The Emperor came to visit the American hospital. The wards were fairly full, but not with war wounded; there were several venereal cases and some of influenza contracted on the journey up (the Imperial Guard seemed to be of lower stamina than the irregular troops); there were a few soldiers who had deserted from Eritrea and got badly cut up by a company of Abyssinian troops deserting in the opposite direction; but there were no heroes upon whom the Emperor could suitably manifest his sympathy. In order to show the equipment of the hospital at its best advantage the doctors staged an operation – the amputation of a gangrened stump of arm. Emperor, Court, and journalists crowded into the theatre; the photographers and cinema men took their shots. The Emperor asked, 'And where did this gallant man lose his hand?'

'Here in Dessye. The Dedjasmach had it cut off for stealing two besas worth of corn.'

Meanwhile in Europe and America the editors and film magnates had begun to lose patience. They had spent large sums of money on the Abyssinian war and were getting very little in return; several journalists had already been recalled; the largest cinema company was beginning to pack up; now a general retreat began. I received my dismissal by cable on the day after the Emperor's arrival. For a few hours I considered staying on independently. That had been my original intention, but now the prospect seemed unendurably dismal. I had long wanted to spend Christmas at Bethlehem. This was the opportunity.

There was a car travelling to Addis Ababa on Red Cross business in which I was able, illegally, to purchase a seat. We had to start before dawn in order to avoid notice from the Red Cross authorities. James cried. It was an uneventful journey. The German driver – an adventurous young airman who had come to

297

look for good fortune after serving in the Paraguayan war – kept a rifle across the wheel and inflicted slight wounds on the passing fauna at point-blank range.

Addis was dead. With the Emperor's departure the public services had settled into the accustomed coma. The bars were open but empty. A handful of journalists from the south were packing up to return to England. The mystery men had faded away.

After a few days I got down to Djibouti. At Dirre-Dowa the French garrison were firmly entrenched; half the town was a French fort. Djibouti was still crowded, still panicky. There were a number of journalists there reporting the war at leisure from their imaginations. Soon after I left, some bombs had been dropped on Dessye and the chief excitement of Djibouti centred on a race to get the films of them back to Europe. Weeks later in Devon I saw them on the news reel. It was difficult to recapture the excitement, secrecy, and competition that had attended their despatch.

News of the Hoare-Laval proposals reached us in the Red Sea; at Port Said we heard of their reception. Next day I was in Jerusalem and visited the Abyssinian monks, perched in their little African village on the roof of the Holy Sepulchre; Christmas morning in Bethlehem; desert and ruined castles in Transjordan; like the rest of the world I began to forget about Abyssinia.